Just Read!

Teacher's Manual

Jenn Clark and Michelle McIntosh

Foreword by Dr Gavin Reid

Just Read! Teacher's Manual

Published by:
Pavilion Publishing and Media Ltd
Blue Sky Offices
25 Cecil Pashley Way
Shoreham by Sea
West Sussex
BN43 5FF
UK

Tel: 01273 434 943
Email: info@pavpub.com
Web: www.pavpub.com

Published 2022

A catalogue record for this book is available from the British Library.

ISBN: 978-1-913414-62-7

Pavilion Publishing and Media is a leading publisher of books, training materials and digital content in mental health, social care and allied fields. Pavilion and its imprints offer must-have knowledge and innovative learning solutions underpinned by sound research and professional values.

Authors: Jenn Clark and Michelle McIntosh
Editor: Mike Benge, Pavilion Publishing and Media
Cover design: Tony Pitt, Pavilion Publishing and Media
Page layout and typesetting: Tony Pitt, Pavilion Publishing and Media
Printing: Ashford Press

Contents

A range of resources for *Just Read!* are available for download at
www.pavpub.com/just-read-teachers-manual-resources

Introduction

Welcome to *Just Read!*, a reading system that aims to promote decoding, reading fluency and reading comprehension.

Just Read! was borne out of a need; a need for a structured and sequential system to support and teach students to learn how to read no matter where they are in their reading journey. We wanted a system where educators and reading specialists could quickly assess their student and begin working with them exactly where they are. As such, this system provides reading fluency practice from letter recognition all the way through to reading comprehension. *Just Read!* is a full-bodied, structured and sequential system that educators can use easily with any student, no matter what their current reading level is.

Just Read! is based on the Multi-sensory Structured language Education (MSLE) approach and, as such, adopts a structured and sequential approach to reading. Each aspect of the system is supported by research and based on currently accepted reading fluency practices. While other excellent reading resources are available to teachers, most of these programs only address a limited or specific area of reading and do not offer a highly structured and sequential teaching of the reading process from the foundational level (phonological awareness) to higher-level processes. What makes *Just Read!* different is that it is a comprehensive system that supports students completely and at any level.

What is *Just Read!* and what will it do?

- *Just Read!* is a highly controlled, sequential, self-contained reading resource, which takes students through the multiple levels of reading from letter recognition to comprehension.
- *Just Read!* enables reading specialists and classroom teachers to design and deliver a structured and sequential approach to reading at an appropriate level for each individual student.
- *Just Read!* is modelled on current evidence-based research and practices that incorporate a Multi-sensory Structured language Education (MSLE) approach to literacy acquisition.
- *Just Read!* builds on developmental reading stages by providing instruction and resources across three separate areas: decoding, reading fluency and reading comprehension.

It is our hope that you can implement *Just Read!* into your classroom or learning support environment and enjoy reading success with your students! Thank you for purchasing *Just Read!* and supporting our love of reading.

Jenn & Michelle

About the Authors

Jennifer Clark

Jennifer is an Orton Gillingham Practitioner and a Structured Literacy Instructor. She holds a Bachelor of Education, a TESOL Diploma, a Family Literacy Certificate and a Trainers Certificate in Adult Education and CCET (Certificate of Competency in Educational Testing-UK). Jenn has had many years of experience teaching students with language-based learning differences and training teachers in a structured and multisensory approach to education. Her publications include: *Practical Activities and Ideas for Parents of Dyslexic Kids and Teens*, and *Dyslexia Tools – Workbook for Teens*. She is a co-founder of the LIT Group Inc. based in Vancouver where she has a private practice. For more information about Jenn, go to www.thelitgroup.ca

Michelle McIntosh

Michelle is also a Certified Orton-Gillingham Supervisor and Practitioner, Structured Literacy Instructor and a Supervising Mentor to other Structured Literacy practitioners. Michelle holds diplomas in Professional Communications and in Broadcasting. Michelle also holds her Associate Teaching Certificate through Trinity College London in Speech and Drama (ATCL). Michelle has many years of experience helping those with language-based learning difficulties. She is the co-founder of the LIT Group Inc. based in Vancouver and she is the co-author of the book *Practical Activities and Ideas for Parents of Dyslexic Kids and Teens*. For more information about Michelle, visit www.thelitgroup.ca

Acknowledgements

This book would not have been possible without the support and encouragement of some amazing people. Our thanks go out to our families and students who helped inspire us to write this book. We would like to express gratitude to Liam Wright for providing illustrations in the student book and finally to Pavilion Publishing for their opportunity to share our vision with educators. We hope *Just Read!* will help your students as much as it has benefitted ours.

Michelle McIntosh and Jenn Clark

Foreword

It is a pleasure to be invited to write a foreword for *Just Read!*. This resource will be invaluable to schools, parents and educators at all levels. The approach to tackling reading issues taken by Michelle McIntosh and Jenn Clark is founded on a combination of robust research in reading and the established principles of structured multi-sensory language instruction.

Both authors have a wealth of practical experience to draw on, and we as parents and teachers, are indebted to them for sharing their expertise in this comprehensive and cleverly designed resource. In my experience as a teacher, parent and psychologist, I know *Just Read!* will be warmly welcomed by all.

I am impressed with the care and presentation the authors and publishers have taken to ensure that *Just Read!* is user friendly. I know for the busy teacher this is invaluable. The Teacher's Manual is clear and concise, yet comprehensive in its perspective. Clearly, a substantial amount of research and creative effort has been extended by the authors. The Reading Screener, a comprehensive screening package, will get the practitioner started with this and the rest follows logically. The manual answers all the questions the teacher might ask and in my mind this reinforces the practitioner-orientated approach taken by the authors, which makes *Just Read!* a first-rate, top-notch resource.

The sections on Decoding Plus!, Fluency Plus! and Comprehension Plus! are surely elements many teachers have been seeking for years, recognising the key roles fluency and comprehension have in the development of competent reading. The reading passages flow well, are interesting and entertaining, and sufficiently diversified to make sense to a multicultural audience. This is a resource that will certainly benefit the reader with dyslexia, but also other children who are still developing their reading skills. This underlines the value to my mind of *Just Read!* – a reading specific-resource with universal application. I am sure parents will want this resource to be utilised in every school.

I would like to conclude this foreword by offering my sincere and heartfelt congratulations to Michelle and Jenn for their endeavours, experience and their expertise, and above all their vision for creating and developing this unique resource that will be a great boost to teachers, parents and all children with reading issues. This surely makes the endeavour more than worthwhile! Congratulations to both authors.

Dr. Gavin Reid
Author and Psychologist

Notes on Reading Fluency

What is Reading Fluency?

When it comes to reading fluency, one thing is certain. The construct of fluency means different things to different researchers, and current models show a large variance in regard to its definition. Historically, fluency as a concept has been of interest from the end of the 19th century in works from James (1886), Cattell (1886) and Huey (1905). From here, research on fluency focused on disparate elements from Laberge and Samuels' 'model of automaticity' (1974) to Doehring (1976), Perfetti (1977; 1985) and on to more modern names such as Fuchs (2001) and Wolf and Katzir-Cohen (2001). These researchers displayed a keen interest in understanding the breadth of fluency and the underlying mechanisms that create, and are responsible for, fluency. This research underpins the complexity of understanding the multifaceted domain of reading and the skills required to become a competent reader.

> The NAEP oral reading substudy (1992) found that fluency instruction in schools is a crucial and neglected bridge from the basics to broader and more complex reading.

While many definitions of fluency currently exist and are dependent on conceptual models, one of the most prevalent and widely accepted definitions looks at both rate and accuracy as key indicators of fluent reading. More recent theories of reading encompass elements such as prosody, rapid naming speed and processing speed but, for the sake of a simple definition, the elements of rate and accuracy have been widely accepted as a defining marker of overall fluency. A more helpful, teacher-friendly definition of reading fluency might be "fluid and accurate reading that mirrors spoken language while adding to the overall comprehension of what has been read." For we know that the aim or purpose of reading is to comprehend what we are reading and interact with text. While decoding and fluency help and are necessary components of this, they may be viewed as the essential stepping stones for comprehension to occur, and a student may need specific attention or training in order to reach the final goal of full comprehension.

According to the National Reading Panel's (NRP) 2000 report on literacy instruction, fluency is one of the top five elements needed for effective literacy instruction. The other elements named were phonemic awareness, phonics, vocabulary and comprehension. All these elements work together to achieve proficient reading. Where most instruction fails is in teaching top down elements such as comprehension before tackling the much needed stepping stones of other components of literacy such as fluency and phonemic awareness.

Fluency Sub-Skills

The skill of fluency is made up of other crucial sub-skills that help form the rapid retrieval of letter names and sounds that are necessary in the early stages of reading. While it is a broader stage of reading, fluency may also be interpreted within other smaller stages of reading. Passage fluency is one element, but so is fluency, or automaticity, in naming speed, letter identification and whole word fluency. Many educators and theorists look for the commonalities between fluency and automaticity and suggest that fluency is a sense of automaticity but also incorporates other elements of reading that are distinctive. For example, prosody is often an element of modern reading fluency definition, however it is distinctly different from the cognitive elements such as processing speed, rapid naming speed, or rapid word identification.

As we approach the teaching of fluency, we can be sure that it will be a laborious stage for both the reader and the teacher, but a necessary one. It is also one that takes a good deal of effort, practice and time. Too often, the teaching of fluency can slide into murky outcomes and fail to recognize some more modern or current concepts of what makes a fluent reader. What might be helpful is to look at fluency as a skill that evolves along an open-ended continuum as a reader weaves in and out of stages of reading. Fluency at some stages is constantly being recycled as readers progress to more demanding tasks of reading, while slowly moving towards the goal of comprehension. For instance, think of the transition between fluent word reading and fluent passage reading. We know that fluent word reading must occur before a student is able to develop a fluent sense of passage reading. The sub-skills that are required for fluent word reading have been mastered and stored as a student moves towards the more demanding tasks that are associated with passage reading.

The focus on rapid sound/symbol fluency has been replaced by other fluency markers, but is still actively used and practiced as students move towards more cognitively challenging markers of fluency or automaticity. The progression of sub-skills moves along the continuum as readers gain a more automatic sense of certain elements of the reading process. This is why fluency teaching must focus on particular aspects of reading in a progressive manner in order to highlight crucial elements within a reading stage. Teachers must recognize what fluency looks like at the 'decoding stage', the 'word stage' and the 'passage stage' in order to instill a set of skills that build on each other and eventually flow together to create a broader sense of reading fluency.

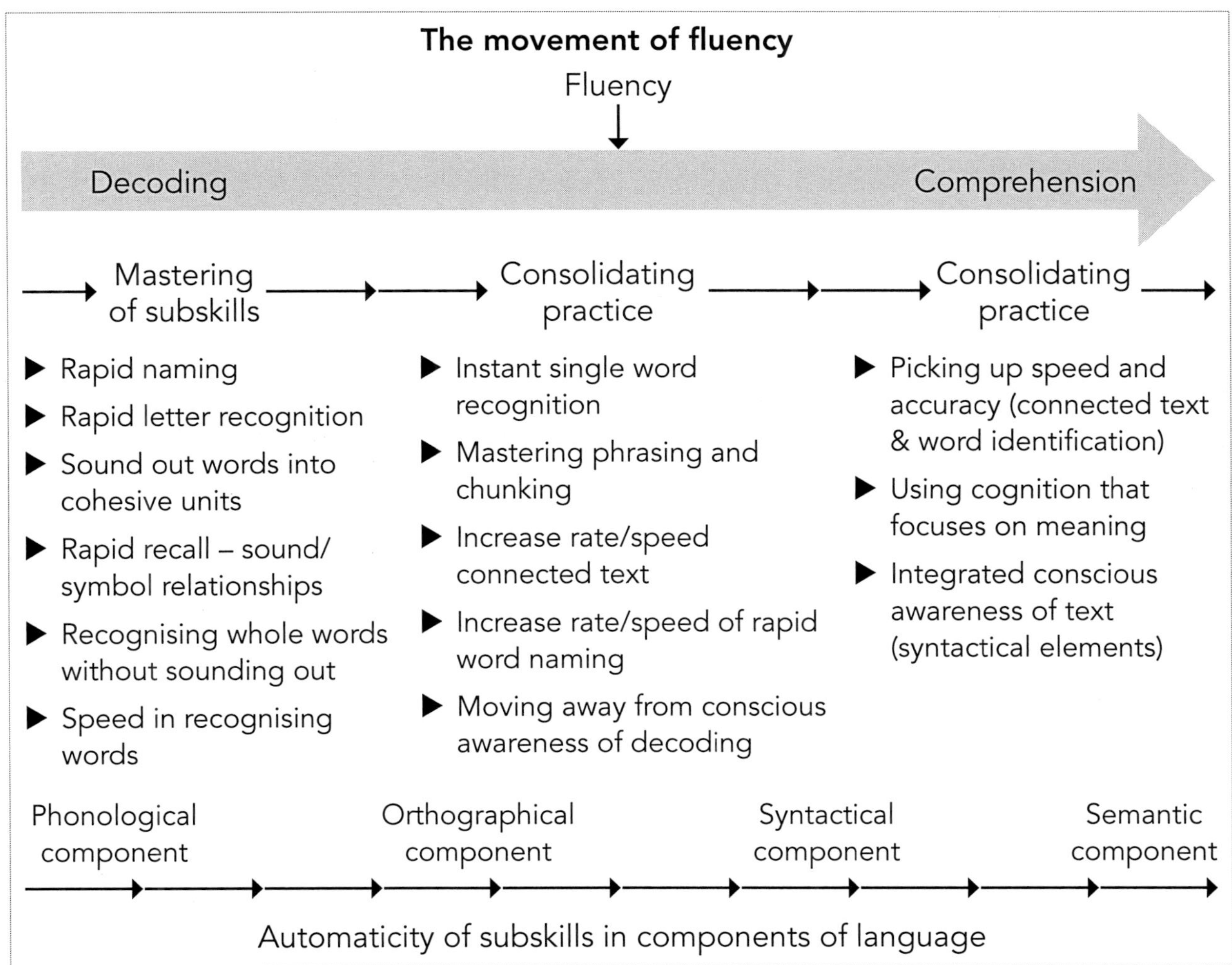

Why is Fluency so Important?

Although the NRP's report named fluency as a definitive marker of effective literacy instruction, educators and practitioners still struggle to understand the importance of fluency to the overall concept of reading instruction. So why exactly is fluency so crucial to our instruction and what do students gain as they begin to master the elements of reading fluency? Most researchers would agree that fluency is the gateway to comprehension. Studies indicate a high degree of correlation between oral reading rate and degree of comprehension – the correlation is .91 in a study conducted by Fuchs, Fuchs & Maxwell, 1988. What this tells us about effective instruction is that if a student has reached the appropriate level of reading rate, then they are likely to be understanding what they read. Often, when fluency is lagging and reading is effortful and cumbersome, we can see how the cognitive processes are focused on the skills needed to interpret and decode text rather than those needed to understand the text itself. When too much time and effort is given to decoding, processing and recognition, not enough time is spent on higher cognitive skills that are crucial for comprehension. This is why the question of oral reading rate is so important in the overall concept of reading, and why effective fluency instruction should focus on achieving a solid reading rate in conjunction with other fluency markers. Fluency is the gateway to comprehension.

Repeated Oral Reading – Implications for Improving Fluency

Current research on fluency has looked at practical implications for teaching practice. The findings suggest that repeated reading is one the best practices used in order to improve fluency markers in children who struggle to read. In 2000, The National Reading Panel concluded that repeated reading is beneficial for improving reading. The NRP contrasted the technique of repeated reading to silent reading, and found no evidence linking silent reading to gains made in overall reading fluency (Meyer, 2012). Not only does repeated oral reading increase overall fluency for a reader, it also may be linked to increases in other areas such as reading comprehension. As children are exposed to multiple rereads of a passage, other elements that fall under the fluency umbrella are also strengthened – such as prosody and attention to semantical features, which will often correlate to an increase in reading comprehension. The beauty of repeated reading is that it allows a student to consolidate the amount of words identified in a passage and increase the speed at which they are able to identify and process these words. Thus, once a word is quickly identified and remembered, these can then be mapped onto other passages and built upon. With repeated reading, students are afforded the opportunity to build and store words automatically while they continue to increase their exposure to other words and build a stronger sense of automaticity and a bigger bank of sight vocabulary. In 1999, Faulkner and Levy produced a study on repeated reading that found this particular technique allowed for poor readers to improve the efficiency with which they processed individual words within a text (Torgensen, 2001).

Most effective repeated reading interventions are characterised by the following criteria:

- Reading and rereading of text a specified number of times or to a specific set of fluency criteria
- An increase in the actual amount of practice time spent reading with a peer or a tutor whereby a student is able to contextualise passage reading
- A program that provides various types of feedback concerning accuracy and fluency in reading

In a recent study where students received repeated reading instruction that focused on reading practice of individual letters, phonograms, words and phrases and connected text, for periods lasting 6-9 months for at least six minutes a day, researchers found substantial gains in reading fluency and accuracy for almost all of the children in the study group (Torgensen, 2001). While it appears that the benefit of repeated reading is on individual word reading efficiency, studies have not been able to definitively link this effect to an increase in the speed of previously unknown words or in the orthographic representation of unknown words. Logically it would appear that both types of effects would be present (Torgensen, 2001).

Another benefit or area of interest to researchers with regard to repeated oral reading is the opportunities and amount of practice time repeated reading affords to those who struggle to read. Studies have shown that differences in reading practice opportunities are not restricted to the period of beginning reading instruction, but may become more pronounced as a child gets older. Nagy and Anderson (1984) estimated that good readers may read as many as one million words a year both in and out of school, while less skilled readers may read less than 100,000 – a substantial difference in the amount of word reading practice (Torgensen, 2001). With the use of repeated reading, less skilled readers become more confident in their reading ability and may therefore become more motivated to read and see themselves as readers. The cycle of "can't do so won't do" can be broken and the overall exposure afforded by repeated reading can provide a substantial opportunity in reading practice, which may then lead to more reading performed both in and out of school.

What does the research on repeated oral reading suggest for fluency intervention? That it is one of the most useful practices to date, with a significant gain in overall fluency and rate, but also that it may impact comprehension. The amount of time, consistency and exposure afforded by multiple reads is the right combination for struggling readers to improve both the speed and efficiency with which they process words and learn to become more fluent readers.

Rapid Naming and Automaticity – Sub-skills that Influence Reading Fluency

Most researchers agree that automaticity is an important factor in becoming a fluent reader. While the terms fluency and automaticity were once believed to be interchangeable, recent research has explored the differences between the two. Characteristics of automaticity include speed, effortlessness, autonomy and lack of conscious awareness (Brenitz, 2012). Often the development of automaticity is most directly linked to an increase in speed – which we know is crucial for processing the rate of words while we are engaged with the reading process. The concept of automaticity is a crucial one. Automaticity as a construct may be viewed as constantly evolving at every stage of reading. For example, during the early stages of decoding we can see how automaticity in letter recognition is directly linked to the speed at which a reader may process this information. This speed evolves as readers move away from the simple sound/symbol match up into automatically learning larger lexical chunks such as sight words and later phrases or sentences. Researchers are quick to point out that skilled readers automatically decode letters, and that this sense of speed or ease of automaticity may been seen at each stage within the reading continuum. As discrete skills become automatic, it frees the reading brain to connect to and engage with other reading processes that in turn will become more automatic. In essence, automaticity is crucial because it allows a reader to free up processing space for more complex cognitive tasks and more sophisticated elements found in reading.

For example, once a student has mastered the basics of automaticity, they are then able to free up space to focus on comprehension because rapid naming and decoding have become effortless and no longer require conscious attention.

Many researchers believe that this sense of automaticity can be attributed to cognitive skills such as processing speed and rapid naming, as both of these cognitive skills are deeply connected to the art of reading. While some researchers see reading or fluency as a wholly linguistic construct, others are quick to point out that many of the causes of disfluency can be attributed and traced back to deficits in cognitive sub-skills as they relate to reading. Wolf and Obregon (1992) found a direct correlation between naming speed and reading measures in dyslexic readers. They found a significant connection between performance on the naming task and that of reading comprehension (Brenitz, 2012). Research consistently shows that dyslexics score poorly on naming tasks and the speed at which they process naming tasks. What does this mean for fluency and its intervention? Clearly, if students are to move through the continuum of fluency and its markers, automaticity is a concept that needs to be mastered from the earliest stages of reading. Letter recognition must be mastered to a certain level, as it is a future predictor of word identification and the speed in which it can be performed. At the earliest stages, reading does require a heavier focus on the mechanics or processes that lead to automaticity such as speed of processing, rapid naming and accuracy. We can see that, at these stages, reading is heavily dependent on these sub-skills and their mastery enables a reader to move up through the ranks of fluency and focus on more developmentally appropriate markers of higher fluency skills. Without a sense of automaticity, the end goal of fluency can become unachievable.

Fluency and its Link to Comprehension

Most researchers agree that there is a link between fluency and reading comprehension, although the exact nature of it is still widely debated. However, while rate and accuracy have a strong link to overall comprehension, fluency's link to comprehension may be harder to tease out. Studies have indicated accurate word recognition does lead to an increase in the speed at which a text is processed; however there are researchers who question the degree to which fluency predicts comprehension. Does word automaticity naturally predict comprehension, or are there other factors along with rate and accuracy that are significant? This question is still being investigated, but some researchers argue that a consistent reading rate, along with an understanding of expressive language and linguistically sophisticated nuances of language, are the top ingredients for successful comprehension.

An important point to note about comprehension is that it is mainly a top down process. Thus the mechanics of reading do not really take effect in this domain. Within this top down process, we are generally thinking about our thinking and employ more sophisticated uses of language to comprehend what we have just read. Going back to the question of fluency as a continuum, we can see that, at the top level, comprehension begins to rely on our understanding of more linguistically sophisticated elements of reading that make us 'fluent' in understanding what we have just read. These advanced linguistic systems – the emphasis on the semantical and syntactical – must be fluent and present if readers are to be secure and understand what they have just read. As Wolf and Katzir-Cohen would argue, these more linguistically advanced components of fluency still must be taught and emphasized if reading comprehension is to be successful. Automaticity or fluency at a more advanced level is recognising semantics and syntax in reading, and integrating them in order to obtain a deeper understanding of fluency and its link to comprehension. We are not finished with the teaching of fluency after the third and fourth grades and their international equivalents; rather, it is important to identify salient linguistic complexities and features, teach them, practice them sufficiently, and integrate these new sub-skills into fluency at higher levels of reading (Garnett, 2011).

Again, the idea that fluency expands well beyond the processing of basic sub-skills such as letter recognition and word recognition is critical. Fluency at each stage will focus on different elements and target specific sub-skills in order to bring a reader to the ultimate goal of comprehension. The importance of processing speed and automaticity at the early stages of reading therefore adds to and builds upon more advanced notions of fluency. They are both equally critical, but the stage at which they occur is vastly different and the cognitive profiles of each stage are developmentally unique. Each stage builds on its predecessors in order that an effortless, automatic unconscious level of awareness can be achieved.

Conclusions and Implications for Fluency Interventions

1. Fluency intervention must approach fluency as a continuum, focusing on and targeting those areas of fluency that correspond to a developmentally appropriate acquisition of sub-skills.
2. Fluency should be mastered from the earliest reading stages – starting from phonological sub-skills, moving up into orthographic sub-skills and then connecting theses skills to higher, more linguistically complex sub-skills found within the semantic systems in our language.
3. Fluency and automaticity within all of the linguistic domains is necessary for the ultimate goal of comprehension.
4. Some studies indicate that a robust oral reading rate can be attributed to higher level of comprehension. The logic behind this is that the faster and more accurately an individual reads, the more cognitive space they have available to engage in higher end functions rather than decoding.
5. Repeated reading techniques help to solidify basic fluency techniques associated with phonological and orthographic systems in our language. Repeated reading helps to promote a sense of automaticity in sub-skills such as processing and retrieval.

6. Effective reading fluency interventions should occur from the earliest stages of reading. Automaticity can and must be built into each stage if fluency is to be realized.
7. Fluency instruction should continue long after the mid-primary grades (third or fourth grade and their international equivalents). The type of interventions will be different, but it is necessary for students to continue with fluency tuition in order to improve their reading comprehension.

The *Just Read!* system has been designed to address all these areas, from the earliest stages of reading all the way through to the higher levels of reading and comprehension. *Just Read!* thereby enables educators to address their students' reading needs wherever they currently are on the reading spectrum.

A range of resources for *Just Read!* are available for download at **www.pavpub.com/just-read-teachers-manual-resources**

Organization and Where to Begin

Just Read! is broken down into three separate sections: Decoding Plus!, Fluency Plus! and Comprehension Plus!

The System Central (pages 27–30) shows how these sections are broken down and what graphemes, spelling rules, syllable types, non-phonetic words and morphological units may be contained in each section and story. This breakdown was created based on research supporting a sequence of reading instruction beginning with the foundational basics of letter recognition and naming and working to more complex reading tasks such as comprehension, critical thinking and inferencing. It is also based on high-frequency, non-phonetic words as they appear in Fry's List of High Frequency Words.

Where you should begin instruction with an individual student will depend on their results from the *Just Read!* Reading Screener (pages 31–51). Once you have performed the Reading Screener with your student, refer to the System Central to determine where to begin.

The assessor and teacher copies contained in this manual are meant for teachers to photocopy or print, as needed, for each individual student. They are intended to be progress tracking records to monitor student progress. These can be downloaded and printed from www.pavpub.com/just-read-teachers-manual-resources The *Just Read!* Student Workbook (sold separately) should be used by the student.

It is important to remember that the *Just Read!* System Central is a general guideline based on current research and a sequential approach to reading instruction. *Just Read!* is intended to be a supplementary resource for educators to use in conjunction with direct and explicit instruction of the sounds, rules, syllables, irregular words and morphological units contained in the System Central. Ideally, your student should not progress to higher levels of this system if they are not familiar with the concepts contained in the story or section. Instructors should maintain this sense of flow and structure, thereby ensuring student self-confidence, sense of achievement, and ultimate success.

How to Use *Just Read!*

Before you get started...

Just Read! is a sequential reading system designed to help you increase your student's overall sense of reading fluency and automaticity. Before you get started using the system, take a thorough look through this Teacher's Manual and familiarize yourself with the different components and, if you haven't already, watch the introduction film that can be found at www.pavpub.com/just-read-resources. The Teacher's Manual contains all the elements you need to track and assess your student's progress. It is very different from the Student Workbook, and it should be strictly used for tracking your student's progress. The Student Workbook has copies of all of the stories you will need, and it may be used by your student during your reading sessions. Each section is clearly laid out, and where you begin with each student should depend on the information you have gathered in the Reading Screener section. Overall, we strongly encourage you to become fully familiar with the system before attempting to use it. General guidelines have been provided at the top of each section in the system to aid you in designing a reading practice with a student. For further information about how to get started with *Just Read!*, please visit us at (www.thelitgroup.ca) for extra tips.

How do I know where to start with my student?

Just Read! contains an informal Reading Screener package intended to assist you with gauging your student's overall reading level. By using this screening package, you will get a quick snapshot of where to begin and then, by using the System Central of the system, you will be able to easily follow the next steps for your student. Once you have established the starting point, you just continue to use the material in a cumulative and sequential fashion as it is laid out in the Teacher's Manual and the Student Workbook. The beauty of following the System Central is that it builds on sequential elements and allows a deep sense of mastery before progressing to the next stage or group of stories. It is also very important to remember that *Just Read!* is a supplementary resource intended to accompany direct and explicit instruction of the elements contained within the stories.

Using the Reading Screener

The Reading Screener is a quick tool to help you place your student within the *Just Read!* system. The screening package includes:

- Rapid letter naming
- Rapid sound/symbol identification
- Irregular word reading
- High frequency word reading
- Pseudo word reading
- Regular word reading
- Fluency passages based on age/grade

All the elements within the Reading Screener should be completed with your student, regardless of age or grade. The purpose of this package is to provide you with a snapshot of your student's overall ability in the various domains of reading. While *Just Read!* does not explicitly teach non-phonetic words or high frequency words, an educator should have a good idea of their student's knowledge of these words as they may affect where you start in the system. It is also good practice to track students' progress in this area as it can help you choose which word lists to teach.

After you have completed the entire package, you will be able record all the information from the various sub-tests on a master page to gain an overall picture of your student's results. By pinpointing their overall sense of fluency in this way, you will then be able to match your results with the information in the System Central.

How do I interpret my student's results?

See the examples on the following pages. There are three examples of students who would fall into different sections of *Just Read!*. Note the descriptions of their results, and how the Reading Screener was used to identify where they would begin in the *Just Read!* system.

Example 1

Reading Fluency Screener

Student information			
Student name: *Sarah Glad*		Age: *7*	Grade: *1*
Testing date: *December 13, 2019*	Assessor's name: *Jane E. Teacher*		

Recording of scores			
Rapid letter naming	Number of letters identified: *35*		Number correct: *29*
Rapid sound identification	Number of sounds identified: *23*		Number correct: *10* (circled)
Non-phonetic reading	Score: *22*	Notes:	
Mixed phonetic pseudo-word reading	Score: *10*	Notes: *short vowels shaky, all blends*	
Mixed real word phonetic reading	Score: *13*	Notes: *short vowels shaky, blend errors*	
Rapid & automatic word recognition	Score: *25*	Notes:	
Oral reading fluency scores			
Reading passage administered:	☑ Fluency 1 (Gr.K-2)	☐ Fluency 2 (Gr.2-4)	
	☐ Fluency 3 (Gr.4-6)	☐ Fluency 4 (Gr.6-8)	
Total words read: *49*	**Number of errors:** *13* (circled)	**WCPM**[1]**:** *36*	**Accuracy rate**[2]**:** *73%*

1. In order to get your WCPM (word count per minute), take the total number of words read minus the total number of errors.
2. In order to get your accuracy reading, divide the WCPM by the total words read.

Behavioural observations related to reading:		
Fluency indicators	**Yes**	**No**
Does the student attend to punctuation?		✓
Does the student read with expression?		✓
Does the student read single words at a time?	✓	
Does the student group words together as they read? (phrasing or chunking)		✓
Does the student track the text with their finger?		✓
Does the student have any word attack strategies? (ie: sound out familiar words)	✓	
Does the student skip over or miss whole words?	✓	
Does the student replace words with similar words?	✓	
Does the student read at a rapid pace with no attention to accuracy?	✓	
Does the student read at a slower and/or laboured pace with no attention to accuracy?	✓	
Does the student make several errors that affect fluency? (ie: bus/dus)	✓	
Other behavioural observations		
Does the student appear nervous while reading?	✓	
Does the student appear to be reluctant to read?	✓	
Does the student appear to be distracted while reading?	✓	
When reading becomes more difficult, does the student persevere?		✓

Example 1 is of a student who struggled at the decoding level. Based on her screener results, she made significant errors at the sound identification level. This student also struggled a great deal at the passage level.

For this student, the teacher would begin working with the student in Decoding Plus! at the rapid sound identification level (Rs-1 to RS-5, see pages 59 and 60), and progress through the subsequent sections of Decoding Plus!. Once the teacher has moved through all of Decoding Plus! and the student has shown significant gains, they are ready to proceed to Fluency Plus!

Example 2

Assessor Copy
(6-8)

Screening Passage 6-8 "The Class Party"

DIRECTIONS: This is a one-minute timed activity. Have your students read the passage below for one- minute. **Mark errors with a slash. Self-corrections do not count as errors.** If a student omits or **skips** a word, put a line through the word and count it as an **error**. If there is a pause of 5 seconds or longer, give the student the word, **put a line through the word** and count it as an **error**. Mark specific errors in the error analysis box below.

It was the last day of class and everyone was so excited. They had worked so 16
hard the entire year and they would now get their class party. Each student 30
was allowed to invite a special guest and bring them to school for the whole 45
day and have them be a part of their class. Cassy was especially excited 59
because she was going to bring her cousin Beth, who was also her best friend. 74
The night before the party, Cassy couldn't sleep because she was so excited. 87
What was the party going to be like? Who would be there? Would her other 102
classmates bring their best friends too? The morning of the party, Cassy's 114
mother made chocolate cupcakes for everyone. On the top of each 125
cupcake was a glow in the dark letter. The letter was for their name. Cassy 140
wanted to walk to school with her cousin Beth, but her mother insisted on 154
driving them because of the heavy load of cupcakes. When they got out of 168
the car and said their goodbyes, both Cassy and Beth saw so many students in 183
line. It was true! Everyone had brought their best friends and the class line was 198
so long and loud. Beth and Cassy stood at the back of the line and tightly 214
held on to their cupcakes. Everyone else had enormous bags of chips and 227
party stuff and everyone was really excited. When the bell rang, they all filed 241
into the classroom and their teacher was standing at the front of the room. 255
She had set up a dance square in the corner of the room and had set up a 273
huge party table in the other corner. The kids arranged all of their food on the 289
table. They were hungry and excited all at the same time. The teacher put on 304
their favourite music and announced that the party had started. It was the 316
best school day ever! 320

Total Words Read: 98	- # of errors: 8	= Words Correct: 90

Enter the number of errors for each concept:

____ short vowels ____ consonant digraphs _5_ vowel digraphs
____ closed syllables _1_ r-controlled syllables ____ open syllables
_2_ non-phonetic words ____ initial blends ____ final blends
____ ng/nk ____ other

Example 2 is of a student who struggled at the fluency stage. Based on his screener results and the error analysis of the passage reading, see next page, struggles were noted in the areas of vowel digraphs and r-controlled vowel sounds. Armed with these results, the teacher would reference the System Central and note that 'Jay's Fishing Trip' in Fluency Plus! is where vowel digraphs are introduced. This is therefore where the teacher would begin instruction with this student.

The Teacher should also note the behaviour observation list and try to address these indicators when working at the Fluency Plus! level.

Reading Fluency Screener

Student information		
Student name: James Smith	Age: 12	Grade: 7
Testing date: January 29, 2019	Assessor's name: Jane E. Teacher	

Recording of scores		
Rapid letter naming	Number of letters identified: 65	Number correct: 64
Rapid sound identification	Number of sounds identified: 52	Number correct: 50
Non-phonetic reading	Score: 82	Notes:
Mixed phonetic pseudo-word reading	Score: 68	Notes: Unfamiliar with vowel digraphs
Mixed real word phonetic reading	Score: 14	Notes: confused aw/ow/ou
Rapid & automatic word recognition	Score: 85	Notes:
Oral reading fluency scores		
Reading passage administered:	☐ Fluency 1 (Gr.K-2)	☑ Fluency 2 (Gr.2-4)
	☐ Fluency 3 (Gr.4-6)	☐ Fluency 4 (Gr.6-8)

Total words read: 98 **Number of errors:** 8 **WCPM[1]:** 90 **Accuracy rate[2]:** 92%

1. In order to get your WCPM (word count per minute), take the total number of words read minus the total number of errors.
2. In order to get your accuracy reading, divide the WCPM by the total words read.

Behavioural observations related to reading:		
Fluency indicators	**Yes**	**No**
Does the student attend to punctuation?	✓	
Does the student read with expression?		✓
Does the student read single words at a time?		✓
Does the student group words together as they read? (phrasing or chunking)		✓
Does the student track the text with their finger?		✓
Does the student have any word attack strategies? (ie: sound out familiar words)	✓	
Does the student skip over or miss whole words?	✓	
Does the student replace words with similar words?	✓	
Does the student read at a rapid pace with no attention to accuracy?	✓	
Does the student read at a slower and/or laboured pace with no attention to accuracy?		✓
Does the student make several errors that affect fluency? (ie: bus/dus)	✓	
Other behavioural observations		
Does the student appear nervous while reading?	✓	
Does the student appear to be reluctant to read?	✓	
Does the student appear to be distracted while reading?		✓
When reading becomes more difficult, does the student persevere?	✓	

Example 3

Reading Fluency Screener

Student information			
Student name: *Aaron Henderson*		Age: *11*	Grade: *6*
Testing date: *November 10, 2019*	Assessor's name: *Jane E. Teacher*		

Recording of scores			
Rapid letter naming	Number of letters identified: *89*		Number correct: *89*
Rapid sound identification	Number of sounds identified: *45*		Number correct: *93*
Non-phonetic reading	Score: *87*	Notes:	
Mixed phonetic pseudo-word reading	Score: *46*	Notes:	
Mixed real word phonetic reading	Score: *70*	Notes:	
Rapid & automatic word recognition	Score: *92*	Notes:	
Oral reading fluency scores			
Reading passage administered:	☑ Fluency 1 (Gr.K-2)	☐ Fluency 2 (Gr.2-4)	
	☐ Fluency 3 (Gr.4-6)	☐ Fluency 4 (Gr.6-8)	
Total words read: *221*	**Number of errors:** *32*	**WCPM[1]:** *218*	**Accuracy rate[2]:** *99%*

1. In order to get your WCPM (word count per minute), take the total number of words read minus the total number of errors.
2. In order to get your accuracy reading, divide the WCPM by the total words read.

Behavioural observations related to reading:		
Fluency indicators	**Yes**	**No**
Does the student attend to punctuation?	✓	
Does the student read with expression?	✓	
Does the student read single words at a time?		✓
Does the student group words together as they read? (phrasing or chunking)	✓	
Does the student track the text with their finger?	✓	
Does the student have any word attack strategies? (ie: sound out familiar words)	✓	
Does the student skip over or miss whole words?		✓
Does the student replace words with similar words?		✓
Does the student read at a rapid pace with no attention to accuracy?		✓
Does the student read at a slower and/or laboured pace with no attention to accuracy?		✓
Does the student make several errors that affect fluency? (ie: bus/dus)		✓
Other behavioural observations		
Does the student appear nervous while reading?		✓
Does the student appear to be reluctant to read?		✓
Does the student appear to be distracted while reading?		✓
When reading becomes more difficult, does the student persevere?	✓	

Example 3 is of a student who did not struggle at the decoding or fluency level. This student is strong in their sound/symbol identification, single word identification and non-phonetic word recognition. According to this student's rate and accuracy in the fluency passage, an appropriate starting point would be the beginning of Comprehension Plus!.

Note that there is no System Central for Comprehension Plus!, and if your student is assessed at this level or has worked through both Decoding Plus! and/or Fluency Plus!, start them at the first story in the section and work through each story and the activities.

Where do I go when I've finished my first story?

Once you have used the reading screener to determine where to start your student, your next step is to follow System Central and use the material as it appears in the book. Once a student has mastered one section, you may move onto the next section and practice the elements within the next story provided your student is familiar with the sound/symbol relationships and irregular words contained in the story. Follow the System Central as it is outlined in this Teacher's Manual and move progressively forward ensuring that your students are familiar with all of the elements contained within a story.

What if my student doesn't know all the concepts contained in a story?

The basic premise of *Just Read!* is that you are using material that reflects the overall capability of your student in order to build fluency. Fluency is built on many factors, but one of the most important is using material that is familiar. If your student is unfamiliar with an aspect of the phonics in a story, take the opportunity to teach it and then use the story to support overall reading practice with a particular sound/symbol relationship. *Just Read!* is not a tool for teaching phonics; rather it is a resource for strengthening sound/symbol relationships as they pertain to reading, and for helping students to master these relationships via reading. If you are unsure as to what elements a story contains, consult the System Central as it details all the phonics elements as well as the irregular words contained in each story.

System Central – Decoding Plus!

Please note: **Bolded items indicate the new concept or material that may be contained in each story.

Section /Story	Decoding Plus! – Breakdown	Sound/Symbol	Non-phonetic Words	Morphological Concept/Unit
Rapid Letter Naming	Rapid Letter Naming (RN-1 - RN-5)			
Rapid Sound Identification	Rapid Sound Identification (RS-1 - RS-5)	a, b, c, d, e, f, g, h, i, j, k, l, m, n, o, p, q, r, s, t, u, v, w, x, y, z		
Phoneme to Phoneme Blending	Phoneme to Phoneme Blending (PSWa-1 - PSWu-5)	a, b, c, d, e, f, g, h, i, j, k, l, m, n, o, p, q, r, s, t, u, v, w, x, y, z		
"Ned the Cop"	CVC (consonant-vowel-consonant words)	a, b, c, d, e, f, g, h, i, j, k, l, m, n, o, p, q, r, s, t, u, v, w, x, y, z	the, was, one, to too	
"Flip and Flop"	CVC (consonant-vowel-consonant words) + Blends	a, b, c, d, e, f, g, h, i, j, k, l, m, n, o, p, q, r, s, t, u, v, w, x, y, z **blends: pl, sp, pt, spl blends: fr, tr, pr, cr, str, scr, dr, nd, gl, gr blends: sw, tw, bl, br**	the, was, one, to too, are, of, put, have, give, two, they, from, are	
"Jan's Quilt"	CVC (consonant-vowel-consonant words), Blends + qu	a, b, c, d, e, f, g, h, i, j, k, l, m, n, o, p, q, r, s, t, u, v, w, x, y, z blends: pl, sp, pt, spl blends: fr, tr, pr, cr, str, scr, dr, nd, gl, gr blends: sw, tw, bl, br **qu**	the, was, one, to too, are, of, put, have, give, two, they, from, are	
"The Quiz". FP-1	CVC, Blends, qu, -**ck**	a, b, c, d, e, f, g, h, i, j, k, l, m, n, o, p, q, r, s, t, u, v, w, x, y, z blends: pl, sp, pt, spl blends: fr, tr, pr, cr, str, scr, dr, nd, gl, gr blends: sw, tw, bl, br, qu, **-ck**	the, was, one, to too, are, of, put, have, give, two, they, from, are, who, done	

Section	Fluency Plus! – Breakdown	Sound/Symbol	Non-phonetic Words	Morphological Concept/Unit
"The Lost Quilt"	CVC, Blends, qu, -ck, **zz/ff/ ss/ll Rule**	a, b, c, d, e, f, g, h, i, j, k, l, m, n, o, p, q, r, s, t, u, v, w, x, y, z blends: pl, sp, pt, spl blends: fr, tr, pr, cr, str, scr, dr, nd, gl, gr blends: sw, tw, bl, br, qu, -ck, **zz/ff/ss/ ll Rule**	the, was, one, to too, are, of, put, have, give, two, they, from, are, who, done, their, said, pull, some, come	
"Seth's Trip on a Ship"	CVC, Blends, qu, -ck, zz/ff/ ss/ll Rule, **th, sh, ch**	a, b, c, d, e, f, g, h, i, j, k, l, m, n, o, p, q, r, s, t, u, v, w, x, y, z blends: pl, sp, pt, spl blends: fr, tr, pr, cr, str, scr, dr, nd, gl, gr blends: sw, tw, bl, br, qu, -ck, zz/ff/ss/ll Rule, th, sh, ch	the, was, one, to too, are, of, put, have, give, two, they, from, are, who, done, their, said, pull, some, come.	
"At the Pond"	CVC, Blends, qu, -ck, zz/ff/ss/ ll Rule, th, sh, ch, **tch, dge, wh**	a, b, c, d, e, f, g, h, i, j, k, l, m, n, o, p, q, r, s, t, u, v, w, x, y, z blends: pl, sp, pt, spl blends: fr, tr, pr, cr, str, scr, dr, nd, gl, gr blends: sw, tw, bl, br, qu, -ck, zz/ff/ss/ll Rule, th, sh, ch, **tch, dge, wh**	the, was, one, to too, are, of, put, have, give, two, they, from, are, who, done, their, said, pull, some, come. once, sure, both, any, could	Suffix: -ing
"Stash the Cash"	CVC, Blends, qu, -ck, zz/ff/ss/ ll Rule, th, sh, ch, tch, dge, wh, ng, nk	a, b, c, d, e, f, g, h, i, j, k, l, m, n, o, p, q, r, s, t, u, v, w, x, y, z blends: pl, sp, pt, spl blends: fr, tr, pr, cr, str, scr, dr, nd, gl, gr blends: sw, tw, bl, br, qu, -ck, zz/ff/ ss/ll Rule, th, sh, ch, tch, dge, wh **th (voiced/unvoiced)**	the, was, one, to too, are, of, put, have, give, two, they, from, are, who, done, their, said, pull, some, come. once, sure, both, any, could, what, would	Suffixes: -ed, -ing
"The Back Lane"	CVC, Blends, qu, -ck, zz/ff/ss/ ll Rule, **th, sh, ch, -tch, -dge, wh, ng, nk, v-e**	a, b, c, d, e, f, g, h, i, j, k, l, m, n, o, p, q, r, s, t, u, v, w, x, y, z blends: pl, sp, pt, spl blends: fr, tr, pr, cr, str, scr, dr, nd, gl, gr blends: sw, tw, bl, br, qu, -ck, zz/ff/ss/ ll Rule, th, sh, ch, -tch, -dge, wh, ng, nk, v-e	the, was, one, to too, are, of, put, have, give, two, they, from, are, who, done, their, said, pull, some, come. once, sure, both, any, could, what, would, friend, because	Suffixes: -ed, -ing
"Mad Ants"	CVC, Blends, qu, -ck, zz/ff/ss/ ll Rule, th, sh, ch, -tch, -dge, wh, ng, nk, v-e, **s/z/**	a, b, c, d, e, f, g, h, i, j, k, l, m, n, o, p, q, r, s, t, u, v, w, x, y, z blends: pl, sp, pt, spl blends: fr, tr, pr, cr, str, scr, dr, nd, gl, gr blends: sw, tw, bl, br, qu, -ck, zz/ff/ss/ll Rule, th, sh, ch, **s/z/**	the, was, one, to too, are, of, put, have, give, two, they, from, are, who, done, their, said, pull, some, come. once, sure, both, any, could, what, would, friend, because, look	Suffixes: -ed, -ing

Section	Fluency Plus! – Breakdown	Sound/Symbol	Non-phonetic Words	Morphological Concept/Unit
"Class Tricks"	CVC, Blends, qu, -ck, zz/ff/ss/ll Rule, th, sh, ch, -tch, -dge, wh, ng, nk, v-e, s/z/, **Open Syllable, 1-1-1 Doubling Rule, all family**	a, b, c, d, e, f, g, h, i, j, k, l, m, n, o, p, q, r, s, t, u, v, w, x, y, z blends: pl, sp, pt, spl blends: fr, tr, pr, cr, str, scr, dr, nd, gl, gr blends: sw, tw, bl, br, qu, -ck, zz/ff/ss/ll Rule, th, sh, ch, s/z/, **Open Syllable, 1-1-1 Doubling Rule**	the, was, one, to too, are, of, put, have, give, two, they, from, are, who, done, their, said, pull, some, come. once, sure, both, any, could, what, would, friend, because, look	Suffixes: -ed, -ing
"Jay's Fishing Trip"	CVC, Blends, qu, -ck, zz/ff/ss/ll Rule, th, sh, ch, -tch, -dge, wh, ng, nk, v-e, s/z/, Open Syllable, 1-1-1 Doubling Rule, all family, **ay, ee, ai, aw, ea, Final 'e' Rule**	a, b, c, d, e, f, g, h, i, j, k, l, m, n, o, p, q, r, s, t, u, v, w, x, y, z blends: pl, sp, pt, spl blends: fr, tr, pr, cr, str, scr, dr, nd, gl, gr blends: sw, tw, bl, br, qu, -ck, zz/ff/ss/ll Rule, th, sh, ch, s/z/, Open Syllable, 1-1-1 Doubling Rule, **ay, ee, ai, aw, ea, Final 'e' Rule**	the, was, one, to too, are, of, put, have, give, two, they, from, are, who, done, their, said, pull, some, come. once, sure, both, any, could, what, would, friend, because, look, thought, answer	Prefixes: un- Suffixes: -ly, -y, -ed, -ing, -en
"Herb the Hermit Crab"	CVC, Blends, qu, -ck, zz/ff/ss/ll Rule, th, sh, ch, -tch, -dge, wh, ng, nk, v-e, s/z/, Open Syllable, 1-1-1 Doubling Rule, all family, ay, ee, ai, aw, ea, Final 'e' Rule, **er, or, ar**	a, b, c, d, e, f, g, h, i, j, k, l, m, n, o, p, q, r, s, t, u, v, w, x, y, z blends: pl, sp, pt, spl blends: fr, tr, pr, cr, str, scr, dr, nd, gl, gr blends: sw, tw, bl, br, qu, -ck, zz/ff/ss/ll Rule, th, sh, ch, s/z/, Open Syllable, 1-1-1 Doubling Rule, ay, ee, ai, aw, ea, Final 'e' Rule, **er, or, ar**	the, was, one, to too, are, of, put, have, give, two, they, from, are, who, done, their, said, pull, some, come. once, sure, both, any, could, what, would, friend, because, look, thought, answer, couldn't, move, tough, love, again	s: -ed, -ing, -ful, -ly, -
"Anne Bonny"	CVC, Blends, qu, -ck, zz/ff/ss/ll Rule, th, sh, ch, -tch, -dge, wh, ng, nk, v-e, s/z/, Open Syllable, 1-1-1 Doubling Rule, all family, ay, ee, ai, aw, ea, Final 'e' Rule, er, or, ar, **oo, ou, ow, oi, oy, oa**	a, b, c, d, e, f, g, h, i, j, k, l, m, n, o, p, q, r, s, t, u, v, w, x, y, z blends: pl, sp, pt, spl blends: fr, tr, pr, cr, str, scr, dr, nd, gl, gr blends: sw, tw, bl, br, qu, -ck, zz/ff/ss/ll Rule, th, sh, ch, s/z/, Open Syllable, 1-1-1 Doubling Rule, **oo, ou, ow, oi, oy, oa**	the, was, one, to too, are, of, put, have, give, two, they, from, are, who, done, their, said, pull, some, come. once, sure, both, any, could, what, would, friend, because, look, thought, answer, couldn't, move, tough, love, again, often, woman, father, four, should	Suffixes: -ed, -ing, -y, -en Prefix: re-

Section	Fluency Plus! – Breakdown	Sound/Symbol	Non-phonetic Words	Morphological Concept/Unit
"The RMS Titanic-A Canadian Connection"	CVC, Blends, qu, -ck, zz/ff/ss/ll Rule, th, sh, ch, -tch, -dge, wh, ng, nk, v-e, s/z/, Open Syllable, 1-1-1 Doubling Rule, all family, ay, ee, ai, aw, ea, Final 'e' Rule, er, or, ar, oo, ou, ow, oi, oy, oa, **ow, ur, ir, ew**	a, b, c, d, e, f, g, h, i, j, k, l, m, n, o, p, q, r, s, t, u, v, w, x, y, z blends: pl, sp, pt, spl blends: fr, tr, pr, cr, str, scr, dr, nd, gl, gr blends: sw, tw, bl, br, qu, -ck, zz/ff/ss/ll Rule, th, sh, ch, s/z/, Open Syllable, 1-1-1 Doubling Rule, oo, ou, ow, oi, oy, oa, **ow, ur, ir, ew**	who, any, put, why eye, buy/ guy, they have/give/live, from the, was, one, to too, are, of, put, have, give, two, they, from, are, who, done, their, said, pull, some, come. once, sure, both, any, could, what, would, friend, because, look, thought, answer, couldn't, move, tough, love, again, often, woman, father, four, should, does, ocean, only, people, bury	Suffixes: -ed, -ing, -y, -ment, -est, - able, -er, -ly, -ion, -ful, -al Prefixes: un-, dis-, im-, ex-, inter-
"The Origin of Castles"	CVC, Blends, qu, -ck, zz/ff/ss/ll Rule, th, sh, ch, -tch, -dge, wh, ng, nk, v-e, s /z/, Open Syllable, 1-1-1 Doubling Rule, ay, ee, ai, aw, ea, Final 'e' Rule, er, or, ar, **oo, ou, ow, oi, oy, oa, ow, ur, ir, ew, 'c'le, ph, igh, ct**	a, b, c, d, e, f, g, h, i, j, k, l, m, n, o, p, q, r, s, t, u, v, w, x, y, z blends: pl, sp, pt, spl blends: fr, tr, pr, cr, str, scr, dr, nd, gl, gr blends: sw, tw, bl, br, qu, -ck, zz/ff/ss/ll Rule, th, sh, ch, s/z/, Open Syllable, 1-1-1 Doubling Rule, ay, ee, ai, aw, ea, Final 'e' Rule, er, or, ar, **oo, ou, ow, oi, oy, oa, ow, ur, ir, ew, 'c'le, ph, igh, ct**	Cumulative Review	Cumulative Review
"Haichi- A Story of Love and Devotion"	Cumulative Review of all previously included elements.	Cumulative Review of all previously included elements.	Cumulative Review of all previously included non- phonetic words.	Cumulative Review of most common morphological units.
"The Lost City of Atlantis-Fact or Fiction?"	Cumulative Review of all previously included elements.	Cumulative Review of all previously included elements.	Cumulative Review of all previously included non- phonetic words.	

Reading Fluency Screener

Student information		
Student name:	Age:	Grade:
Testing date:	Assessor's name:	

Recording of scores			
Rapid letter naming	Number of letters identified:		Number correct:
Rapid sound identification	Number of sounds identified:		Number correct:
Non-phonetic reading	Score:	Notes:	
Mixed phonetic pseudo-word reading	Score:	Notes:	
Mixed real word phonetic reading	Score:	Notes:	
Rapid & automatic word recognition	Score:	Notes:	
Oral reading fluency scores			
Reading passage administered:	☐ Fluency 1 (Gr.K-2)	☐ Fluency 2 (Gr.2-4)	
	☐ Fluency 3 (Gr.4-6)	☐ Fluency 4 (Gr.6-8)	
Total words read:	**Number of errors:**	**WCPM[1]:**	**Accuracy rate[2]:**

1. In order to get your WCPM (word count per minute), take the total number of words read minus the total number of errors.
2. In order to get your accuracy reading, divide the WCPM by the total words read.

Behavioural observations related to reading:		
Fluency indicators	**Yes**	**No**
Does the student attend to punctuation?		
Does the student read with expression?		
Does the student read single words at a time?		
Does the student group words together as they read? (phrasing or chunking)		
Does the student track the text with their finger?		
Does the student have any word attack strategies? (ie: sound out familiar words)		
Does the student skip over or miss whole words?		
Does the student replace words with similar words?		
Does the student read at a rapid pace with no attention to accuracy?		
Does the student read at a slower and/or laboured pace with no attention to accuracy?		
Does the student make several errors that affect fluency? (ie: bus/dus)		
Other behavioural observations		
Does the student appear nervous while reading?		
Does the student appear to be reluctant to read?		
Does the student appear to be distracted while reading?		
When reading becomes more difficult, does the student persevere?		

Rapid Letter Naming

DIRECTIONS: This is a one-minute timed activity. Have your students identify as many letters as they can in one minute. **Mark errors with a slash. Self-corrections do not count as errors.** If a student omits or **skips** a letter, circle the letter and count it as an **error**. If there is a pause of 5 seconds or longer, give the student the letter name, **circle the letter** and count it as an **error**.

Q	w	x	k	M	t	i	H	j	s	10
F	b	a	d	G	R	e	u	O	y	20
V	c	B	Y	S	U	o	P	A	o	30
p	M	l	r	i	X	T	W	b	z	40
g	f	L	h	J	z	n	m	q	Y	50
q	r	f	l	g	V	i	K	I	H	60
e	i	V	d	t	p	o	X	C	z	70
y	G	U	r	D	q	y	H	J	u	80
Q	w	x	k	M	t	i	H	j	s	90
F	b	a	d	G	R	e	u	O	y	100

Total Named:	- # of errors:	= Letters Correct:

Assessor Notes & Observations:

Rapid Sound Identification

DIRECTIONS: This is a one-minute timed activity. Have your students identify as many sounds as they can in one minute. **Score 1 point for every correct sound and 0 points for sounds missed or skipped**. Tally the total number of correct sounds made in each of the following 4 columns and then tally the final score.

Score	Letter	Sound	Keyword
Vowel Sounds			
	a	/ă/	apple
		/ā/	cake
		/ə/	above
		/ŏ/	walrus
	e	/ĕ/	elephant
		/ē/	we
	i	/ĭ/	insect
		/ī/	bike
		/ē/	radio
	o	/ŏ/	octopus
		/ō/	go
	u	/ŭ/	up
		/yū/	cube
		/ü/	flute
		/ů/	bull
	y	/ī/	cry
		/ē/	candy
		/ĭ/	gym
Consonant Sounds			
	b	/b/	bat
	c	/k/	cookie
		/s/	city
	d	/d/	dog
	f	/f/	feather
	g	/g/	goat
		/j/	gentle

Column 1 Total ________

Score	Letter	Sound	Keyword
	h	/h/	horse
	j	/j/	jam
	k	/k/	kite
	l	/l/	leg
	m	/m/	mat
	n	/n/	nap
	p	/p/	pig
	qu	/kw/	quick
	r	/r/	rat
	s	/s/	snake
		/z/	nose
	t	/t/	table
	v	/v/	van
	w	/w/	wagon
	x	/x/	ax
	y	/y/	yo-yo
	z	/z/	zebra
Digraphs and Trigraphs			
	ck	/ck/	black
	sh	/sh/	ship
	ch	/ch/	chin
		/sh/	chef
		/k/	chord
	th	/th/	thumb
		/th/	bathe
	wh	/w/	when
		/hw/	wheat

Column 2 Total ________

Rapid Sound Identification (continued)

Score	Letter	Sound	Keyword
	dge	/j/	badge
	tch	/ch/	witch
	ph	/f/	phone
Vowel Digraphs/r-controlled vowel sounds			
	er	/ər/	her
	ar	/är/	car
		/ȯr/	war
		/ər/	regular
	or	/ȯr/	corn
		/ər/	humor
	ir	/ər/	bird
	ur	/ər/	church
	ai	/ā/	nail
	ay	/ā/	hay
	ee	/ē/	tree
	ey	/ē/	key
	oa	/ō/	goat
	oe	/ō/	toe
	ue	/ü/	glue
		/yū/	cue
	oi	/oi/	oil
	oy	/oi/	boy
	aw	/Ŏ/	saw
	au	/Ŏ/	faucet
	ow	/Ŏ/	snow
		/aů/	cow
	ou	/aů/	house

Score	Letter	Sound	Keyword
	ou	/ü/	soup
	oo	/ü/	spoon
		/ů/	look
	ea	/ē/	treat
		/ĕ/	bread
		/ā/	steak
	eu	/ů/	neuron
		/yū/	eulogy
	ew	/yū/	few
		/ü/	screw
	ui	/ü/	fruit
	ie	/ē/	field
		/ī/	pie
	ei	/ē/	ceiling
		/ā/	feign
	igh	/ī/	sigh
	eigh	/ā/	eight
Other Sound Patterns			
	ang	/aŋ/	hang
	ing	/iŋ/	sing
	ong	/oŋ/	song
	ung	/oŋ/	hung
	ank	/aŋk/	bank
	ink	/iŋk/	sink
	onk	/oŋk/	bonk
	unk	/uŋk/	sunk

Column 1 Total _________

Column 2 Total _________

Sound Identification Total Score: _________

Irregular Word Reading

DIRECTIONS: This is a one-minute timed activity. Have your students identify as many words as they can in one minute. **Mark errors with a slash. Self-corrections do not count as errors.** If a student omits or **skips** a word, circle the word and count it as an **error**. If there is a pause of 5 seconds or longer, give the student the word, **circle the word** and count it as an **error**.

I	of	to	do	the	you	was	are	one	two	10
too	who	any	many	put	why	they	have	give	live	20
from	what	were	your	you're	said	some	come	only	very	30
much	such	very	sure	here	there	where	does	goes	don't	40
won't	both	four	once	busy	gone	push	bush	look	took	50
pull	full	bull	done	none	pretty	their	they're	which	every	60
love	above	would	could	should	often	again	against	heart	friend	70
other	mother	another	brother	laugh	month	nothing	people	because	answer	80
front	among	build	built	usual	usually	blood	flood	sugar	listen	90
glisten	woman	women	orange	father	rough	tough	enough	eye	during	100

Non-Phonetic Word Reading Total Score: _____ /100

Assessor Notes & Observations:

Mixed Phonetic Pseudo-Word Reading

DIRECTIONS: This is a one-minute timed activity. Have your students identify as many pseudo-words as they can in one minute. **Mark errors with a slash. Self-corrections do not count as errors**. If a student omits or **skips** a word, circle the word and count it as an **error**. If there is a pause of 5 seconds or longer, give the student the word, **circle the word** and count it as an **error**. Mark the types of errors and the number of those errors on the error analysis box below.

yub	caz	lom	fiv	rej	kib	zat	mej	puz	gov	10
ped	baz	ruv	sig	hej	kem	lod	vup	yax	fet	20
glub	prex	skib	remp	pust	glusk	splast	strift	twand	sweft	30
frob	plend	hest	streg	swimp	blesp	jelt	bluft	prist	vont	40
strock	quip	blutch	vidge	bleck	squiv	pelch	shast	potch	mudge	50
vexrip	ponjub	rixvem	pidfoz	prixcot	slibfuz	swigrop	glutfib	bistpub	helbix	60
strame	plibe	vope	rube	gordilp	lang	ponkrid	tring	larpeet	benflab	70
brimeful	lorpoot	spute	hibely	monepill	swi	blu	plotube	trigabe	fring	80
bucle	vife	brafle	vockle	mickest	twickle	punkle	hestle	cratube	zemple	90
jougrip	blaypin	quaip	strewbix	strigh	yixtume	splinge	beurop	jieb	fleigh	100

Mixed Phonetic Pseudo-Word Reading Total Score : _____ /100

Error Analysis:

____ Single consonants ____ ng, nk, all ____ Closed Syllable ____ c'le Syllable

____ Short Vowels ____ qu ____ v-e Syllable ____ Vowel Team Syllable

____ Beginning Blends ____ v-e Error ____ Open Syllable

____ Final Blends ____ Digraphs ____ r-controlled Syllable

Assessor Notes & Observations:

Assessor Copy

Mixed Phonetic Real Word Reading

DIRECTIONS: This is a one-minute timed activity. Have your students identify as many pseudo-words as they can in one minute. **Mark errors with a slash. Self-corrections do not count as errors**. If a student omits or **skips** a word, circle the word and count it as an **error**. If there is a pause of 5 seconds or longer, give the student the word, **circle the word** and count it as an **error**. Mark the types of errors and the number of those errors on the error analysis box below.

fun	cab	fax	kiss	dug	pin	jazz	fed	cod	lap	10
bless	brisk	spot	end	lamp	bond	dusk	swept	mist	flat	20
limp	strand	swift	splint	jump	bask	cuff	twist	punt	blunt	30
quack	botch	wedge	shop	chimp	clock	thud	latch	squid	shed	40
bake	tube	pitch	lodge	pine	spoke	lathe	game	theme	kite	50
ring	trunk	strung	link	bonk	thank	stall	long	pink	bring	60
quake	try	horn	spite	first	he	purse	farm	probe	term	70
sky	sweet	house	crow	boot	treat	mail	tray	coil	toy	80
crackle	rifle	marble	whistle	table	simple	candle	maple	thimble	bottle	90
boiler	played	twinkle	jousting	happy	jumped	boastful	swiftly	bursting	hunted	100

Mixed Phonetic Real Word Reading Total Score : _____ /100

Error Analysis:

____ Single consonants ____ ng, nk, all ____ Closed Syllable ____ c'le Syllable

____ Short Vowels ____ qu ____ v-e Syllable ____ Vowel Team Syllable

____ Beginning Blends ____ v-e Error ____ Open Syllable

____ Final Blends ____ Digraphs ____ r-controlled Syllable

Assessor Notes & Observations:

High Frequency Instant Word Reading

DIRECTIONS: This is a one-minute timed activity. Have your students identify as many high frequency words as they can in one minute. **Mark errors with a slash. Self-corrections do not count as errors.** If a student omits or **skips** a word, circle the word and count it as an **error**. If there is a pause of 5 seconds or longer, give the student the word, **circle the word** and count it as an **error**.

the	of	and	a	to	in	is	you	it	he	10
was	for	on	are	as	with	his	they	I	at	20
be	this	have	from	or	one	had	by	word	but	30
not	what	were	we	when	your	can	said	there	use	40
an	each	which	she	do	how	their	if	will	up	50
other	about	out	many	then	them	so	some	her	would	60
make	like	him	into	time	has	look	two	more	write	70
go	see	number	no	way	could	people	my	than	first	80
been	call	who	oil	its	now	find	long	down	day	90
did	get	come	made	may	part	over	new	take	only	100

Mixed High-Frequency Word Reading Total Score : _____ /100

Assessor Notes & Observations:

* Sourced from "*The Reading Teacher's Book of Lists*" Pg.95 Fry's List of High Frequency Words

Rapid Letter Naming

Q	w	x	k	M	t	i	H	j	s
F	b	a	d	G	R	e	u	O	y
V	c	B	Y	S	U	o	P	A	o
p	M	l	r	i	X	T	W	b	z
g	f	L	h	J	z	n	m	q	Y
q	r	f	l	g	V	i	K	I	H
e	i	V	d	t	p	o	X	C	z
y	G	U	r	D	q	y	H	J	u
Q	w	x	k	M	t	i	H	j	s
F	b	a	d	G	R	e	u	O	y

Rapid Sound Identification

a	e	i	o	u	y	b	c	d	f
g	h	j	k	l	m	n	p	qu	r
s	t	v	w	x	z	ck	sh	ch	th
wh	tch	dge	ph	er	ar	or	ir	ur	aw
ai	ay	ee	ey	oa	oe	ue	oi	oy	aw
au	ow	ou	oo	ee	eu	ew	ui	ie	ei
igh	eigh	ang	ing	ong	ung	ank	ink	onk	unk

Student Copy

Irregular Word Reading

I	of	to	do	the	you	was	are	one	two
too	who	any	many	put	why	they	have	give	live
from	what	were	your	you're	said	some	come	only	very
much	such	very	sure	here	there	where	does	goes	don't
won't	both	four	once	busy	gone	push	bush	look	took
pull	full	bull	done	none	pretty	their	they're	which	every
love	above	would	could	should	often	again	against	heart	friend
other	mother	another	brother	laugh	month	nothing	people	because	answer
front	among	build	built	usual	usually	blood	flood	sugar	listen
glisten	woman	women	orange	father	rough	tough	enough	eye	during

Mixed Phonetic Pseudo-Word Reading

yub	caz	lom	fiv	rej	kib	zat	mej	puz	gov
ped	baz	ruv	sig	hej	kem	lod	vup	yax	fet
glub	prex	skib	remp	pust	glusk	splast	strift	twand	sweft
frob	plend	hest	streg	swimp	blesp	jelt	bluft	prist	vont
strock	quip	blutch	vidge	bleck	squiv	pelch	shast	potch	mudge
vexrip	ponjub	rixvem	pidfoz	prixcot	slibfuz	swigrop	glutfib	bistpub	helbix
strame	plibe	vope	rube	gordilp	lang	ponkrid	tring	larpeet	benflab
brimeful	lorpoot	spute	hibely	monepill	swi	blu	plotube	trigabe	fring
bucle	vife	brafle	vockle	mickest	twickle	punkle	hestle	cratube	zemple
jougrip	blaypin	quaip	strewbix	strigh	yixtume	splinge	beurop	jieb	fleigh

Mixed Phonetic Real Word Reading

fun	cab	fax	kiss	dug	pin	jazz	fed	cod	lap
bless	brisk	spot	end	lamp	bond	dusk	swept	mist	flat
limp	strand	swift	splint	jump	bask	cuff	twist	punt	blunt
quack	botch	wedge	shop	chimp	clock	thud	latch	squid	shed
bake	tube	pitch	lodge	pine	spoke	lathe	game	theme	kite
ring	trunk	strung	link	bonk	thank	stall	long	pink	bring
quake	try	horn	spite	first	he	purse	farm	probe	term
sky	sweet	house	crow	boot	treat	mail	tray	coil	toy
crackle	rifle	marble	whistle	table	simple	candle	maple	thimble	bottle
boiler	played	twinkle	jousting	happy	jumped	boastful	swiftly	bursting	hunted

High Frequency Instant Word Reading

the	of	and	a	to	in	is	you	it	he
was	for	on	are	as	with	his	they	I	at
be	this	have	from	or	one	had	by	word	but
not	what	were	we	when	your	can	said	there	use
an	each	which	she	do	how	their	if	will	up
other	about	out	many	then	them	so	some	her	would
make	like	him	into	time	has	look	two	more	write
go	see	number	no	way	could	people	my	than	first
been	call	who	oil	its	now	find	long	down	day
did	get	come	made	may	part	over	new	take	only

Screening Passage K-2 "Spot the Lost Dog"

DIRECTIONS: This is a one-minute timed activity. Have your students read the passage below for one-minute. **Mark errors with a slash. Self-corrections do not count as errors**. If a student omits or **skips** a word, put a line through the word and count it as an **error**. If there is a pause of 5 seconds or longer, give the student the word, **put a line through the word** and count it as an **error**. Mark specific errors in the error analysis box below.

Spot the dog was lost. Spot ran to his back deck but his mom and dad 16
were lost too. He did sniff the deck and did fret but at last he did hunt 33
for some prints. He set off on a quest to help find his mom and dad. 49
Quick and fast, Spot did run up the hill of the back to a flat spot. He did 67
tramp in the muck. He was hot and stiff but did not quit. At last, he met 84
his bud Quack who said he sent Spot's mom and dad back to his deck. 99
Spot did rant and yell, but ran back quick and fast. On the back deck, 114
Spot did smell and sniff his mom and dad. He felt his bum wag and he 130
did hum. At last, his mom and dad did stand next to him on the deck. 146
They were glad at last to see Spot. 154

Total Words Read:	- # of errors:	= Words Correct:

Enter the number of errors for each concept:

____ ck ____ short vowels ____ non-phonetic words ____ qu

____ initial blends ____ final blends ____ other

Check all the boxes that apply to your student:

☐ student has no word attack strategies

☐ student sounds out every letter in a word

☐ student can read whole words automatically

☐ student disregards punctuation

☐ student reads with very little expression

☐ student has some phrasing and chunking

If a student makes 5 or more errors on any one concept listed above in the box, start working with them at the Decoding Plus Story 1.

Spot the Lost Dog

Spot the dog was lost. Spot ran to his back deck but his mom and dad were lost too. He did sniff the deck and did fret but at last he did hunt for some prints. He set off on a quest to help find his mom and dad. Quick and fast, Spot did run up the hill of the back to a flat spot. He did tramp in the muck. He was hot and stiff but did not quit. At last, he met his bud Quack who said he sent Spot's mom and dad back to his deck. Spot did rant and yell, but ran back quick and fast. On the back deck, Spot did smell and sniff his mom and dad. He felt his bum wag and he did hum. At last, his mom and dad did stand next to him on the deck. They were glad at last to see Spot.

Screening Passage 2-4 "A Fish Wish"

DIRECTIONS: This is a one-minute timed activity. Have your students read the passage below for one-minute. **Mark errors with a slash. Self-corrections do not count as errors**. If a student omits or **skips** a word, put a line through the word and count it as an **error**. If there is a pause of 5 seconds or longer, give the student the word, **put a line through the word** and count it as an **error**. Mark specific errors in the error analysis box below.

Slash is a fish with just one wish. He would like to swim in a big pond. In 18
his very small tank, Slash swims all day long. He is glum and sad but will 34
not give up his wish to swim in a big pond. With a big push, Slash and his 52
bud Chad the crab bump and fall when they jump up from the tank. 67
The tank is too tall to jump from, and they fall back into the small tank. 83
One day, Slash plans a big jump. He tells all of his pals and they think it is 101
the best plan. Chad the crab sits on the small rock and all of the other 117
pals stack on top of him. One by one, they sit still and do not fuss until 134
Slash can get on top.The small tank shifts and spills and all of them think 151
it will tip and spill. They think they must stop but Slash will not. At last, 166
Slash catches himself and sits on the very top of the bunch. He can just 181
tap the top of the dish when he shifts and lands on all of his pals. They 198
jump off the rock and end up in a big clump of sand and dust. They are 215
all very sad that the plan had to stop and that Slash did not get his wish. 231
They all said that one day Slash's wish must come to be. 243

Total Words Read:	- # of errors:	= Words Correct:

Enter the number of errors for each concept:

____ short vowels ____ consonant digraphs ____ non-phonetic words

____ initial blends ____ final blends ____ ng/nk ____ other

Check all the boxes that apply to your student:

☐ student has no word attack strategies

☐ student sounds out every letter in a word

☐ student can read whole words automatically

☐ student disregards punctuation

☐ student reads with very little expression

☐ student has some phrasing and chunking

If a student makes 5 or more errors on any one concept listed above in the box, start at story ______ in Fluency Plus!

A Fish Wish

Slash is a fish with just one wish. He would like to swim in a big pond. In his very small tank, Slash swims all day long. He is glum and sad but will not give up his wish to swim in a big pond. With a big push, Slash and his bud Chad the crab bump and fall when they jump up from the tank. The tank is too tall to jump from, and they fall back into the small tank. One day, Slash plans a big jump. He tells all of his pals and they think it is the best plan. Chad the crab sits on the small rock and all of the other pals stack on top of him. One by one, they sit still and do not fuss until Slash can get on top. The small tank shifts and spills and all of them think it will tip and spill. They think they must stop but Slash will not. At last, Slash catches himself and sits on the very top of the bunch. He can just tap the top of the dish when he shifts and lands on all of his pals. They jump off the rock and end up in a big clump of sand and dust. They are all very sad that the plan had to stop and that Slash did not get his wish. They all said that one day Slash's wish must come to be.

Screening Passage 4-6 "The Lone Hawk"

DIRECTIONS: This is a one-minute timed activity. Have your students read the passage below for one-minute. **Mark errors with a slash. Self-corrections do not count as errors**. If a student omits or **skips** a word, put a line through the word and count it as an **error**. If there is a pause of 5 seconds or longer, give the student the word, **put a line through the word** and count it as an **error**. Mark specific errors in the error analysis box below.

Fleet was a man who prayed all day long in an extremely quiet hallway. 14
When he would pray, he would often get a pain in his neck as it was 30
tilted for too long. One day, while Fleet was praying, he saw an amazing 44
thing in front of his eyes. He realized that a hawk had gained its way into 60
the hallway and landed on top of an old green box. Fleet had not ever 76
seen the hawk, but it was pretty unusual to see birds inside buildings. Fleet 89
sat still and waited for the hawk to fly away. The hawk remained quite 105
still and watched Fleet. Fleet made an attempt to remain in prayer but 117
he became a bit confused and couldn't regain his focus. The hawk sat 129
completely still and watched Fleet as he prayed. It just waited and 141
waited. At last, Fleet became stiff from so much praying and he got up 155
to leave. The hawk sensed his moving and shifting and lifted up its wings 169
to fly away. From the back of the hallway, Fleet watched the hawk fly to 184
the front lawn. It landed in a tree close by and gazed at the distant sea. 200

Total Words Read:	- # of errors:	= Words Correct:

Enter the number of errors for each concept:

____ short vowels ____ consonant digraphs ____ vowel digraphs

____ open syllables ____ non-phonetic words ____ initial blends

____ final blends ____ ng/nk ____ other

Check all the boxes that apply to your student:

☐ student has no word attack strategies

☐ student sounds out every letter in a word

☐ student can read whole words automatically

☐ student disregards punctuation

☐ student reads with very little expression

☐ student has some phrasing and chunking

If a student makes 5 or more errors on any one concept listed above in the box, start at story 1, The Quiz, in Fluency Plus!

The Lone Hawk

Fleet was a man who prayed all day long in an extremely quiet hallway. When he would pray, he would often get a pain in his neck as it was tilted for too long. One day, while Fleet was praying, he saw an amazing thing in front of his eyes. He realized that a hawk had gained its way into the hallway and landed on top of an old green box. Fleet had not ever seen the hawk, but it was pretty unusual to see birds inside buildings. Fleet sat still and waited for the hawk to fly away. The hawk remained quite still and watched Fleet. Fleet made an attempt to remain in prayer but he became a bit confused and couldn't regain his focus. The hawk sat completely still and watched Fleet as he prayed. It just waited and waited. At last, Fleet became stiff from so much praying and he got up to leave. The hawk sensed his moving and shifting and lifted up its wings to fly away. From the back of the hallway, Fleet watched the hawk fly to the front lawn. It landed in a tree close by and gazed at the distant sea.

Screening Passage 6-8 "The Class Party"

DIRECTIONS: This is a one-minute timed activity. Have your students read the passage below for one-minute. **Mark errors with a slash. Self-corrections do not count as errors**. If a student omits or **skips** a word, put a line through the word and count it as an **error**. If there is a pause of 5 seconds or longer, give the student the word, **put a line through the word** and count it as an **error**. Mark specific errors in the error analysis box below.

It was the last day of class and everyone was so excited. They had worked so 16
hard the entire year and they would now get their class party. Each student 30
was allowed to invite a special guest and bring them to school for the whole 45
day and have them be a part of their class. Cassy was especially excited 59
because she was going to bring her cousin Beth, who was also her best friend. 74
The night before the party, Cassy couldn't sleep because she was so excited. 87
What was the party going to be like? Who would be there? Would her other 102
classmates bring their best friends too? The morning of the party, Cassy's 114
mother made chocolate cupcakes for everyone. On the top of each 125
cupcake was a glow in the dark letter. The letter was for their name. Cassy 140
wanted to walk to school with her cousin Beth, but her mother insisted on 154
driving them because of the heavy load of cupcakes. When they got out of 168
the car and said their goodbyes, both Cassy and Beth saw so many students in 183
line. It was true! Everyone had brought their best friends and the class line was 198
so long and loud. Beth and Cassy stood at the back of the line and tightly 214
held on to their cupcakes. Everyone else had enormous bags of chips and 227
party stuff and everyone was really excited. When the bell rang, they all filed 241
into the classroom and their teacher was standing at the front of the room. 255
She had set up a dance square in the corner of the room and had set up a 273
huge party table in the other corner. The kids arranged all of their food on the 289
table. They were hungry and excited all at the same time. The teacher put on 304
their favourite music and announced that the party had started. It was the 316
best school day ever! 320

Total Words Read:	- # of errors:	= Words Correct:

Enter the number of errors for each concept:

____ short vowels ____ consonant digraphs ____ vowel digraphs

____ closed syllables ____ r-controlled syllables ____ open syllables

____ non-phonetic words ____ initial blends ____ final blends

____ ng/nk ____ other

Check all the boxes that apply to your student:

☐ student has no word attack strategies

☐ student sounds out every letter in a word

☐ student can read whole words automatically

☐ student disregards punctuation

☐ student reads with very little expression

☐ student has some phrasing and chunking

If a student makes 5 or more errors on any one concept listed above in the box, start at story ______ in Fluency Plus!

The Class Party

It was the last day of class and everyone was so excited. They had worked so hard the entire year and they would now get their class party. Each student was allowed to invite a special guest and bring them to school for the whole day and have them be a part of their class. Cassy was especially excited because she was going to bring her cousin Beth, who was also her best friend. The night before the party, Cassy couldn't sleep because she was so excited. What was the party going to be like? Who would be there? Would her other classmates bring their best friends too? The morning of the party, Cassy's mother made chocolate cupcakes for everyone. On the top of each cupcake was a glow in the dark letter. The letter was for their name. Cassy wanted to walk to school with her cousin Beth, but her mother insisted on driving them because of the heavy load of cupcakes. When they got out of the car and said their goodbyes, both Cassy and Beth saw so many students in line. It was true! Everyone had brought their best friends and the class line was so long and loud. Beth and Cassy stood at the back of the line and tightly held on to their cupcakes. Everyone else had enormous bags of chips and party stuff and everyone was really excited. When the bell rang, they all filed into the classroom and their teacher was standing at the front of the room. She had set up a dance square in the corner of the room and had set up a huge party table in the other corner. The kids arranged all of their food on the table. They were hungry and excited all at the same time. The teacher put on their favourite music and announced that the party had started. It was the best school day ever!

Decoding Plus!

Where to Begin

Assessor Instructions

If you have completed the Reading Fluency Screener and have determined that your student is at the Decoding Plus! level, you can start here. You will find assessor copies of all the Decoding Plus! sections here; these are for you to copy as needed and refer to when your student is performing the drills. You can find the corresponding student copies in the Student Workbook. All pages and sections are labeled and named.

There are five versions of each drill in Decoding Plus! Once you have determined where your student should begin working (e.g.: rapid letter naming, rapid sound detection), find the first page of that section and begin your student drills. Ideally, one drill is performed for each lesson or day that you are working with your student. All drills are one-minute timed drills. You should have your student make five attempts at each version. The student tracks his or her progress on the corresponding tracking sheet, and the assessor monitors and tracks progress on their assessor copy and keeps this in the student's file.

Move through the Decoding Plus! drills until your student consistently achieves 98% or higher on their Mixed Phonetic Reading drills (the final drills of the Decoding Plus!) section. Once your student reaches this milestone, you are ready to progress onto the first three stories in the Decoding Plus! section. See page 89 for instructions on how to progress through the passages.

Rapid Letter Naming

Teacher Copy

Student Name: ____________________

RN-1

b	F	a	G	d	e	R	y	u	O	10
w	Q	x	M	k	i	t	s	H	j	20
c	V	B	S	Y	o	U	o	P	A	30
f	g	L	J	h	n	z	Y	m	q	40
M	p	l	i	r	T	X	z	W	b	50
r	q	f	g	l	i	V	H	K	l	60
G	y	U	D	r	y	q	u	H	J	70
i	e	V	t	d	o	p	z	X	C	80
b	F	a	G	d	e	R	y	u	O	90
w	Q	x	M	k	i	t	s	H	j	100

1 Total blended:
- # of errors:
= Correct blends:
2 Total blended:
- # of errors:
= Correct blends:
3 Total blended:
- # of errors:
= Correct blends:
4 Total blended:
- # of errors:
= Correct blends:
5 Total blended:
- # of errors:
= Correct blends:

RN-2

V	b	n	s	D	f	j	l	K	z	10
B	y	W	r	p	t	i	o	X	z	20
t	q	e	R	d	h	P	a	F	V	30
z	w	U	m	C	s	e	r	O	n	40
n	i	a	u	B	f	y	z	M	V	50
t	q	e	R	d	h	P	a	F	V	60
V	b	n	s	D	f	j	l	K	z	70
A	y	x	T	p	Q	g	H	k	L	80
z	w	U	m	C	s	e	r	O	n	90
t	q	e	R	d	h	P	a	F	V	100

1 Total blended:
- # of errors:
= Correct blends:
2 Total blended:
- # of errors:
= Correct blends:
3 Total blended:
- # of errors:
= Correct blends:
4 Total blended:
- # of errors:
= Correct blends:
5 Total blended:
- # of errors:
= Correct blends:

RN-3

V	b	n	s	D	f	j	l	K	z	10
B	y	W	r	p	t	i	o	X	z	20
t	q	e	R	d	h	P	a	F	V	30
z	w	U	m	C	s	e	r	O	n	40
n	i	a	u	B	f	y	z	M	V	50
t	q	e	R	d	h	P	a	F	V	60
V	b	n	s	D	f	j	l	K	z	70
A	y	x	T	p	Q	g	H	k	L	80
z	w	U	m	C	s	e	r	O	n	90
t	q	e	R	d	h	P	a	F	V	100

1 Total blended:
- # of errors:
= Correct blends:
2 Total blended:
- # of errors:
= Correct blends:
3 Total blended:
- # of errors:
= Correct blends:
4 Total blended:
- # of errors:
= Correct blends:
5 Total blended:
- # of errors:
= Correct blends:

RN-4

R	e	a	d	h	q	V	P	F	t	10
r	W	o	p	t	y	z	i	X	B	20
m	U	r	C	s	w	n	e	O	z	30
s	n	l	D	f	b	z	j	K	V	40
R	e	a	d	h	q	V	P	F	t	50
T	x	H	p	Q	y	L	g	k	A	60
s	n	l	D	f	b	z	j	K	V	70
R	e	a	d	h	q	V	P	F	t	80
m	U	r	C	s	w	n	e	O	z	90
R	e	a	d	h	q	V	P	F	t	100

1 Total blended:
- # of errors:
= Correct blends:
2 Total blended:
- # of errors:
= Correct blends:
3 Total blended:
- # of errors:
= Correct blends:
4 Total blended:
- # of errors:
= Correct blends:
5 Total blended:
- # of errors:
= Correct blends:

RN-5

W	r	p	o	z	t	i	y	B	X	10
U	m	C	r	n	s	e	w	z	O	20
e	R	d	a	V	h	P	q	t	F	30
x	T	p	H	L	Q	g	y	A	k	40
n	s	D	l	z	f	j	b	V	K	50
U	m	C	r	n	s	e	w	z	O	60
e	R	d	a	V	h	P	q	t	F	70
U	m	C	r	n	s	e	w	z	O	80
n	s	D	l	z	f	j	b	V	K	90

1 Total blended:
- # of errors:
= Correct blends:
2 Total blended:
- # of errors:
= Correct blends:
3 Total blended:
- # of errors:
= Correct blends:
4 Total blended:
- # of errors:
= Correct blends:
5 Total blended:
- # of errors:
= Correct blends:

Rapid Sound Identification

Teacher Copy

Student Name: ______________________________

RS-1

m	U	r	n	C	e	w	s	O	z	10
r	W	o	z	p	i	y	t	X	B	20
T	x	H	L	p	g	y	W	k	A	30
R	e	a	V	d	P	i	h	F	t	40
m	U	r	n	C	e	w	s	O	z	50
s	n	l	z	D	j	b	f	K	V	60
T	e	a	V	d	P	k	h	F	t	70
m	U	r	n	C	e	w	s	O	z	80
R	e	a	V	d	P	o	h	F	t	90
s	n	l	z	D	j	b	f	K	V	100

1 Total blended:
- # of errors:
= Correct blends:

2 Total blended:
- # of errors:
= Correct blends:

3 Total blended:
- # of errors:
= Correct blends:

4 Total blended:
- # of errors:
= Correct blends:

5 Total blended:
- # of errors:
= Correct blends:

RS-2

W	r	z	o	i	p	t	y	B	X	10
U	m	n	r	e	C	s	w	z	O	20
e	R	V	a	P	d	h	q	t	F	30
x	T	L	H	g	p	W	y	A	k	40
n	s	z	l	j	D	f	b	V	K	50
U	m	n	r	e	C	s	w	z	O	60
e	R	V	a	P	d	h	y	t	F	70
n	s	z	l	j	D	f	b	V	K	80
e	T	V	a	P	d	h	u	t	F	90
n	s	z	l	j	D	f	b	V	K	100

1 Total blended:
- # of errors:
= Correct blends:

2 Total blended:
- # of errors:
= Correct blends:

3 Total blended:
- # of errors:
= Correct blends:

4 Total blended:
- # of errors:
= Correct blends:

5 Total blended:
- # of errors:
= Correct blends:

RS-3

X	o	z	p	i	y	t	B	r	W	10
O	r	n	C	e	w	s	z	m	U	20
F	a	V	d	P	q	h	t	R	e	30
j	H	L	p	g	y	K	A	T	x	40
K	l	z	D	j	b	f	V	s	n	50
O	r	n	C	e	w	s	z	m	U	60
K	l	z	D	j	b	f	V	s	n	70
F	a	V	d	P	i	h	t	R	e	80
K	l	z	D	j	b	f	V	s	n	90
F	a	V	d	P	d	h	t	T	e	100

1 Total blended:
- # of errors:
= Correct blends:
2 Total blended:
- # of errors:
= Correct blends:
3 Total blended:
- # of errors:
= Correct blends:
4 Total blended:
- # of errors:
= Correct blends:
5 Total blended:
- # of errors:
= Correct blends:

RS-4

O	n	r	e	C	w	z	m	s	U	10
X	z	o	i	p	y	B	r	t	W	20
j	L	H	g	p	y	A	T	J	x	30
F	V	a	P	d	i	t	R	h	e	40
K	z	l	j	D	b	V	s	f	n	50
O	n	r	e	C	w	z	m	s	U	60
F	V	a	P	d	j	t	R	h	e	70
K	z	l	j	D	b	V	s	f	n	80
F	V	a	P	d	y	t	T	h	e	90
O	n	r	e	C	w	z	m	s	U	100

1 Total blended:
- # of errors:
= Correct blends:
2 Total blended:
- # of errors:
= Correct blends:
3 Total blended:
- # of errors:
= Correct blends:
4 Total blended:
- # of errors:
= Correct blends:
5 Total blended:
- # of errors:
= Correct blends:

RS-5

y	X	o	i	z	p	B	t	r	W	10
w	O	r	e	n	C	z	s	m	U	20
y	j	H	g	L	p	A	K	T	x	30
w	F	a	P	V	d	t	h	R	e	40
b	K	l	j	z	D	V	f	s	n	50
p	F	a	P	V	d	t	h	T	e	60
w	o	r	e	n	C	z	s	m	U	70
t	F	a	P	V	d	t	h	R	e	80
b	K	l	j	z	D	V	f	s	n	90
w	O	r	e	n	C	z	s	m	U	100

1 Total blended:
- # of errors:
= Correct blends:
2 Total blended:
- # of errors:
= Correct blends:
3 Total blended:
- # of errors:
= Correct blends:
4 Total blended:
- # of errors:
= Correct blends:
5 Total blended:
- # of errors:
= Correct blends:

Phoneme to Phoneme Blending (ă)

Teacher Copy

Student Name: ______________________________

PBa-1

ap	ab	ak	af	ag	ak	ax	az	an	ad	10
am	an	ab	av	ax	az	al	ak	ag	af	20
ap	at	az	ax	ac	av	an	ap	ag	ak	30
aj	af	ap	ad	ac	av	ax	ac	aj	al	40
ap	ab	ak	af	ag	ak	ax	az	an	ad	50
aj	af	ap	ad	ac	av	ax	ac	aj	al	60
am	an	ab	av	ax	az	al	ak	ag	af	70
aj	af	ap	ad	ac	av	ax	ac	aj	al	80
ap	at	az	ax	ac	av	an	ap	ag	ak	90
ag	aj	ak	ap	ac	av	az	an	al	am	100

1 Total blended:
- # of errors:
= Correct blends:
2 Total blended:
- # of errors:
= Correct blends:
3 Total blended:
- # of errors:
= Correct blends:
4 Total blended:
- # of errors:
= Correct blends:
5 Total blended:
- # of errors:
= Correct blends:

PBa-2

ap	at	az	ax	ac	av	an	ap	ag	ak	10
ap	ab	ak	af	ag	ak	ax	az	an	ad	20
aj	af	ap	ad	ac	av	ax	ac	aj	al	30
am	an	ab	av	ax	az	al	ak	ag	af	40
ap	at	az	ax	ac	av	an	ap	ag	ak	50
am	an	ab	av	ax	az	al	ak	ag	af	60
aj	af	ap	ad	ac	av	ax	ac	aj	al	70
aj	af	ap	ad	ac	av	ax	ac	aj	al	80
ag	aj	ak	ap	ac	av	az	an	al	am	90
ap	ab	ak	af	ag	ak	ax	az	an	ad	100

1 Total blended:
- # of errors:
= Correct blends:
2 Total blended:
- # of errors:
= Correct blends:
3 Total blended:
- # of errors:
= Correct blends:
4 Total blended:
- # of errors:
= Correct blends:
5 Total blended:
- # of errors:
= Correct blends:

PBa-3

at	ax	ap	av	az	ac	an	ag	ap	ak	10
ab	af	ap	ak	ak	ag	ax	an	az	ad	20
an	av	am	az	ab	ax	al	ag	ak	af	30
af	ad	aj	av	ap	ac	ax	aj	ac	al	40
at	ax	ap	av	az	ac	an	ag	ap	ak	50
af	ad	aj	av	ap	ac	ax	aj	ac	al	60
an	av	am	az	ab	ax	al	ag	ak	af	70
af	ad	aj	av	ap	ac	ax	aj	ac	al	80
ab	af	ap	ak	ak	ag	ax	an	az	ad	90
aj	ap	ag	av	ak	ac	az	al	an	am	100

1 Total blended:
- # of errors:
= Correct blends:
2 Total blended:
- # of errors:
= Correct blends:
3 Total blended:
- # of errors:
= Correct blends:
4 Total blended:
- # of errors:
= Correct blends:
5 Total blended:
- # of errors:
= Correct blends:

PBa-4

am	an	ab	ax	al	av	af	ak	ag	az	10
ap	ab	ak	ag	ax	af	ad	az	an	ak	20
ap	at	az	ac	an	ax	ak	ap	ag	av	30
ap	ab	ak	ag	ax	af	ad	az	an	ak	40
aj	af	ap	ac	ax	ad	al	ac	aj	av	50
am	an	ab	ax	al	av	af	ak	ag	az	60
aj	af	ap	ac	ax	ad	al	ac	aj	av	70
ap	at	az	ac	an	ax	ak	ap	ag	av	80
aj	af	ap	ac	ax	ad	al	ac	aj	av	90
ag	aj	ak	ac	az	ap	am	an	al	av	100

1 Total blended:
- # of errors:
= Correct blends:
2 Total blended:
- # of errors:
= Correct blends:
3 Total blended:
- # of errors:
= Correct blends:
4 Total blended:
- # of errors:
= Correct blends:
5 Total blended:
- # of errors:
= Correct blends:

PBa-5

an	am	av	ab	al	ag	af	az	ak	ax	10
at	ap	ax	az	an	ag	ak	av	ap	ac	20
ab	ap	af	ak	ax	an	ad	ak	az	ag	30
aj	ag	ap	ak	az	al	am	av	an	ac	40
af	aj	ad	ap	ax	aj	al	av	ac	ac	50
an	am	av	ab	al	ag	af	az	ak	ax	60
af	aj	ad	ap	ax	aj	al	av	ac	ac	70
ab	ap	af	ak	ax	an	ad	ak	az	ag	80
at	ap	ax	az	an	ag	ak	av	ap	ac	90
af	aj	ad	ap	ax	aj	al	av	ac	ac	100

1 Total blended:
- # of errors:
= Correct blends:
2 Total blended:
- # of errors:
= Correct blends:
3 Total blended:
- # of errors:
= Correct blends:
4 Total blended:
- # of errors:
= Correct blends:
5 Total blended:
- # of errors:
= Correct blends:

Phoneme to Phoneme Blending (ĕ)

Teacher Copy

Student Name: ______________________________

PBe-1

et	ep	ed	ef	eg	ej	ek	el	ez	ex	10	1 Total blended: - # of errors:
em	en	eb	ec	ex	ek	el	ez	ej	eg	20	= Correct blends:
es	ep	et	ed	eb	ec	el	ez	ex	eg	30	2 Total blended: - # of errors:
ev	en	ez	et	em	ek	ef	ej	el	ep	40	= Correct blends:
em	en	eb	ec	ex	ek	el	ez	ej	eg	50	3 Total blended: - # of errors:
et	ep	ed	ef	eg	ej	ek	el	ez	ex	60	= Correct blends:
es	ep	et	ed	eb	ec	el	ez	ex	eg	70	4 Total blended: - # of errors:
em	en	eb	ec	ex	ek	el	ez	ej	eg	80	= Correct blends:
ev	en	ez	et	em	ek	ef	ej	el	ep	90	5 Total blended: - # of errors:
et	ep	ed	ef	eg	ej	ek	el	ez	ex	100	= Correct blends:

PBe-2

et	ed	ex	ep	ej	ef	el	ek	ez	eg	10	1 Total blended: - # of errors:
em	eb	eg	en	ek	ec	ez	el	ej	ex	20	= Correct blends:
ev	ez	ep	en	ek	et	ej	ef	el	em	30	2 Total blended: - # of errors:
es	et	eg	ep	ec	ed	ez	el	ex	eb	40	= Correct blends:
em	eb	eg	en	ek	ec	ez	el	ej	ex	50	3 Total blended: - # of errors:
et	ed	ex	ep	ej	ef	el	ek	ez	eg	60	= Correct blends:
es	et	eg	ep	ec	ed	ez	el	ex	eb	70	4 Total blended: - # of errors:
et	ed	ex	ep	ej	ef	el	ek	ez	eg	80	= Correct blends:
ev	ez	ep	en	ek	et	ej	ef	el	em	90	5 Total blended: - # of errors:
em	eb	eg	en	ek	ec	ez	el	ej	ex	100	= Correct blends:

PBe-3

eb	em	eg	ek	en	ec	el	ej	ez	ex	10
et	es	eg	ec	ep	ed	el	ex	ez	eb	20
eb	em	eg	ek	en	ec	el	ej	ez	ex	30
ez	ev	ep	ek	en	et	ef	el	ej	em	40
ed	et	ex	ej	ep	ef	ek	ez	el	eg	50
et	es	eg	ec	ep	ed	el	ex	ez	eb	60
ed	et	ex	ej	ep	ef	ek	ez	el	eg	70
eb	em	eg	ek	en	ec	el	ej	ez	ex	80
ez	ev	ep	ek	en	et	ef	el	ej	em	90
ed	et	ex	ej	ep	ef	ek	ez	el	eg	100

1 Total blended:
- # of errors:
= Correct blends:
2 Total blended:
- # of errors:
= Correct blends:
3 Total blended:
- # of errors:
= Correct blends:
4 Total blended:
- # of errors:
= Correct blends:
5 Total blended:
- # of errors:
= Correct blends:

PBe-4

em	eg	ek	el	ec	en	ej	ez	eb	ex	10
ev	ep	ek	ef	et	en	el	ej	ez	em	20
em	eg	ek	el	ec	en	ej	ez	eb	ex	30
es	eg	ec	el	ed	ep	ex	ez	et	eb	40
et	ex	ej	ek	ef	ep	ez	el	ed	eg	50
es	eg	ec	el	ed	ep	ex	ez	et	eb	60
et	ex	ej	ek	ef	ep	ez	el	ed	eg	70
et	ex	ej	ek	ef	ep	ez	el	ed	eg	80
ev	ep	ek	ef	et	en	el	ej	ez	em	90
em	eg	ek	el	ec	en	ej	ez	eb	ex	100

1 Total blended:
- # of errors:
= Correct blends:
2 Total blended:
- # of errors:
= Correct blends:
3 Total blended:
- # of errors:
= Correct blends:
4 Total blended:
- # of errors:
= Correct blends:
5 Total blended:
- # of errors:
= Correct blends:

PBe-5

ev	ek	ef	et	ep	en	el	ej	ez	em	10
em	ek	el	ec	eg	en	ej	ez	eb	ex	20
et	ej	ek	ef	ex	ep	ez	el	ed	eg	30
es	ec	el	ed	eg	ep	ex	ez	et	eb	40
em	ek	el	ec	eg	en	ej	ez	eb	ex	50
et	ej	ek	ef	ex	ep	ez	el	ed	eg	60
es	ec	el	ed	eg	ep	ex	ez	et	eb	70
et	ej	ek	ef	ex	ep	ez	el	ed	eg	80
em	ek	el	ec	eg	en	ej	ez	eb	ex	90
ev	ek	ef	et	ep	en	el	ej	ez	em	100

1 Total blended:
- # of errors:
= Correct blends:
2 Total blended:
- # of errors:
= Correct blends:
3 Total blended:
- # of errors:
= Correct blends:
4 Total blended:
- # of errors:
= Correct blends:
5 Total blended:
- # of errors:
= Correct blends:

Phoneme to Phoneme Blending (ĭ)

Teacher Copy

Student Name: ______________________________

PBi-1

ip	it	is	id	if	ig	ij	ik	il	iz	10
ic	iv	ib	in	im	iz	ic	it	ip	ig	20
il	ij	ip	ig	iv	ik	id	ib	iz	ix	30
ip	it	is	id	if	ig	ij	ik	il	iz	40
ip	it	is	id	if	ig	ij	ik	il	iz	50
il	ij	ip	ig	iv	ik	id	ib	iz	ix	60
ip	it	is	id	if	ig	ij	ik	il	iz	70
ic	iv	ib	in	im	iz	ic	it	ip	ig	80
iv	ig	ij	ip	it	id	iz	in	ij	il	90
ip	it	is	id	if	ig	ij	ik	il	iz	100

1 Total blended:
- # of errors:
= Correct blends:
2 Total blended:
- # of errors:
= Correct blends:
3 Total blended:
- # of errors:
= Correct blends:
4 Total blended:
- # of errors:
= Correct blends:
5 Total blended:
- # of errors:
= Correct blends:

PBi-2

iv	ic	ib	im	in	ic	ij	iz	it	ig	10
ig	iv	ij	it	ip	iz	im	id	in	il	20
ij	il	ip	iv	ig	id	if	ik	ib	ix	30
it	ip	is	if	id	ij	ix	ig	ik	iz	40
ig	iv	ij	it	ip	iz	im	id	in	il	50
it	ip	is	if	id	ij	ix	ig	ik	iz	60
iv	ic	ib	im	in	ic	ij	iz	it	ig	70
it	ip	is	if	id	ij	ix	ig	ik	iz	80
ig	iv	ij	it	ip	iz	im	id	in	il	90
ij	il	ip	iv	ig	id	if	ik	ib	ix	100

1 Total blended:
- # of errors:
= Correct blends:
2 Total blended:
- # of errors:
= Correct blends:
3 Total blended:
- # of errors:
= Correct blends:
4 Total blended:
- # of errors:
= Correct blends:
5 Total blended:
- # of errors:
= Correct blends:

PBi-3

iv	ib	ic	im	ic	in	iz	ij	ig	it	10
ig	ij	iv	it	iz	ip	id	im	il	in	20
it	is	ip	if	ij	id	ig	ix	iz	ik	30
ij	ip	il	iv	id	ig	ik	if	ix	ib	40
ig	ij	iv	it	iz	ip	id	im	il	in	50
iv	ib	ic	im	ic	in	iz	ij	ig	it	60
it	is	ip	if	ij	id	ig	ix	iz	ik	70
it	is	ip	if	ij	id	ig	ix	iz	ik	80
ij	ip	il	iv	id	ig	ik	if	ix	ib	90
ig	ij	iv	it	iz	ip	id	im	il	in	100

1 Total blended:
- # of errors:
= Correct blends:
2 Total blended:
- # of errors:
= Correct blends:
3 Total blended:
- # of errors:
= Correct blends:
4 Total blended:
- # of errors:
= Correct blends:
5 Total blended:
- # of errors:
= Correct blends:

PBi-4

ic	iv	in	it	ib	im	ij	iz	ic	ig	10
iz	ig	ip	in	ij	it	im	id	iv	il	20
ij	it	id	ik	is	if	ix	ig	ip	iz	30
id	ij	ig	ib	ip	iv	if	ik	il	ix	40
iz	ig	ip	in	ij	it	im	id	iv	il	50
ij	it	id	ik	is	if	ix	ig	ip	iz	60
ic	iv	in	it	ib	im	ij	iz	ic	ig	70
id	ij	ig	ib	ip	iv	if	ik	il	ix	80
ij	it	id	ik	is	if	ix	ig	ip	iz	90
iz	ig	ip	in	ij	it	im	id	iv	il	100

1 Total blended:
- # of errors:
= Correct blends:
2 Total blended:
- # of errors:
= Correct blends:
3 Total blended:
- # of errors:
= Correct blends:
4 Total blended:
- # of errors:
= Correct blends:
5 Total blended:
- # of errors:
= Correct blends:

PBi-5

ig	ic	iz	iv	ib	in	im	ic	it	ij	10
iz	ij	ig	it	is	id	if	ip	ik	ix	20
il	iz	id	ig	ij	ip	it	iv	in	im	30
ix	id	ik	ij	ip	ig	iv	il	ib	if	40
iz	ij	ig	it	is	id	if	ip	ik	ix	50
il	iz	id	ig	ij	ip	it	iv	in	im	60
ig	ic	iz	iv	ib	in	im	ic	it	ij	70
iz	ij	ig	it	is	id	if	ip	ik	ix	80
ix	id	ik	ij	ip	ig	iv	il	ib	if	90
il	iz	id	ig	ij	ip	it	iv	in	im	100

1 Total blended:
- # of errors:
= Correct blends:
2 Total blended:
- # of errors:
= Correct blends:
3 Total blended:
- # of errors:
= Correct blends:
4 Total blended:
- # of errors:
= Correct blends:
5 Total blended:
- # of errors:
= Correct blends:

Phoneme to Phoneme Blending (ŏ)

Teacher Copy

Student Name: ______________________________

PBo-1

ot	op	os	od	og	oj	ok	ol	oz	ox	10
ov	ob	on	om	oc	ox	oz	ol	oj	ok	20
ot	op	os	od	og	oj	ol	om	on	ox	30
ov	ob	on	ot	op	os	od	og	ol	on	40
oz	ok	ol	od	ob	os	og	oj	oc	ol	50
ov	ox	on	ot	op	os	od	og	ol	on	60
ot	op	os	od	og	oj	ol	om	on	ox	70
oz	ok	ol	od	ob	os	og	oj	oc	ol	80
ov	ob	on	om	oc	ox	oz	ol	oj	ok	90
ot	op	os	od	og	oj	ok	ol	oz	ox	100

1 Total blended:
- # of errors:
= Correct blends:
2 Total blended:
- # of errors:
= Correct blends:
3 Total blended:
- # of errors:
= Correct blends:
4 Total blended:
- # of errors:
= Correct blends:
5 Total blended:
- # of errors:
= Correct blends:

PBo-2

ob	on	oc	ok	om	ol	ox	oz	ov	oj	10
op	os	og	ox	od	om	oj	ol	ot	on	20
ob	on	op	on	ot	og	os	od	ov	ol	30
op	os	og	ox	od	ol	oj	ok	ot	oz	40
ok	ol	ob	ol	od	oj	os	og	oz	oc	50
ox	on	op	on	ot	og	os	od	ov	ol	60
op	os	og	ox	od	ol	oj	ok	ot	oz	70
ok	ol	ob	ol	od	oj	os	og	oz	oc	80
op	os	og	ox	od	om	oj	ol	ot	on	90
ob	on	oc	ok	om	ol	ox	oz	ov	oj	100

1 Total blended:
- # of errors:
= Correct blends:
2 Total blended:
- # of errors:
= Correct blends:
3 Total blended:
- # of errors:
= Correct blends:
4 Total blended:
- # of errors:
= Correct blends:
5 Total blended:
- # of errors:
= Correct blends:

PBo-3

ov	om	on	ox	oz	ob	oj	ol	ok	oc	10
ot	od	os	oj	ol	op	on	om	ox	og	20
oz	od	ol	os	og	ok	oc	oj	ol	ob	30
ot	od	os	oj	ok	op	oz	ol	ox	og	40
ov	ot	on	os	od	ox	ol	og	on	op	50
ot	od	os	oj	ol	op	on	om	ox	og	60
ov	ot	on	os	od	ob	ol	og	on	op	70
oz	od	ol	os	og	ok	oc	oj	ol	ob	80
ov	om	on	ox	oz	ob	oj	ol	ok	oc	90
ot	od	os	oj	ok	op	oz	ol	ox	og	100

1 Total blended:
- # of errors:
= Correct blends:
2 Total blended:
- # of errors:
= Correct blends:
3 Total blended:
- # of errors:
= Correct blends:
4 Total blended:
- # of errors:
= Correct blends:
5 Total blended:
- # of errors:
= Correct blends:

PBo-4

oz	od	os	ol	ok	og	ol	oj	oc	ob	10
ot	od	oj	os	op	ok	ox	ol	oz	og	20
ov	ot	os	on	ox	od	on	og	ol	op	30
ot	od	oj	os	op	ol	ox	om	on	og	40
ov	ot	os	on	ob	od	on	og	ol	op	50
ot	od	oj	os	op	ok	ox	ol	oz	og	60
ov	om	ox	on	ob	oz	ok	ol	oj	oc	70
oz	od	os	ol	ok	og	ol	oj	oc	ob	80
ov	om	ox	on	ob	oz	ok	ol	oj	oc	90
ot	od	oj	os	op	ol	ox	om	on	og	100

1 Total blended:
- # of errors:
= Correct blends:
2 Total blended:
- # of errors:
= Correct blends:
3 Total blended:
- # of errors:
= Correct blends:
4 Total blended:
- # of errors:
= Correct blends:
5 Total blended:
- # of errors:
= Correct blends:

PBo-5

ol	ok	od	oz	os	ol	oc	oj	ob	og	10
on	ob	om	ov	ox	ok	oj	ol	oc	oz	20
on	ox	ot	ov	os	on	ol	og	op	od	30
os	op	od	ot	oj	ox	on	om	og	ol	40
on	ob	ot	ov	os	on	ol	og	op	od	50
os	op	od	ot	oj	ox	oz	ol	og	ok	60
on	ob	om	ov	ox	ok	oj	ol	oc	oz	70
os	op	od	ot	oj	ox	oz	ol	og	ok	80
ol	ok	od	oz	os	ol	oc	oj	ob	og	90
os	op	od	ot	oj	ox	on	om	og	ol	100

1 Total blended:
- # of errors:
= Correct blends:
2 Total blended:
- # of errors:
= Correct blends:
3 Total blended:
- # of errors:
= Correct blends:
4 Total blended:
- # of errors:
= Correct blends:
5 Total blended:
- # of errors:
= Correct blends:

Phoneme to Phoneme Blending (ŭ)

Teacher Copy

Student Name: ____

PBu-1

ut	up	us	ud	uf	ug	uj	uk	ul	uz	10
um	un	uv	uc	ux	uz	ul	uk	uj	ug	20
ud	us	up	ut	ud	uv	ub	ux	uj	uk	30
ut	ud	uj	uk	uc	uz	um	ub	uk	ul	40
uv	up	us	ud	uf	ug	uj	uk	ul	uz	50
um	un	uv	uc	ux	uz	ul	uk	uj	ug	60
ub	un	uz	up	ut	ud	ug	uk	ul	ud	70
ud	us	up	ut	ud	uv	ub	ux	uj	uk	80
uv	ud	uj	uk	uc	uz	um	ub	uk	ul	90
ut	up	us	ud	uf	ug	uj	uk	ul	uz	100

1 Total blended:
- # of errors:
= Correct blends:
2 Total blended:
- # of errors:
= Correct blends:
3 Total blended:
- # of errors:
= Correct blends:
4 Total blended:
- # of errors:
= Correct blends:
5 Total blended:
- # of errors:
= Correct blends:

PBu-2

ud	uk	uz	uj	uc	um	uk	ub	ul	uv	10
un	uc	uz	uv	ux	ul	uj	uk	ug	um	20
us	ut	uv	up	ud	ub	uj	ux	uk	ud	30
up	ud	ug	us	uf	uj	ul	uk	uz	uv	40
un	uc	uz	uv	ux	ul	uj	uk	ug	um	50
ud	uk	uz	uj	uc	um	uk	ub	ul	ut	60
up	ud	ug	us	uf	uj	ul	uk	uz	ut	70
un	up	ud	uz	ut	ug	ul	uk	ud	ub	80
us	ut	uv	up	ud	ub	uj	ux	uk	ud	90
up	ud	ug	us	uf	uj	ul	uk	uz	ut	100

1 Total blended:
- # of errors:
= Correct blends:
2 Total blended:
- # of errors:
= Correct blends:
3 Total blended:
- # of errors:
= Correct blends:
4 Total blended:
- # of errors:
= Correct blends:
5 Total blended:
- # of errors:
= Correct blends:

PBu-3

uc	un	uv	uz	ul	ux	uk	uj	um	ug	10
uk	ud	uj	uz	um	uc	ub	uk	uv	ul	20
ud	up	us	ug	uj	uf	uk	ul	uv	uz	30
ut	us	up	uv	ub	ud	ux	uj	ud	uk	40
uk	ud	uj	uz	um	uc	ub	uk	ut	ul	50
uc	un	uv	uz	ul	ux	uk	uj	um	ug	60
up	un	uz	ud	ug	ut	uk	ul	ub	ud	70
ud	up	us	ug	uj	uf	uk	ul	ut	uz	80
ut	us	up	uv	ub	ud	ux	uj	ud	uk	90
ud	up	us	ug	uj	uf	uk	ul	ut	uz	100

1 Total blended:
- # of errors:
= Correct blends:
2 Total blended:
- # of errors:
= Correct blends:
3 Total blended:
- # of errors:
= Correct blends:
4 Total blended:
- # of errors:
= Correct blends:
5 Total blended:
- # of errors:
= Correct blends:

PBu-4

uk	up	ud	uf	us	uj	ug	ul	ut	uz	10
uk	un	uc	ux	uv	ul	uz	uj	um	ug	20
ux	us	ut	ud	up	ub	uv	uj	ud	uk	30
uk	up	ud	uf	us	uj	ug	ul	uv	uz	40
ub	ud	uk	uc	uj	um	uz	uk	ut	ul	50
uk	un	uc	ux	uv	ul	uz	uj	um	ug	60
uk	un	up	ut	uz	ug	ud	ul	ub	ud	70
ub	ud	uk	uc	uj	um	uz	uk	uv	ul	80
ux	us	ut	ud	up	ub	uv	uj	ud	uk	90
uk	up	ud	uf	us	uj	ug	ul	ut	uz	100

1 Total blended:
- # of errors:
= Correct blends:
2 Total blended:
- # of errors:
= Correct blends:
3 Total blended:
- # of errors:
= Correct blends:
4 Total blended:
- # of errors:
= Correct blends:
5 Total blended:
- # of errors:
= Correct blends:

PBu-5

ul	uc	un	ux	ul	uv	uz	um	uj	ug	10
um	ud	up	uf	uj	us	ug	uv	ul	uz	20
ux	ut	us	ud	ub	up	uv	ud	uj	uk	30
ub	uk	ud	uc	um	uj	uz	ut	uk	ul	40
uk	ud	up	uf	uj	us	ug	ut	ul	uz	50
uf	uc	un	ux	ul	uv	uz	um	uj	ug	60
ub	uk	ud	uc	um	uj	uz	uv	uk	ul	70
uk	up	un	ut	ug	uz	ud	ub	ul	ud	80
ux	ut	us	ud	ub	up	uv	ud	uj	uk	90
uj	ud	up	uf	uj	us	ug	ut	ul	uz	100

1 Total blended:
- # of errors:
= Correct blends:
2 Total blended:
- # of errors:
= Correct blends:
3 Total blended:
- # of errors:
= Correct blends:
4 Total blended:
- # of errors:
= Correct blends:
5 Total blended:
- # of errors:
= Correct blends:

Phoneme to Phoneme Blending (Mixed)

Teacher Copy

Student Name: ______________________________

PBm-1

av	et	ut	ob	ek	iv	og	id	af	oc	10
ib	um	ol	ad	ev	ex	ic	ok	al	ov	20
ig	ud	ej	ox	iv	ap	ub	ik	os	ec	30
of	es	id	eg	av	ak	uz	ix	ap	od	40
am	on	eb	ud	iz	ux	at	im	op	ix	50
ab	og	uz	om	it	ec	il	ox	ez	uf	60
ig	uj	az	ov	eb	im	ux	oz	ac	ol	70
el	uk	in	ez	oj	aj	ib	ov	ep	iz	80
ol	ug	ij	ak	ec	ud	oc	iv	ag	ef	90
ob	ig	ap	ed	ux	ev	ib	od	uz	ik	100

Score
1 Total blended:
- # of errors:
= Correct blends:
2 Total blended:
- # of errors:
= Correct blends:
3 Total blended:
- # of errors:
= Correct blends:
4 Total blended:
- # of errors:
= Correct blends:
5 Total blended:
- # of errors:
= Correct blends:

PBm-2

um	ib	ad	ol	ex	ev	ok	ic	ov	al	10
et	av	ob	ut	iv	ek	id	og	oc	af	20
es	of	eg	id	ak	av	ix	uz	od	ap	30
ud	ig	ox	ej	ap	iv	ik	ub	ec	os	40
og	ab	om	uz	ec	it	ox	il	uf	ez	50
on	am	ud	eb	ux	iz	im	at	ix	op	60
uk	el	ez	in	aj	oj	ov	ib	iz	ep	70
uj	ig	ov	az	im	eb	oz	ux	ol	ac	80
ig	ob	ed	ap	ev	ux	od	ib	ik	uz	90
ug	ol	ak	ij	ud	ec	iv	oc	ef	ag	100

Score
1 Total blended:
- # of errors:
= Correct blends:
2 Total blended:
- # of errors:
= Correct blends:
3 Total blended:
- # of errors:
= Correct blends:
4 Total blended:
- # of errors:
= Correct blends:
5 Total blended:
- # of errors:
= Correct blends:

PBm-3

av	et	ob	iv	ut	id	ek	og	af	oc	10
ib	um	ad	ex	ol	ok	ev	ic	al	ov	20
ig	ud	ox	ap	ej	ik	iv	ub	os	ec	30
of	es	eg	ak	id	ix	av	uz	ap	od	40
ab	og	om	ec	uz	ox	it	il	ez	uf	50
el	uk	ez	aj	in	ov	oj	ib	ep	iz	60
am	on	ud	ux	eb	im	iz	at	op	ix	70
ob	ig	ed	ev	ap	od	ux	ib	uz	ik	80
ig	uj	ov	im	az	oz	eb	ux	ac	ol	90
ol	ug	ak	ud	ij	iv	ec	oc	ag	ef	100

1 Total blended:
- # of errors:
= Correct blends:
2 Total blended:
- # of errors:
= Correct blends:
3 Total blended:
- # of errors:
= Correct blends:
4 Total blended:
- # of errors:
= Correct blends:
5 Total blended:
- # of errors:
= Correct blends:

PBm-4

ol	ib	ad	um	ex	ok	ic	ev	ov	al	10
id	of	eg	es	ak	ix	uz	av	od	ap	20
az	ig	ov	uj	im	oz	ux	eb	ol	ac	30
ej	ig	ox	ud	ap	ik	ub	iv	ec	os	40
uz	ab	om	og	ec	ox	il	it	uf	ez	50
in	el	ez	uk	aj	ov	ib	oj	iz	ep	60
eb	am	ud	on	ux	im	at	iz	ix	op	70
ij	ol	ak	ug	ud	iv	oc	ec	ef	ag	80
ap	ob	ed	ig	ev	od	ib	ux	ik	uz	90
ut	av	ob	et	iv	id	og	ek	oc	af	100

1 Total blended:
- # of errors:
= Correct blends:
2 Total blended:
- # of errors:
= Correct blends:
3 Total blended:
- # of errors:
= Correct blends:
4 Total blended:
- # of errors:
= Correct blends:
5 Total blended:
- # of errors:
= Correct blends:

PBm-5

of	id	eg	ak	ix	av	es	uz	ap	od	10
av	ut	ob	iv	id	ek	et	og	af	oc	20
ig	ej	ox	ap	ik	iv	ud	ub	os	ec	30
ab	uz	om	ec	ox	it	og	il	ez	uf	40
el	in	ez	aj	ov	oj	uk	ib	ep	iz	50
ig	az	ov	im	oz	eb	uj	ux	ac	ol	60
am	eb	ud	ux	im	iz	on	at	op	ix	70
ol	ij	ak	ud	iv	ec	ug	oc	ag	ef	80
ob	ap	ed	ev	od	ux	ig	ib	uz	ik	90
ib	ol	ad	ex	ok	ev	um	ic	al	ov	100

1 Total blended:
- # of errors:
= Correct blends:
2 Total blended:
- # of errors:
= Correct blends:
3 Total blended:
- # of errors:
= Correct blends:
4 Total blended:
- # of errors:
= Correct blends:
5 Total blended:
- # of errors:
= Correct blends:

Pseudo-Word (CVC) Reading (ă)

Teacher Copy

Student Name: ____

PSWa-1

bap	caf	gat	mak	pab	jad	mab	laj	zak	hax	10
baz	dag	maj	vap	zat	sav	rax	lav	taj	wam	20
jat	lan	waj	vax	naf	faz	gan	lak	pav	zad	30
hab	jal	cax	yan	vad	gad	waz	paj	kak	mal	40
raf	yax	hal	nan	cav	bab	rav	gat	haf	laz	50
das	wab	yad	kax	nas	dac	bap	baf	nam	ral	60
san	mas	fam	hac	kal	laz	baj	dab	vaz	dag	70
wad	fab	jac	pag	raf	wat	gax	san	tak	cam	80
zat	baz	paz	jan	bac	gat	hac	gad	raz	daf	90
sab	fac	dax	paz	vam	pag	sab	kak	cav	gam	100

1 Words read:
- # of errors:
= Words correct:
2 Words read:
- # of errors:
= Words correct:
3 Words read:
- # of errors:
= Words correct:
4 Words read:
- # of errors:
= Words correct:
5 Words read:
- # of errors:
= Words correct:

PSWa-2

baz	wam	maj	dag	zat	vap	rax	sav	taj	lav	10
bap	hax	gat	caf	pab	mak	mab	jad	zak	laj	20
hab	mal	cax	jal	vad	yan	waz	gad	kak	paj	30
jat	zad	waj	lan	naf	vax	gan	faz	pav	lak	40
das	ral	yad	wab	nas	kax	bap	dac	nam	baf	50
raf	laz	hal	yax	cav	nan	rav	bab	haf	gat	60
san	dag	fam	mas	kal	hac	baj	laz	vaz	dab	70
zat	daf	paz	baz	bac	jan	hac	gat	raz	gad	80
wad	cam	jac	fab	raf	pag	gax	wat	tak	san	90
sab	gam	dax	fac	vam	paz	sab	pag	cav	kak	100

1 Words read:
- # of errors:
= Words correct:
2 Words read:
- # of errors:
= Words correct:
3 Words read:
- # of errors:
= Words correct:
4 Words read:
- # of errors:
= Words correct:
5 Words read:
- # of errors:
= Words correct:

PSWa-3

pab	bap	gat	hax	caf	mab	jad	mak	laj	zak	10
vad	hab	cax	mal	jal	waz	gad	yan	paj	kak	20
zat	baz	maj	wam	dag	rax	sav	vap	lav	taj	30
naf	jat	waj	zad	lan	gan	faz	vax	lak	pav	40
nas	das	yad	ral	wab	bap	dac	kax	baf	nam	50
vam	sab	dax	gam	fac	sab	pag	paz	kak	cav	60
cav	raf	hal	laz	yax	rav	bab	nan	gat	haf	70
kal	san	fam	dag	mas	baj	laz	hac	dab	vaz	80
raf	wad	jac	cam	fab	gax	wat	pag	san	tak	90
bac	zat	paz	daf	baz	hac	gat	jan	gad	raz	100

1 Words read:
- # of errors:
= Words correct:
2 Words read:
- # of errors:
= Words correct:
3 Words read:
- # of errors:
= Words correct:
4 Words read:
- # of errors:
= Words correct:
5 Words read:
- # of errors:
= Words correct:

PSWa-4

raf	hac	mab	bap	laf	maz	zab	rax	pac	cav	10
zad	daf	gan	pak	yax	jaf	pap	laz	mam	nad	20
lal	baf	fac	laj	jax	wad	mag	gad	bab	dag	30
haz	zaj	dax	wak	mak	rab	wab	maf	faj	jat	40
dap	wav	lak	dag	zaf	hab	rab	tac	mak	dav	50
lat	bav	rab	bap	kat	naj	vab	wap	sab	baf	60
nac	dac	waz	jak	pak	sab	mag	baj	wav	caz	70
paj	lav	raj	rax	nad	waj	vaf	faz	mak	lac	80
tam	jax	cav	jaj	lan	nan	waf	paj	laz	tav	90
vab	ral	caj	vab	saf	pas	mam	jad	sas	yab	100

1 Words read:
- # of errors:
= Words correct:
2 Words read:
- # of errors:
= Words correct:
3 Words read:
- # of errors:
= Words correct:
4 Words read:
- # of errors:
= Words correct:
5 Words read:
- # of errors:
= Words correct:

PSWa-5

hac	zab	bap	laf	mab	maz	raf	cav	rax	pac	10
jax	waf	jaj	lan	cav	nan	tam	tav	paj	laz	20
baf	mag	laj	jax	fac	wad	lal	dag	gad	bab	30
wav	rab	dag	zaf	lak	hab	dap	dav	tac	mak	40
zaj	wab	wak	mak	dax	rab	haz	jat	maf	faj	50
daf	pap	pak	yax	gan	jaf	zad	nad	laz	mam	60
bav	vab	bap	kat	rab	naj	lat	baf	wap	sab	70
dac	mag	jak	pak	waz	sab	nac	caz	baj	wav	80
lav	vaf	rax	nad	raj	waj	paj	lac	faz	mak	90
ral	mam	vab	saf	caj	pas	vab	yab	jad	sas	100

1 Words read:
- # of errors:
= Words correct:
2 Words read:
- # of errors:
= Words correct:
3 Words read:
- # of errors:
= Words correct:
4 Words read:
- # of errors:
= Words correct:
5 Words read:
- # of errors:
= Words correct:

Pseudo-Word (CVC) Reading (ĕ)

Teacher Copy

Student Name: ______________________________

PSWe-1

fek	yed	tev	pex	yev	bes	seb	jep	pef	fen	10
mez	ket	lec	ven	nen	hez	lep	pel	rel	tex	20
ved	mez	neb	beb	jek	dej	jeb	pev	jez	nef	30
yez	mev	lex	kek	lev	mes	sep	heb	bef	leb	40
wec	reb	tez	yej	pec	sef	deg	fek	hev	jex	50
kev	lep	zeg	ved	bex	nej	mef	fef	zec	seb	60
mez	nex	yed	jef	pej	vev	hep	dek	fex	zep	70
yem	jez	les	reg	tep	jej	nep	zes	ved	lex	80
tef	yek	pec	sez	dex	fev	heb	jed	rel	weg	90
mev	nep	zev	bek	ved	mem	pel	hev	kem	lep	100

1 Words read:
- # of errors:
= Words correct:
2 Words read:
- # of errors:
= Words correct:
3 Words read:
- # of errors:
= Words correct:
4 Words read:
- # of errors:
= Words correct:
5 Words read:
- # of errors:
= Words correct:

PSWe-2

ket	mez	ven	lec	hez	nen	pel	lep	tex	rel	10
yed	fek	pex	tev	bes	yev	jep	seb	fen	pef	20
mev	yez	kek	lex	mes	lev	heb	sep	leb	bef	30
mez	ved	beb	neb	dej	jek	pev	jeb	nef	jez	40
lep	kev	ved	zeg	nej	bex	fef	mef	seb	zec	50
reb	wec	yej	tez	sef	pec	fek	deg	jex	hev	60
jez	yem	reg	les	jej	tep	zes	nep	lex	ved	70
nex	mez	jef	yed	vev	pej	dek	hep	zep	fex	80
nep	mev	bek	zev	mem	ved	hev	pel	lep	kem	90
yek	tef	sez	pec	fev	dex	jed	heb	weg	rel	100

1 Words read:
- # of errors:
= Words correct:
2 Words read:
- # of errors:
= Words correct:
3 Words read:
- # of errors:
= Words correct:
4 Words read:
- # of errors:
= Words correct:
5 Words read:
- # of errors:
= Words correct:

PSWe-3

fek	yed	tev	feg	kev	wef	rep	weg	jem	ken	10
wep	rep	tef	bep	tej	pes	kep	reb	sep	rez	20
bev	deg	reb	dev	pem	bec	zet	feg	pej	reg	30
kel	jep	rep	sez	pek	sed	pem	meg	wez	leb	40
deg	zed	heb	nes	fep	det	feg	sev	peb	hed	50
kes	jek	pef	fec	bef	ket	yev	nen	wes	jeg	60
ved	sez	kef	zep	feg	lem	mex	hev	nev	wep	70
bex	mep	ped	het	yex	zes	ved	jel	bej	wec	80
lrp	mem	pex	lef	fet	veg	hek	lep	mez	zej	90
jev	nef	mez	pek	tev	beb	kem	jex	keb	feb	100

1 Words read:
- # of errors:
= Words correct:
2 Words read:
- # of errors:
= Words correct:
3 Words read:
- # of errors:
= Words correct:
4 Words read:
- # of errors:
= Words correct:
5 Words read:
- # of errors:
= Words correct:

PSWe-4

nef	pek	beb	tev	jex	keb	kem	mez	feb	jev	10
yed	feg	wef	kev	weg	jem	rep	tev	ken	fek	20
deg	dev	bec	pem	feg	pej	zet	reb	reg	bev	30
jep	sez	sed	pek	meg	wez	pem	rep	leb	kel	40
rep	bep	pes	tej	reb	sep	kep	tef	rez	wep	50
zed	nes	det	fep	sev	peb	feg	heb	hed	deg	60
mem	lef	veg	fet	lep	mez	hek	pex	zej	lrp	70
jek	fec	ket	bef	nen	wes	yev	pef	jeg	kes	80
mep	het	zes	yex	jel	bej	ved	ped	wec	bex	90
sez	zep	lem	feg	hev	nev	mex	kef	wep	ved	100

1 Words read:
- # of errors:
= Words correct:
2 Words read:
- # of errors:
= Words correct:
3 Words read:
- # of errors:
= Words correct:
4 Words read:
- # of errors:
= Words correct:
5 Words read:
- # of errors:
= Words correct:

PSWe-5

feg	yed	kev	wef	jem	weg	tev	rep	fek	ken	10
pek	nef	tev	beb	keb	jex	mez	kem	jev	feb	20
sez	jep	pek	sed	wez	meg	rep	pem	kel	leb	30
dev	deg	pem	bec	pej	feg	reb	zet	bev	reg	40
nes	zed	fep	det	peb	sev	heb	feg	deg	hed	50
bep	rep	tej	pes	sep	reb	tef	kep	wep	rez	60
fec	jek	bef	ket	wes	nen	pef	yev	kes	jeg	70
lef	mem	fet	veg	mez	lep	pex	hek	lrp	zej	80
zep	sez	feg	lem	nev	hev	kef	mex	ved	wep	90
het	mep	yex	zes	bej	jel	ped	ved	bex	wec	100

1 Words read:
- # of errors:
= Words correct:
2 Words read:
- # of errors:
= Words correct:
3 Words read:
- # of errors:
= Words correct:
4 Words read:
- # of errors:
= Words correct:
5 Words read:
- # of errors:
= Words correct:

Pseudo-Word (CVC) Reading (ĭ)

Teacher Copy

Student Name: ____

PSWi-1

pip	lim	nip	pim	fiv	vid	diz	vix	kib	bik	10	1 Words read:
mim	nid	dit	tig	hif	fip	sid	wip	tib	lis	20	- # of errors: = Words correct:
sib	vin	pix	rij	kix	bis	wiz	rif	tik	yix	30	2 Words read:
piz	sij	div	fim	hic	jik	kiv	liz	zib	viv	40	- # of errors: = Words correct:
bip	nix	mif	wix	rij	tiv	yip	nin	kij	jix	50	3 Words read:
mij	lig	hib	biv	ziv	dil	fid	wik	yit	vit	60	- # of errors: = Words correct:
fif	jiv	wip	jix	mil	kiv	rix	miz	bij	dif	70	4 Words read:
sib	nif	kij	mig	vib	zig	hiv	pik	liv	dil	80	- # of errors: = Words correct:
hib	fiv	nig	jil	ziz	sig	nix	vig	bix	rif	90	5 Words read:
lib	bip	siz	hix	kib	dil	liz	hij	piv	rix	100	- # of errors: = Words correct:

PSWi-2

fiv	vid	diz	pim	lim	vix	kib	nip	bik	pip	10	1 Words read:
kix	bis	wiz	rij	vin	rif	tik	pix	yix	sib	20	- # of errors: = Words correct:
hic	jik	kiv	fim	sij	liz	zib	div	viv	piz	30	2 Words read:
rij	tiv	yip	wix	nix	nin	kij	mif	jix	bip	40	- # of errors: = Words correct:
hif	fip	sid	tig	nid	wip	tib	dit	lis	mim	50	3 Words read:
ziv	dil	fid	biv	lig	wik	yit	hib	vit	mij	60	- # of errors: = Words correct:
kib	dil	liz	hix	bip	hij	piv	siz	rix	lib	70	4 Words read:
mil	kiv	rix	jix	jiv	miz	bij	wip	dif	fif	80	- # of errors: = Words correct:
vib	zig	hiv	mig	nif	pik	liv	kij	dil	sib	90	5 Words read:
ziz	sig	nix	jil	fiv	vig	bix	nig	rif	hib	100	- # of errors: = Words correct:

PSWi-3

ziz	nix	sig	fiv	jil	bix	vig	nig	hib	rif	10
hic	kiv	jik	sij	fim	zib	liz	div	piz	viv	20
kix	wiz	bis	vin	rij	tik	rif	pix	sib	yix	30
hif	sid	fip	nid	tig	tib	wip	dit	mim	lis	40
ziv	fid	dil	lig	biv	yit	wik	hib	mij	vit	50
rij	yip	tiv	nix	wix	kij	nin	mif	bip	jix	60
kib	liz	dil	bip	hix	piv	hij	siz	lib	rix	70
vib	hiv	zig	nif	mig	liv	pik	kij	sib	dil	80
mil	rix	kiv	jiv	jix	bij	miz	wip	fif	dif	90
fiv	diz	vid	lim	pim	kib	vix	nip	pip	bik	100

1 Words read:
- # of errors:
= Words correct:
2 Words read:
- # of errors:
= Words correct:
3 Words read:
- # of errors:
= Words correct:
4 Words read:
- # of errors:
= Words correct:
5 Words read:
- # of errors:
= Words correct:

PSWi-4

jig	pik	hif	vix	lif	pib	viz	lin	kiv	lig	10
bim	tiv	kij	pif	biv	tic	div	sid	dix	piv	20
jik	liz	dib	bik	piz	fip	miz	fip	zin	miv	30
vig	hib	nif	mip	pik	kib	vip	zid	sid	wib	40
vib	sif	fid	diz	hij	jix	ric	nig	kiz	vip	50
mim	pij	lig	tib	bis	div	vid	zij	bim	pip	60
zix	pib	kij	jiv	div	hix	mip	piz	yim	vit	70
tid	fid	sij	fik	lif	ris	liz	hix	biv	wip	80
rix	kif	lij	zig	hiv	jik	kib	liz	pib	bif	90
hig	jip	bix	niv	zid	kif	sib	tiz	lif	pif	100

1 Words read:
- # of errors:
= Words correct:
2 Words read:
- # of errors:
= Words correct:
3 Words read:
- # of errors:
= Words correct:
4 Words read:
- # of errors:
= Words correct:
5 Words read:
- # of errors:
= Words correct:

PSWi-5

vig	hib	mip	pik	zid	kib	vip	wib	sid	nif	10
mim	pij	tib	bis	zij	div	vid	pip	bim	lig	20
vib	sif	diz	hij	nig	jix	ric	vip	kiz	fid	30
zix	pib	jiv	div	piz	hix	mip	vit	yim	kij	40
tid	fid	fik	lif	hix	ris	liz	wip	biv	sij	50
jik	liz	bik	piz	fip	fip	miz	miv	zin	dib	60
rix	kif	zig	hiv	liz	jik	kib	bif	pib	lij	70
bim	tiv	pif	biv	sid	tic	div	piv	dix	kij	80
hig	jip	niv	zid	tiz	kif	sib	pif	lif	bix	90
jig	pik	vix	lif	lin	pib	viz	lig	kiv	hif	100

1 Words read:
- # of errors:
= Words correct:
2 Words read:
- # of errors:
= Words correct:
3 Words read:
- # of errors:
= Words correct:
4 Words read:
- # of errors:
= Words correct:
5 Words read:
- # of errors:
= Words correct:

Pseudo-Word (CVC) Reading (ŏ)

Teacher Copy

Student Name: ______________________________

PSWo-1

wob	rov	tox	wol	yob	poz	sov	dox	fon	goj	10
hoz	jop	cos	lod	zon	coj	vop	lol	bom	nop	20
wof	hol	rop	bol	tob	yog	pog	sox	dob	fov	30
gov	hox	joz	lod	zob	cof	vom	bop	nof	mox	40
wov	rog	tod	yoz	pos	sov	doc	tol	fof	yot	50
yom	mol	pob	soz	dod	fop	gof	nol	hod	nop	60
mon	bol	yop	vog	hon	lod	zoz	jox	fot	jok	70
rov	bok	dof	gog	fod	sov	cos	loz	fos	lon	80
gop	fod	jod	mog	coz	nop	pok	doz	rox	bov	90
dop	foj	rol	vod	yov	zol	tof	moj	dop	bok	100

1 Words read:
- # of errors:
= Words correct:
2 Words read:
- # of errors:
= Words correct:
3 Words read:
- # of errors:
= Words correct:
4 Words read:
- # of errors:
= Words correct:
5 Words read:
- # of errors:
= Words correct:

PSWo-2

jop	hoz	lod	cos	coj	zon	lol	vop	nop	bom	10
rov	wob	wol	tox	poz	yob	dox	sov	goj	fon	20
hox	gov	lod	joz	cof	zob	bop	vom	mox	nof	30
hol	wof	bol	rop	yog	tob	sox	pog	fov	dob	40
mol	yom	soz	pob	fop	dod	nol	gof	nop	hod	50
rog	wov	yoz	tod	sov	pos	tol	doc	yot	fof	60
bok	rov	gog	dof	sov	fod	loz	cos	lon	fos	70
bol	mon	vog	yop	lod	hon	jox	zoz	jok	fot	80
foj	dop	vod	rol	zol	yov	moj	tof	bok	dop	90
fod	gop	mog	jod	nop	coz	doz	pok	bov	rox	100

1 Words read:
- # of errors:
= Words correct:
2 Words read:
- # of errors:
= Words correct:
3 Words read:
- # of errors:
= Words correct:
4 Words read:
- # of errors:
= Words correct:
5 Words read:
- # of errors:
= Words correct:

PSWo-3

gop	pok	mog	rox	jod	nop	coz	doz	bov	fod	10
gov	vom	lod	nof	joz	cof	zob	bop	mox	hox	20
wof	pog	bol	dob	rop	yog	tob	sox	fov	hol	30
wob	sov	wol	fon	tox	poz	yob	dox	goj	rov	40
yom	gof	soz	hod	pob	fop	dod	nol	nop	mol	50
wov	doc	yoz	fof	tod	sov	pos	tol	yot	rog	60
rov	cos	gog	fos	dof	sov	fod	loz	lon	bok	70
mon	zoz	vog	fot	yop	lod	hon	jox	jok	bol	80
hoz	vop	lod	bom	cos	coj	zon	lol	nop	jop	90
dop	tof	vod	foj	rol	zol	yov	moj	bok	foj	100

1 Words read:
- # of errors:
= Words correct:
2 Words read:
- # of errors:
= Words correct:
3 Words read:
- # of errors:
= Words correct:
4 Words read:
- # of errors:
= Words correct:
5 Words read:
- # of errors:
= Words correct:

PSWo-4

poc	hos	gob	rof	pok	roz	zot	dop	toz	wob	10
tod	wof	fot	lok	rog	poc	lom	mog	wok	pog	20
loj	sog	mox	dob	com	roz	fov	vox	jom	lov	30
zop	mov	pon	hoj	lok	mox	cof	fos	woj	jon	40
cov	bom	yod	jol	poj	hox	vov	zok	los	wof	50
pof	yog	vob	zoz	hon	pok	sop	jox	dop	bos	60
los	fot	boz	coj	wov	nof	gox	roj	lok	sov	70
yox	woz	rop	tob	pon	sof	dov	foz	gog	hok	80
joc	loz	zop	cof	vod	bol	nok	mov	wox	roj	90
toc	yod	pol	sov	dox	fov	gom	hos	jol	loc	100

1 Words read:
- # of errors:
= Words correct:
2 Words read:
- # of errors:
= Words correct:
3 Words read:
- # of errors:
= Words correct:
4 Words read:
- # of errors:
= Words correct:
5 Words read:
- # of errors:
= Words correct:

PSWo-5

pok	hos	rof	roz	zot	poc	dop	wob	toz	gob	10
rog	wof	lok	poc	lom	tod	mog	pog	wok	fot	20
lok	mov	hoj	mox	cof	zop	fos	jon	woj	pon	30
poj	bom	jol	hox	vov	cov	zok	wof	los	yod	40
dox	yod	sov	fov	gom	toc	hos	loc	jol	pol	50
com	sog	dob	roz	fov	loj	vox	lov	jom	mox	60
hon	yog	zoz	pok	sop	pof	jox	bos	dop	vob	70
wov	fot	coj	nof	gox	los	roj	sov	lok	boz	80
vod	loz	cof	bol	nok	joc	mov	roj	wox	zop	90
pon	woz	tob	sof	dov	yox	foz	hok	gog	rop	100

1 Words read:
- # of errors:
= Words correct:
2 Words read:
- # of errors:
= Words correct:
3 Words read:
- # of errors:
= Words correct:
4 Words read:
- # of errors:
= Words correct:
5 Words read:
- # of errors:
= Words correct:

Pseudo-Word (CVC) Reading (ŭ)

Teacher Copy

Student Name: ______________________________

PSWu-1

wup	ruv	tuc	yun	puz	sup	duc	fub	gug	jup	10
lud	suz	zub	cun	vuf	bup	nud	mus	wul	ruc	20
yud	puj	sug	duf	fuv	guc	hux	jus	lup	zuz	30
cuf	vud	buj	nup	muf	rul	tun	yud	puc	sux	40
duf	fuz	gup	huv	jum	luz	zug	cul	vum	bup	50
wul	rup	yut	tut	pux	suj	duk	fuv	gul	huz	60
bux	wun	ruf	tuv	yud	pux	sut	duz	fub	gup	70
huc	jun	lup	zuv	cux	vud	buj	nup	mut	wub	80
lup	rux	yud	pud	fuf	gud	huc	jub	luz	zup	90
mun	bup	wud	zuz	pum	juf	fut	zux	sup	nug	100

1 Words read:
- # of errors:
= Words correct:
2 Words read:
- # of errors:
= Words correct:
3 Words read:
- # of errors:
= Words correct:
4 Words read:
- # of errors:
= Words correct:
5 Words read:
- # of errors:
= Words correct:

PSWu-2

ruv	wup	tuc	puz	yun	sup	fub	duc	jup	gug	10
puj	yud	sug	fuv	duf	guc	jus	hux	zuz	lup	20
suz	lud	zub	vuf	cun	bup	mus	nud	ruc	wul	30
fuz	duf	gup	jum	huv	luz	cul	zug	bup	vum	40
vud	cuf	buj	muf	nup	rul	yud	tun	sux	puc	50
wun	bux	ruf	yud	tuv	pux	duz	sut	gup	fub	60
rup	wul	yut	pux	tut	suj	fuv	duk	huz	gul	70
rux	lup	yud	fuf	pud	gud	jub	huc	zup	luz	80
jun	huc	lup	cux	zuv	vud	nup	buj	wub	mut	90
bup	mun	wud	pum	zuz	juf	zux	fut	nug	sup	100

1 Words read:
- # of errors:
= Words correct:
2 Words read:
- # of errors:
= Words correct:
3 Words read:
- # of errors:
= Words correct:
4 Words read:
- # of errors:
= Words correct:
5 Words read:
- # of errors:
= Words correct:

PSWu-3

wut	rud	wup	tud	gub	nug	luz	cuz	juv	sux	10
yud	bux	zub	num	mux	sut	vum	nuv	puj	luk	20
zup	vux	huf	gup	yub	rul	lup	huv	mup	suz	30
puj	lun	wug	hux	zuk	sul	guv	ruf	fup	gug	40
zub	buv	wud	yug	gud	fug	nup	pud	dut	nuz	50
jud	suz	bux	vud	lup	ruj	nul	juv	muz	yux	60
tuv	wup	zum	mub	jun	mux	vub	rup	suz	tun	70
pux	buv	sus	hux	yub	nud	luz	huf	bub	yub	80
duf	jun	muv	yun	nug	dup	jub	lum	nux	wuv	90
buz	lub	wud	zuj	bub	dux	jud	sug	lum	mup	100

1 Words read:
- # of errors:
= Words correct:
2 Words read:
- # of errors:
= Words correct:
3 Words read:
- # of errors:
= Words correct:
4 Words read:
- # of errors:
= Words correct:
5 Words read:
- # of errors:
= Words correct:

PSWu-4

cun	nud	mus	jus	lup	fuv	zub	suz	ruc	puj	10
yun	duc	fub	fub	gug	puz	wup	ruv	jup	juv	20
duf	hux	jus	mus	wul	vuf	huf	puj	zuz	mup	30
huv	zug	cul	yud	puc	muf	wud	fuz	bup	dut	40
nup	tun	yud	cul	vum	jum	wug	vud	sux	fup	50
tut	duk	fuv	duz	fub	yud	bux	rup	huz	muz	60
zuv	buj	nup	jub	luz	fuf	sus	jun	wub	bub	70
tuv	sut	duz	fuv	gul	pux	zum	wun	gup	suz	80
zuz	fut	zux	zux	sup	pum	wud	bup	nug	lum	90
pud	huc	jub	nup	mut	cux	muv	rux	zup	nux	100

1 Words read:
- # of errors:
= Words correct:
2 Words read:
- # of errors:
= Words correct:
3 Words read:
- # of errors:
= Words correct:
4 Words read:
- # of errors:
= Words correct:
5 Words read:
- # of errors:
= Words correct:

PSWu-5

yud	puz	zub	cun	sut	yub	guc	mux	juv	jup	10
wut	fuv	tuc	yun	nug	wup	sup	gub	puj	ruc	20
zup	vuf	sug	duf	rul	lud	bup	yub	mup	zuz	30
puj	muf	buj	nup	sul	duf	luz	zuk	dut	bup	40
zub	jum	gup	huv	fug	cuf	rul	gud	fup	sux	50
tuv	fuf	ruf	tuv	mux	wul	suj	jun	bub	wub	60
jud	yud	yut	tut	ruj	bux	pux	lup	muz	huz	70
pux	pux	lup	zuv	nud	lup	gud	yub	suz	gup	80
buz	cux	wud	zuz	dux	mun	juf	bub	nux	zup	90
duf	pum	yud	pud	dup	huc	vud	nug	lum	nug	100

1 Words read:
- # of errors:
= Words correct:
2 Words read:
- # of errors:
= Words correct:
3 Words read:
- # of errors:
= Words correct:
4 Words read:
- # of errors:
= Words correct:
5 Words read:
- # of errors:
= Words correct:

Real Word (CVC) Reading (Mixed Vowels)

Teacher Copy

Student Name: ______________________________

RWm-1

got	egg	hug	dib	dip	met	con	big	fed	hen	10
bid	don	did	cod	bed	cog	cot	cad	cud	bus	20
bin	bit	dig	din	fun	dud	gut	dim	dug	hut	30
dot	leg	beg	Ben	bet	den	cub	get	fab	Ed	40
fog	hit	bad	Ken	hip	jet	god	men	med	cut	50
fob	fox	fig	dog	gob	fin	his	him	hog	fit	60
Gus	gun	bot	bog	hub	jut	Bob	cob	cop	box	70
hid	gig	yap	fib	gal	wax	bat	dam	fan	bam	80
bam	can	bag	dad	cap	ban	dab	cab	cat	fat	90
led	hex	bug	bun	Ned	bud	Meg	cup	but	bum	100

1 Words read:
- # of errors:
= Words correct:
2 Words read:
- # of errors:
= Words correct:
3 Words read:
- # of errors:
= Words correct:
4 Words read:
- # of errors:
= Words correct:
5 Words read:
- # of errors:
= Words correct:

RWm-2

had	lop	hap	gag	lax	hop	set	lox	hag	ham	10
lob	mid	pub	gab	fax	lap	reg	fad	gas	gap	20
hot	jug	job	lip	lug	mud	sit	mix	pug	sun	30
jog	jot	jig	kit	kid	log	lid	lot	lit	kin	40
mum	rug	mug	mutt	pup	nut	rum	pun	hem	pod	50
run	lam	sum	mob	wed	sub	non	nod	ref	ten	60
mod	web	nip	nib	bib	red	Zen	nix	pit	pep	70
nil	peg	pig	pet	pin	net	rip	rib	pen	rep	80
mom	vet	mop	Ted	nog	not	hog	wet	yes	yen	90
had	lop	hap	gag	lax	hop	set	lox	hag	ham	100

1 Words read:
- # of errors:
= Words correct:
2 Words read:
- # of errors:
= Words correct:
3 Words read:
- # of errors:
= Words correct:
4 Words read:
- # of errors:
= Words correct:
5 Words read:
- # of errors:
= Words correct:

RWm-3

bin	egg	tot	win	sip	men	lax	Ned	jet	get	10	1 Words read:
											- # of errors:
sit	cud	hen	rod	fed	med	tin	mad	leg	nab	20	= Words correct:
man	hex	sin	sit	six	led	pun	jab	tix	lag	30	2 Words read:
											- # of errors:
wig	zig	rob	fix	bug	but	rot	cub	sod	bud	40	= Words correct:
nap	nag	pad	pub	nun	rig	rug	rim	rid	tip	50	3 Words read:
											- # of errors:
mag	mat	map	max	tug	yum	nub	hum	gum	hub	60	= Words correct:
Ken	hat	has	met	lad	Meg	lab	lam	jam	lap	70	4 Words read:
											- # of errors:
pom	Tim	Sid	pot	win	pop	zip	pox	Ron	sob	80	= Words correct:
bum	beg	bed	bet	cut	Ben	odd	gob	den	Ed	90	5 Words read:
											- # of errors:
sog	bun	tog	bus	cup	top	ox	tom	sop	tot	100	= Words correct:

RWm-4

rap	ten	sag	ram	ran	cup	sod	pom	tin	gig	10	1 Words read:
											- # of errors:
cog	bot	lug	him	red	met	but	jug	pug	sap	20	= Words correct:
hip	his	fit	leg	med	six	cot	hex	jet	Ned	30	2 Words read:
											- # of errors:
box	fig	van	sob	cod	cop	hid	fin	fib	hit	40	= Words correct:
pub	bum	bun	mum	pan	rad	pal	cut	rag	sad	50	3 Words read:
											- # of errors:
pox	Bob	tad	rob	Ron	bog	tax	vat	con	cob	60	= Words correct:
Ken	men	led	rid	rim	Meg	sit	sip	rep	ref	70	4 Words read:
											- # of errors:
rig	sin	pen	net	peg	pep	tip	pet	tix	set	80	= Words correct:
pot	pop	sat	sax	rod	tag	rot	tan	tap	tab	90	5 Words read:
											- # of errors:
mud	nut	mug	bud	mutt	bus	pun	cub	cud	bug	100	= Words correct:

RWm-5

vat	hex	led	got	tin	jet	men	fab	hog	tix	10	1 Words read:
											- # of errors:
Meg	sip	sun	med	rut	pod	sun	run	pup	fat	20	= Words correct:
sum	dog	dot	sit	gob	fox	tad	tap	fog	hog	30	2 Words read:
											- # of errors:
rut	rug	dad	tub	rid	sin	rig	rim	six	tip	40	= Words correct:
don	sat	fob	god	tag	tan	tab	sax	tax	van	50	3 Words read:
											- # of errors:
rub	rum	sub	cad	cat	can	cap	dab	dam	fan	60	= Words correct:
met	Ken	kid	leg	sit	lip	mid	Ned	jig	lit	70	4 Words read:
											- # of errors:
kin	kit	pup	lid	rub	mix	sum	mop	wet	run	80	= Words correct:
rum	rug	vet	Ted	hem	sub	yen	tub	non	not	90	5 Words read:
											- # of errors:
web	mod	wed	Zen	mom	yes	reg	mob	nog	nod	100	= Words correct:

Real Word Reading (Mixed Vowels)

Teacher Copy

Student Name: ______________________________

RWblm-1

pond	slump	step	camp	frost	slum	went	stamp	glass	fast	10	1 Words read: - # of errors:
swift	truck	wept	grand	fled	soft	crisp	plum	test	blunt	20	= Words correct:
frog	vast	stand	blot	sand	drop	print	belt	cram	grin	30	2 Words read: - # of errors:
rest	drift	skin	jump	stunt	trot	mist	frost	sled	weld	40	= Words correct:
tramp	clock	silk	slant	cross	risk	plump	stop	bond	flint	50	3 Words read: - # of errors:
grip	golf	brisk	bran	land	grunt	flop	lost	blend	stem	60	= Words correct:
fond	scamp	grab	ramp	trust	smog	list	clump	still	help	70	4 Words read: - # of errors:
stilt	track	desk	gland	flap	nest	flask	snip	limp	brand	80	= Words correct:
smug	melt	strict	plan	bend	graft	plan	past	skimp	trick	90	5 Words read: - # of errors:
tent	grant	bled	damp	plug	bland	lend	slip	draft	drill	100	= Words correct:

RWblm-2

mint	trap	blimp	bent	stuff	glint	vest	black	trump	felt	10	1 Words read: - # of errors:
flag	scalp	held	spin	crust	sent	drum	spent	west	glad	20	= Words correct:
blast	lamp	brag	frisk	ant	cliff	plant	dust	grim	swept	30	2 Words read: - # of errors:
bump	stick	twist	vent	snag	grasp	yelp	frill	squint	hand	40	= Words correct:
flip	swept	dent	trim	strand	welt	spell	clasp	mast	plus	50	3 Words read: - # of errors:
splint	black	cram	drab	flip	grub	lump	mast	welt	bend	60	= Words correct:
grand	plus	scrap	wind	just	splint	blunt	lend	dump	pest	70	4 Words read: - # of errors:
lift	quest	melt	went	swift	lint	held	plump	flask	send	80	= Words correct:
cast	hump	primp	clasp	spot	grunt	snap	felt	tusk	grump	90	5 Words read: - # of errors:
plop	gulp	raft	floss	desk	frock	blimp	rant	task	drip	100	= Words correct:

RWblm-3

ramp	bond	blog	risk	pelt	crab	jest	clam	crust	husk	10
band	strand	gust	flask	past	vest	trim	scalp	blond	last	20
smug	fast	plod	dusk	primp	loft	clasp	melt	grim	trot	30
scrimp	clack	squid	twig	nest	drag	spend	brag	punt	frisk	40
ramp	crisp	crag	bland	flux	clamp	stub	pump	bust	vend	50
fret	glug	flint	hunt	slept	twin	mint	bond	swim	twin	60
stop	blend	grasp	must	bent	font	gland	help	just	milk	70
plant	splot	yelp	draft	flock	jump	trust	skip	fled	weld	80
mast	drip	rasp	skit	melt	trod	gloss	stump	land	test	90
grim	rest	drag	stomp	flat	left	glad	went	mask	best	100

1 Words read:
- # of errors:
= Words correct:
2 Words read:
- # of errors:
= Words correct:
3 Words read:
- # of errors:
= Words correct:
4 Words read:
- # of errors:
= Words correct:
5 Words read:
- # of errors:
= Words correct:

RWblm-4

clump	grand	mast	still	moss	drip	grub	brand	drip	clog	10
drug	help	twin	brisk	just	lump	primp	flint	vast	kept	20
grab	bless	clog	melt	swig	kelp	scrap	strip	prod	clamp	30
blend	flat	grab	silt	drug	kilt	crust	hand	brick	plant	40
lamp	mend	belt	risk	step	pram	glint	scalp	strand	swift	50
smug	trick	plum	frog	cliff	drum	flap	brand	skin	black	60
lisp	jump	blunt	blimp	graft	slant	list	soft	limp	help	70
vest	bust	fond	bluff	quell	stunt	grant	slept	swill	slum	80
trust	glass	spell	grass	blast	plug	glad	smog	snag	slip	90
just	crop	wept	lump	cuff	crag	twig	west	slid	desk	100

1 Words read:
- # of errors:
= Words correct:
2 Words read:
- # of errors:
= Words correct:
3 Words read:
- # of errors:
= Words correct:
4 Words read:
- # of errors:
= Words correct:
5 Words read:
- # of errors:
= Words correct:

RWblm-5

jest	clap	flan	Clem	glib	plot	glen	sled	scab	crib	10
drab	brat	glint	punt	print	rust	cusp	blimp	fend	gland	20
frump	brisk	sniff	flax	mint	brass	skill	crest	truss	scrimp	30
gift	dress	kilt	rapt	sect	hilt	sculpt	cleft	cull	wilt	40
scrub	nest	bulk	snuff	flick	track	plop	crack	tuft	gulp	50
sulk	cram	prod	spend	trust	smelt	trap	plug	lisp	heft	60
twin	crop	just	brisk	clasp	gulf	risk	text	mask	slack	70
welt	stress	slick	drop	drab	hemp	brag	sprat	meld	tram	80
swill	jest	pulp	glom	rest	vast	struck	kelp	still	stomp	90
wisp	fund	flop	crept	welp	flux	rift	tempt	bond	stack	100

1 Words read:
- # of errors:
= Words correct:
2 Words read:
- # of errors:
= Words correct:
3 Words read:
- # of errors:
= Words correct:
4 Words read:
- # of errors:
= Words correct:
5 Words read:
- # of errors:
= Words correct:

Fluency Passages (CVC)

Decoding Plus: Fluency Passages

1. Have your student read the fluency passage to get a baseline WCPM (word count per minute) score. Record the baseline on the teacher's copy. Have your student record their baseline score on the Reading Fluency Tracking sheet. Discuss reading goals with your student based on their scores. Have your student record their personal goals on their tracking sheet.
2. Have your student perform isolated phonogram, nonsense word reading, and real word reading in that order and record scores (Section 1). The student records their progress on their tracking sheet. These drills should not be done in one sitting. The isolated phonogram, nonsense word, and real word reading should be done one time during one session.
3. After the timed sequence of drills above have been completed, have your student practice identifying the non-phonetic words in the non-phonetic word recognition section (Section 2). This is NOT a timed activity. Once that is complete, the student can then practice the sentence stacks. The sentence stacks are also an UNTIMED activity.
4. After your student has completed the sequence of drills (Section 1) five times (over five sessions), have your student read the full passage five times over another five sessions and record the results. The final fifth reading is the student's final passage reading.
5. Record results of baseline reading and final (fifth) reading to view summarized progress.

Decoding Story 1.1: "Ned the Cop"

DIRECTIONS: • When beginning a new story, have your student read the whole story and time them for 1 minute. Record their results in the Baseline reading section and have your student record their baseline results on their tracking sheet. • Each Reading in Section 1 is a 15-second timed activity. Have your student do one timed reading of each in one sitting. Track your results on your assessor copy and have your students track their progress on their tracking sheet. • Section 2 contains passages that contain nonsense words with non-phonetic words embedded within the story. Have your student scan the passage and find the non-phonetic words. This is NOT a timed activity. • Section 3 contains sentence stacks. These are sentences from the passage that are broken down into chunks. • Have your student read each chunk and then the next using the scoops (having them run their finger along the scoops as they read) in order to build fluency and prosody. Perform these activities once during one session. • Once your student has completed all readings 5 times over 5 sessions, have them read the story for one final time and record their results and have your student track their results.

Section 1 (Time: 15 seconds for each exercise)

Isolated Phonogram Reading

c	n	s	f	p
a	b	l	e	u
t	h	s	a	b
d	i	e	o	g
j	u	k	v	d

	1	2	3	4	5
Date					
Total Sounds Read					
- Errors					
= Total Sounds Correct					

Nonsense Word Reading

deb	cag	hep	tiv	jux
loz	yem	mif	guv	kib
nis	wep	pid	boj	nem
saf	pag	sav	mag	lig
wug	pob	suz	zib	nop

	1	2	3	4	5
Date					
Total Sounds Read					
- Errors					
= Total Sounds Correct					

Real Word Reading

wed	cop	van	jut	not
cab	bad	run	lid	met
did	bet	pad	job	lap
pal	rob	him	mug	set
fed	top	lad	pug	leg

	1	2	3	4	5
Date					
Total Sounds Read					
- Errors					
= Total Sounds Correct					

Decoding Story 1.1: "Ned the Cop"

Section 2 (Untimed exercises)

Non-phonetic Word Recognition

Only read the real words in these paragraphs.

Fex con tup are git to pex the tup
You fip feb was un kib med two fis
One paf lix rit the kiz
Oh weg coz of lil the yop

Hep one to lin qop to tup You won
feb Pon feb vit are fis des fow
Lix was you Qop sig tyop
Sav lig yen the gim saf cag

Was gim gol fop dit ros
Bab biz two you was
Kijvhiy rop the dup cirt
Nis dupol waz cuvit oh

pid hyu thi pol iy tyim
Guv mag xot em lit
hep tiw you nit ruy il
mif qep nis los zit nop

vol pliy rplo afplooi dit
one are hiplo yilk hlop
sav zin bviuy kib molk
poki mif hust ghuop ir

Decoding Story 1.1: "Ned the Cop"

Section 3 (Untimed exercises)

Sentence Stacks

Ned was sad

Ned was sad at his

Ned was sad at his pal Sam.

Ned and Sam

Ned and Sam sat in

Ned and Sam sat in the van.

Ned had to run

Ned had to run to the cab

Ned had to run to the cab to get Sam.

Ten men met Sam

Ten men met Sam and led him

Ten men met Sam and led him to the pen.

Decoding Story 1.1: "Ned the Cop"

Section 4 (1 minute timed activity)

Ned was a cop. Ned had fun as a cop. Ned had one pal. His pal was 17
Sam. Sam was not a cop. Sam was a bad man on the run. Sam did rob 34
one man. Ned was sad at his pal Sam. Sam had a bad rap. Ned had to 50
nab his pal Sam. Ned the cop was on the job. Ned had to run to the 68
cab to get Sam. Ned did nab Sam. Sam was too sad. His pal Ned did 84
get him. Ned and Sam sat in the van. Ten men met Sam and led him to 101
the pen. Ned had a mad pal. Ned was a sad lad. 113

Baseline
Total Words Read:
- # of errors:
= Words Correct:

1. Total Words Read:
- # of errors:
= Words Correct:

2. Total Words Read:
- # of errors:
= Words Correct:

3. Total Words Read:
- # of errors:
= Words Correct:

4. Total Words Read:
- # of errors:
= Words Correct:

5. Total Words Read:
- # of errors:
= Words Correct:

Baseline	5	10	15	20	25	30	35	40	45	50	55	60	65	70	75	80
	85	90	95	100	105	110	115	120	125	130	135	140	145	150	155	160
	165	170	175	180	185	190	195	200	205	210	215	220	225	230	235	240

Final Reading	5	10	15	20	25	30	35	40	45	50	55	60	65	70	75	80
	85	90	95	100	105	110	115	120	125	130	135	140	145	150	155	160
	165	170	175	180	185	190	195	200	205	210	215	220	225	230	235	240

Baseline Score (WPM): ___________ Final Reading (WPM): ___________ Final WPM (+/-): ___________

Decoding Story 1.2: "Flip and Flop"

DIRECTIONS: • When beginning a new story, have your student read the whole story and time them for 1 minute. Record their results in the Baseline reading section and have your student record their baseline results on their tracking sheet. • Each Reading in Section 1 is a 15-second timed activity. Have your student do one timed reading of each in one sitting. Track your results on your assessor copy and have your students track their progress on their tracking sheet. • Section 2 contains passages that contain nonsense words with non-phonetic words embedded within the story. Have your student scan the passage and find the non-phonetic words. This is NOT a timed activity. • Section 3 contains sentence stacks. These are sentences from the passage that are broken down into chunks. • Have your student read each chunk and then the next using the scoops (having them run their finger along the scoops as they read) in order to build fluency and prosody. Perform these activities once during one session. • Once your student has completed all readings 5 times over 5 sessions, have them read the story for one final time and record their results and have your student track their results.

Section 1 (Time: 15 seconds for each exercise)

Isolated Phonogram Reading

bl	a	gl	u	fl
n	d	g	w	p
fl	l	t	g	e
o	i	pl	cl	h
b	r	c	fl	sl

	1	2	3	4	5
Date					
Total Sounds Read					
- Errors					
= Total Sounds Correct					

Nonsense Word Reading

flug	grib	flam	frin	blod
glub	wid	dem	heg	bap
vix	ed	glup	plob	wen
flob	trin	plid	swen	frix
jeld	vind	simp	gox	lub

	1	2	3	4	5
Date					
Total Words Read					
- Errors					
= Total Words Correct					

Real Word Reading

Bob	sad	plan	jam	glad
yelp	blip	flax	beg	get
pal	yet	pin	met	box
lid	grab	plod	help	belt
vest	nut	tux	red	slop

	1	2	3	4	5
Date					
Total Words Read					
- Errors					
= Total Words Correct					

Decoding Story 1.2: "Flip and Flop"

Section 2 (Untimed exercises)

Non-phonetic Word Recognition

Only read the real words in these paragraphs.

Wix fen the gliv frens glap too fip.
One grix brap two vens ix frep are int.
Flen grib from the jend fisp.
Cran frim have yub tilp wext.
Silb what dran give plit.

Swip yub the grix pid too fip.
One yub prab two lems id porf are ont.
Gren julb from the pisk felp.
Grom trux have nuv pilt twend.
Bild what groz give plax.

Yuv pex the drig frib ploz too gov.
One lif yorp two ud ont trib are und.
Plen brax from the yelb twixt.
Pilt grav have yoj kilf rund.
Sav what prax give selt.

Mox the too wext trest what give.
One frop liolpo have from dewn fisppp
Plen brax from the yelb twixt.
Hu hup yoildf one the int hytrf fcolvk
Ru clof have njghuy fspoil are what

Simps ott cdriu too the yuipol
Glup ed xim from the goiyt ug
Lub niou two adkje gtiop one ir
Fitly drkiuyt too one fut iw
Grin ute rtiut was the Rio lpoi

Decoding Story 1.2: "Flip and Flop"

Sentence Stacks

Flip and Flop

Flip and Flop were pals

Flip and Flop were pals from a

Flip and Flop were pals from a grand land.

Flip was glad

Flip was glad but

Flip was glad but Flop was

Flip was glad but Flop was sad.

Flop was

Flop was glad

Flop was glad to have

Flop was glad to have a lot of dogs.

Flip got

Flip got his pal Flop

Flip got his pal Flop to hop

Flip got his pal Flop to hop up and run.

Flip got

Flip got his pal Flop

Flip got his pal Flop to hop

Flip got his pal Flop to hop up and run.

Decoding Story 1.2: "Flip and Flop"

Flip and Flop are pals from a grand land. In the land, Flip has a lot 16
of dogs. Flip was a lad who put his dogs at the top. Flop had one 32
dog. Flip was glad but Flop was sad as Flip did not have a lot of 48
dogs. Flip went to get Flop to run with his dogs but Flop was too 63
sad to run. Flip did give his pal Flop two dogs. Flip got his pal Flop to 80
hop up and run. Flop was not sad. Flop was glad to have a lot of 96
dogs. Flop got up to run with Flip and his dogs. What fun Flip and 111
Flop had as they ran from spot to spot. Flop had the best dogs in 126
the land. Flip and Flop are pals who are glad. 136

Baseline
Total Words Read:
- # of errors:
= Words Correct:

2. Total Words Read:
- # of errors:
= Words Correct:

4. Total Words Read:
- # of errors:
= Words Correct:

1. Total Words Read:
- # of errors:
= Words Correct:

3. Total Words Read:
- # of errors:
= Words Correct:

5. Total Words Read:
- # of errors:
= Words Correct:

Baseline	5	10	15	20	25	30	35	40	45	50	55	60	65	70	75	80
	85	90	95	100	105	110	115	120	125	130	135	140	145	150	155	160
	165	170	175	180	185	190	195	200	205	210	215	220	225	230	235	240

Final Reading	5	10	15	20	25	30	35	40	45	50	55	60	65	70	75	80
	85	90	95	100	105	110	115	120	125	130	135	140	145	150	155	160
	165	170	175	180	185	190	195	200	205	210	215	220	225	230	235	240

Baseline Score (WPM): ____________ Final Reading (WPM): ____________ Final WPM (+/-): ______________

Decoding Story 1.3: "Jan's Quilt"

DIRECTIONS: • When beginning a new story, have your student read the whole story and time them for 1 minute. Record their results in the Baseline reading section and have your student record their baseline results on their tracking sheet. • Each Reading in Section 1 is a 15-second timed activity. Have your student do one timed reading of each in one sitting. Track your results on your assessor copy and have your students track their progress on their tracking sheet. • Section 2 contains passages that contain nonsense words with non-phonetic words embedded within the story. Have your student scan the passage and find the non-phonetic words. This is NOT a timed activity. • Section 3 contains sentence stacks. These are sentences from the passage that are broken down into chunks. • Have your student read each chunk and then the next using the scoops (having them run their finger along the scoops as they read) in order to build fluency and prosody. Perform these activities once during one session. • Once your student has completed all readings 5 times over 5 sessions, have them read the story for one final time and record their results and have your student track their results.

Section 1 (Time: 15 seconds for each exercise)

Isolated Phonogram Reading

gr	qu	fl	sp	cr
bl	st	f	mp	u
pl	sn	dr	qu	nd
lt	ft	st	r	e
nt	pt	tr	pl	fl

	1	2	3	4	5
Date					
Total Sounds Read					
- Errors					
= Total Sounds Correct					

Nonsense Word Reading

quab	grox	lemp	fust	brasp
bint	snup	fruz	wemp	lund
lopt	brist	telp	treft	kisp
cruft	hund	squift	plox	reft
muxt	jept	grap	quelp	bisk

	1	2	3	4	5
Date					
Total Sounds Read					
- Errors					
= Total Sounds Correct					

Real Word Reading

quilt	dog	mud	grab	jump
sad	red	pal	fast	lamp
grub	past	craft	graft	last
tub	bag	crab	dump	just
quit	flip	squid	lug	had

	1	2	3	4	5
Date					
Total Sounds Read					
- Errors					
= Total Sounds Correct					

Decoding Story 1.3: "Jan's Quilt"

Section 2 (Untimed exercises)

Non-phonetic Word Recognition

Only read the real words in these paragraphs.

Trix wen have frin ip jost. Jelp was
un gat ep the glist.
Mesp brix gren to plid.
Twisp are drig was em frid.

Ftiyu piox clkiop was are whi uyt
iap Trough trie st to are the fgty
ot Fust tyue frist to are the lakrei
fi Kijhg typo have blopid are the yu

Drolp fiouist fip to the was
Saqwse fil ghto have the
to Wlklri frot the have bijgke ty
treft ghuj xewsd have polk pooit

Quelp the roiuty to the redfs
Thirfy to nmcnvb the serety
Ghvbcet to the have dfgopit ij
Dredsc ti seq wolpi are to glij

gholoiu have swa the to rfklj
fro jumolk to the roliuyj have muyte ut
klop the to yutyip gilet bvxesd foq
the nvboplit was the to have qoejkn

Decoding Story 1.3: "Jan's Quilt"

Section 3 (Untimed exercises)

Sentence Stacks

Sid had

Sid had the quilt

Sid had the quilt and did jump on it.

Sid ran to grab

Sid ran to grab Jan but Sid did not

Sid ran to grab Jan but Sid did not run fast.

Sid did

Sid did jump and jump

Sid did jump and jump and Jan was fed up.

Jan did grab

Jan did grab the quilt

Jan did grab the quilt and ran.

The quilt

The quilt had mud

The quilt had mud and Jan

The quilt had mud and Jan did not have

The quilt had mud and Jan did not have a pal in Sid.

Decoding Story 1.3: "Jan's Quilt"

Section 4 (1 minute timed activity)

Jan had a quilt. This quilt was the best. It had a red dog on it. 16
Jan's mom did craft the quilt for Jan. Jan did grab the quilt to sit 31
on. Jan's pal Sid did grab the quilt. Jan was sad. Sid had the quilt 46
and did jump on it. The red dog on the quilt had mud on it. Jan was 62
mad. Sid did jump and jump and Jan was fed up. Jan did grab the 76
quilt and ran. Sid ran to grab Jan but Sid did not run fast. Sid did not 92
grab Jan. Jan quit the run. Sid and Jan are not pals. The quilt 108
had mud and Jan did not have a pal in Sid. Sid and Jan felt sad. 124
126

Baseline
Total Words Read:
- # of errors:
= Words Correct:

1. Total Words Read:
- # of errors:
= Words Correct:

2. Total Words Read:
- # of errors:
= Words Correct:

3. Total Words Read:
- # of errors:
= Words Correct:

4. Total Words Read:
- # of errors:
= Words Correct:

5. Total Words Read:
- # of errors:
= Words Correct:

Baseline	5	10	15	20	25	30	35	40	45	50	55	60	65	70	75	80
	85	90	95	100	105	110	115	120	125	130	135	140	145	150	155	160
	165	170	175	180	185	190	195	200	205	210	215	220	225	230	235	240

Final Reading	5	10	15	20	25	30	35	40	45	50	55	60	65	70	75	80
	85	90	95	100	105	110	115	120	125	130	135	140	145	150	155	160
	165	170	175	180	185	190	195	200	205	210	215	220	225	230	235	240

Baseline Score (WPM): ___________ Final Reading (WPM): ___________ Final WPM (+/-): ___________

Fluency Plus!

Where to Begin

Assessor Instructions

Once you have completed the Reading Fluency Screener and have determined that your student is at the Fluency Plus! level, you can start here. Refer to the System Central to determine the best starting point for your student. The System Central lays out what concepts may be contained in each story. Refer to the Error Analysis section of your student's Reading Screener.

Compare the student's passage reading results to the results of the individual letters, sounds and word results and determine the most suitable starting point for your individual student.

The stories contained in Fluency Plus! are sequential and cumulative and build upon each other. It is very important to be mindful of not introducing stories with advanced concepts prior to the student being introduced to these concepts. Bearing this in mind helps maintain a sense of accomplishment and confidence for your student.

Here are some detailed instructions on how to proceed through the Fluency Plus! stories.

Fluency Passages

1. Have the student read the fluency passage to get a baseline WCPM (word count per minute) score. Record the baseline on the teacher's copy. Have your student record their baseline score on the Reading Fluency Tracking sheet (see page 201). Discuss with your student about their reading goals based on what their baseline scores were. Have the student record their personal goals on their tracking sheet.
2. Have the student perform isolated phonogram, nonsense word reading, and real word reading in that order, and record their scores (Section 1). The student records their progress on their tracking sheet. These drills should not be done in one sitting. The isolated phonogram, nonsense word, and real word reading should be done one time during one session.
3. After the timed sequence of drills above have been completed, have student practice identifying the non-phonetic words in the non-phonetic word recognition section. Once that is complete, the student can then practice the sentence stacks.
4. After the student has completed the sequence of drills five times (over five sessions), have student read the full passage reading five times over another five sessions and record results. The final fifth reading is the student's final passage reading.
5. Record results of baseline reading and final (fifth) reading to view summarized progress.

Story FP-1.1: "The Quiz"

DIRECTIONS: • When beginning a new story, have your student read the whole story and time them for 1 minute. Record their results in the Baseline reading section and have your student record their baseline results on their tracking sheet. • Each Reading in Section 1 is a 15-second timed activity. Have your student do one timed reading of each in one sitting. Track your results on your assessor copy and have your students track their progress on their tracking sheet. • Section 2 contains passages that contain nonsense words with non-phonetic words embedded within the story. Have your student scan the passage and find the non-phonetic words. This is NOT a timed activity. • Section 3 contains sentence stacks. These are sentences from the passage that are broken down into chunks. • Have your student read each chunk and then the next using the scoops (having them run their finger along the scoops as they read) in order to build fluency and prosody. Perform these activities once during one session. • Once your student has completed all readings 5 times over 5 sessions, have them read the story for one final time and record their results and have your student track their results.

Section 1 (Time: 15 seconds for each exercise)

Isolated Phonogram Reading

qu	cl	pl	cr	gr
ck	qu	fr	br	sm
pl	gl	ck	tr	sw
bl	qu	fr	cr	dr
pr	tw	sk	ft	mp

	1	2	3	4	5
Date					
Total Sounds Read					
- Errors					
= Total Sounds Correct					

Nonsense Word Reading

quet	vuck	bromp	quop	crund
splock	strind	flaz	brift	plon
quix	vick	quend	creft	sprip
wend	twib	juck	vind	quelp
cleck	strift	prump	jelp	drick

	1	2	3	4	5
Date					
Total Words Read					
- Errors					
= Total Words Correct					

Real Word Reading

struck	clamp	quell	brick	back
plan	loft	quest	deck	clock
quiz	grand	grab	cram	jump
plot	stop	black	muck	quid
split	struck	lost	strip	quack

	1	2	3	4	5
Date					
Total Words Read					
- Errors					
= Total Words Correct					

Story FP-1.1: "The Quiz"

Section 2 (Untimed exercises)

Non-phonetic Word Recognition

Only read the real words in these paragraphs.

crund flox tremp was grix
jund frimp have pord grusk lopt
trind fip give tru plemp to dilp
delp wux done wift fop hund

quia frimp to jud forg
swind brep milp have frut
trelp fid give turp to barx
wex frig tump brig was belp

Was rituyr tpolout done was to the ip
Dipole you qasdt foiuty was plaiasw you
Cilklmn dipole you from to the was you
Giuit ghytuo of the to from you have ew

Barxz cgfhyt was done tyeieh ewer driploiu
Vyterd from the to you djro iejou shof jrj to
Voojuty flooiuyt kwade qwiao gvie ytu powes
Molkji ahjoiy have grwaqst giuyt yuryt erst fro

rweyurt to the give noplert to the
have the give to the roisutp mollie your
myofia uint was the roiuty the hvae huy
qwsder folopi done the was to req to nedt

Story FP-1.1: "The Quiz"

Section 3 (Untimed exercises)

Sentence Stacks

Quin was quick
Quin was quick to grab
Quin was quick to grab his pen
Quin was quick to grab his pen and run
Quin was quick to grab his pen and run up to his loft
Quin was quick to grab his pen and run up to his loft to print a map
Quin was quick to grab his pen and run up to his loft to print a map of his plan.

Quin's plan
Quin's plan was to
Quin's plan was to jam his plan
Quin's plan was to jam his plan in his bag
Quin's plan was to jam his plan in his bag and give it
Quin's plan was to jam his plan in his bag and give it to his pal Dan.

Quin had
Quin had a plan
Quin had a plan to cram
Quin had a plan to cram for the quiz.

Quin felt
Quin felt the quiz
Quin felt the quiz was
Quin felt the quiz was in the bag.

Quin did
Quin did not get
Quin did not get to the top
Quin did not get to the top of his class.

Story FP-1.1: "The Quiz"

Section 4 (1 minute timed activity)

Quin was a guy who was on a quest. Quin's quest was to get to the 17
top of his class. Quin had a plan to cram for the quiz. Quin was quick 33
to grab his pen and run up to his loft to print a map of his plan. On 50
his desk sat a big clock. The clock was from a pal. Quin's plan was 67
to jam his plan in his bag and give it to his pal Dan. Quin had to 84
map his big plan at the back of his loft. Quin was quick to map the 101
plan. The plan was done. Quin felt the quiz was in the bag. Quin 118
got to his class and met Dan. Dan did pat Quin on the back. The 134
quiz was not on the plan. Mrs Jun had to pass on the plan to have 152
a quiz. Quin did not get to the top of his class. Bad luck Quin. 169
183

Baseline	2. Total Words Read:	4. Total Words Read:
Total Words Read:	- # of errors:	- # of errors:
- # of errors:	= Words Correct:	= Words Correct:
= Words Correct:		

1. Total Words Read:	3. Total Words Read:	5. Total Words Read:
- # of errors:	- # of errors:	- # of errors:
= Words Correct:	= Words Correct:	= Words Correct:

Baseline																
	5	10	15	20	25	30	35	40	45	50	55	60	65	70	75	80
	85	90	95	100	105	110	115	120	125	130	135	140	145	150	155	160
	165	170	175	180	185	190	195	200	205	210	215	220	225	230	235	240

Final Reading																
	5	10	15	20	25	30	35	40	45	50	55	60	65	70	75	80
	85	90	95	100	105	110	115	120	125	130	135	140	145	150	155	160
	165	170	175	180	185	190	195	200	205	210	215	220	225	230	235	240

Baseline Score (WPM): ____________ Final Reading (WPM): ____________ Final WPM (+/-): ____________

Comprehension Questions

1. What was Quin's quest?
2. Where did Quin map his plan?
3. Did Quin feel good about his plan?
4. Why did Quin have bad luck?
5. Why did Quin's pal Dan pat Quin on the back?
6. Have you ever planned for a test and then not had to do it?

Story FP-2.1: "The Lost Quilt"

DIRECTIONS: • When beginning a new story, have your student read the whole story and time them for 1 minute. Record their results in the Baseline reading section and have your student record their baseline results on their tracking sheet. • Each Reading in Section 1 is a 15-second timed activity. Have your student do one timed reading of each in one sitting. Track your results on your assessor copy and have your students track their progress on their tracking sheet. • Section 2 contains passages that contain nonsense words with non-phonetic words embedded within the story. Have your student scan the passage and find the non-phonetic words. This is NOT a timed activity. • Section 3 contains sentence stacks. These are sentences from the passage that are broken down into chunks. • Have your student read each chunk and then the next using the scoops (having them run their finger along the scoops as they read) in order to build fluency and prosody. Perform these activities once during one session. • Once your student has completed all readings 5 times over 5 sessions, have them read the story for one final time and record their results and have your student track their results.

Section 1 (Time: 15 seconds for each exercise)

Isolated Phonogram Reading

qu	spl	str	mp	dr
a	ck	c	pl	k
e	sp	st	u	squ
l	ft	nd	nt	gl
scr	tw	st	sk	sw

	1	2	3	4	5
Date					
Total Sounds Read					
- Errors					
= Total Sounds Correct					

Nonsense Word Reading

squip	fack	plom	med	plust
quif	yod	climp	nug	glon
spom	swif	flomp	frist	clof
flist	crill	Vost	quot	blist
drog	pron	Plant	snoft	lop

	1	2	3	4	5
Date					
Total Words Read					
- Errors					
= Total Words Correct					

Real Word Reading

quest	squid	nob	bluff	floss
frog	track	dock	stump	pond
spot	tell	skip	glad	quilt
fast	trump	mess	squint	pick
rocks	black	twig	last	muck

	1	2	3	4	5
Date					
Total Words Read					
- Errors					
= Total Words Correct					

Story FP-2.1: "The Lost Quilt"

Section 2 (Untimed exercises)

Non-phonetic Word Recognition

Only read the real words in these paragraphs.

Kipet unplo many narth plet
Only vab axd some fups hox
Come trub flin to speg
Skol some dexho tef pauy oj

Many raztim nolf kunch some
Ofent pog only uhert many
Only feag ykip how come
Tepit arjphat many fab veb

Some of the many to you was frif drgtop
Fjkhsjykt guidjfj many to the was frjhiuth
Jshtohrouh only Tod sjeh josijrij jhueh to
to ksjktj kzk thr skljt ir olmo done to the

Thujijar of the to you njfhth eu tref ploi
Diejr sht the some ahdf to the was you
The furhf jirh gyup do to the fro jhskjh
Fhiur to the was only jhsuht tfsj of

deaswqer only some rihsjdh come to you
was the kftuior to jskjytrj only frhtkh su tajs
the come some jdhtuhkjhjy jihfjskhur irwks
saberte ksjfrun kjshjkh come jiuhekj some

Story FP-2.1: "The Lost Quilt"

Section 3 (Untimed exercises)

Sentence Stacks

They were so mad

They were so mad at the muck but

They were so mad at the muck but Quin got a twig

They were so mad at the muck but Quin got a twig and did pick it off.

Quin fled

Quin fled up the big hill

Quin fled up the big hill as fast as Quin did run

Quin fled up the big hill as fast as Quin did run and did belt a big yell.

Bess was

Bess was on a quest

Bess was on a quest to pick

Bess was on a quest to pick a black fleck rock

Bess was on a quest to pick a black fleck rock but Tess felt mad

Bess was on a quest to pick a black fleck rock but Tess felt mad and did a big yell.

Bess and Tess

Bess and Tess did squint

Bess and Tess did squint at him

Bess and Tess did squint at him and they ran back

Bess and Tess did squint at him and they ran back to the pond.

As luck did come,

As luck did come, Bess did put

As luck did come, Bess did put the quilt

As luck did come, Bess did put the quilt in a big clump

As luck did come, Bess did put the quilt in a big clump of black muck!

Story FP-2.1: "The Lost Quilt"

Section 4 (1 minute timed activity)

Bess, Tess and Quin sat on the red quilt in the sun. They felt very cold and 17
were to pick up many rocks for the pond in the back. Bess was on a 33
quest for a black fleck rock but Tess felt mad and did a big yell. Quin felt 50
they were too quick to pick up rocks and did skip back to the quilt, but it 67
was lost! Quick, Quin fled up the big hill as fast as the wind and he did 84
belt a big yell "The red quilt is lost!!" Bess and Tess did squint at him and 101
they ran back to the pond. As luck did come, Bess did put the quilt in a 118
big clump of black muck! It was a big mess! Who put the quilt in the muck? 134
Bess did drop and roll it in the grass to get the muck off, but it was 152
stuck! They were so mad at the muck but Quin got a twig and did pick it 169
off. They were back on the red quilt and felt the sun at last. 183

Baseline
Total Words Read:
- # of errors:
= Words Correct:

2. Total Words Read:
- # of errors:
= Words Correct:

4. Total Words Read:
- # of errors:
= Words Correct:

1. Total Words Read:
- # of errors:
= Words Correct:

3. Total Words Read:
- # of errors:
= Words Correct:

5. Total Words Read:
- # of errors:
= Words Correct:

Baseline	5	10	15	20	25	30	35	40	45	50	55	60	65	70	75	80
	85	90	95	100	105	110	115	120	125	130	135	140	145	150	155	160
	165	170	175	180	185	190	195	200	205	210	215	220	225	230	235	240

Final Reading	5	10	15	20	25	30	35	40	45	50	55	60	65	70	75	80
	85	90	95	100	105	110	115	120	125	130	135	140	145	150	155	160
	165	170	175	180	185	190	195	200	205	210	215	220	225	230	235	240

Baseline Score (WPM): ____________ Final Reading (WPM): ____________ Final WPM (+/-): ____________

Comprehension Questions

1. What colour was the quilt?
2. Who found the lost quilt?
3. What was the quilt covered with?
4. What were they collecting rocks for?
5. Who do you think took it? Why?

Story FP-3.1: "Seth's Trip on a Ship"

DIRECTIONS: • When beginning a new story, have your student read the whole story and time them for 1 minute. Record their results in the Baseline reading section and have your student record their baseline results on their tracking sheet. • Each Reading in Section 1 is a 15-second timed activity. Have your student do one timed reading of each in one sitting. Track your results on your assessor copy and have your students track their progress on their tracking sheet. • Section 2 contains passages that contain nonsense words with non-phonetic words embedded within the story. Have your student scan the passage and find the non-phonetic words. This is NOT a timed activity. • Section 3 contains sentence stacks. These are sentences from the passage that are broken down into chunks. • Have your student read each chunk and then the next using the scoops (having them run their finger along the scoops as they read) in order to build fluency and prosody. Perform these activities once during one session. • Once your student has completed all readings 5 times over 5 sessions, have them read the story for one final time and record their results and have your student track their results.

Section 1 (Time: 15 seconds for each exercise)

Isolated Phonogram Reading

th	sh	tr	ch	gr
bl	nd	ch	lt	mp
nt	th	pl	tw	shr
thr	bl	gr	fl	st
pt	sh	pt	sw	fr

	1	2	3	4	5
Date					
Total Sounds Read					
- Errors					
= Total Sounds Correct					

Nonsense Word Reading

chud	thrip	flum	shub	trux
shrag	jund	prib	twuv	wolp
flej	venft	swib	thiz	vind
sprox	brub	glopt	thag	prilk
wemp	prax	glud	dimp	rext

	1	2	3	4	5
Date					
Total Words Read					
- Errors					
= Total Words Correct					

Real Word Reading

lunch	grab	with	rush	jump
that	help	told	gal	ship
did	stop	man	back	bump
bench	stub	flop	branch	fix
bath	kelp	dump	lock	welt

	1	2	3	4	5
Date					
Total Words Read					
- Errors					
= Total Words Correct					

Story FP-3.1: "Seth's Trip on a Ship"

Section 2 (Untimed exercises)

Non-phonetic Word Recognition

Only read the real words in these paragraphs.

sprif grib many twix crub
groft premp trif only druj klib
sprox frend truj pluv come
swiv trib frox many brins

frib veng drex croz come trij
wex criv blon only frim
reb brid frup some twibs
spleft wanch wuld many

f Many to come ahjthi u to the freh
Fitly osjg gtup one many some have
Fieshhj jail only some shukrkn the to
Janjkf cfut ajnjf j was to the you of

Jgnoshh to many jetjshd jej kje kj
Hjfkshekrh to shish kjhs you jshiuteh
Kjehkjh too usyrjn jhherukh are roi
jshgurhjn ksnlkeh ksjrie to the jhkjh many some

kjshktuh to done to have teuhrkjf hkjshj you ksjh
hrhuhone have to the jaheiuhru htiu skwull you
shituh done to sjkhtuehj k kjahk you noutnj jolrj
bjhsuhr was are rhtkuhut to hsiue bihroiuh obj to

Story FP-3.1: "Seth's Trip on a Ship"

Section 3 (Untimed exercises)

Sentence Stacks

Seth and Chad

Seth and Chad sat

Seth and Chad sat on the bench

Seth and Chad sat on the bench to have their lunch.

Seth told Chad

Seth told Chad that some guys

Seth told Chad that some guys were on the ship

Seth told Chad that some guys were on the ship and they did help Seth.

The man

The man did wish

The man did wish to have a swim

The man did wish to have a swim but went back

The man did wish to have a swim but went back to his flat

The man did wish to have a swim but went back to his flat on the ship.

Seth and the gal

Seth and the gal did pat

Seth and the gal did pat the man's back

Seth and the gal did pat the man's back and were glad

Seth and the gal did pat the man's back and were glad that the man

Seth and the gal did pat the man's back and were glad that the man did not jump ship.

The man

The man did wish

The man did wish to have a swim

The man did wish to have a swim but went back

The man did wish to have a swim but went back to his flat

Chad was glad that Seth and the gal did help the man.

Story FP-3.1: "Seth's Trip on a Ship"

Section 4 (1 minute timed activity)

Seth met Chad for lunch. Seth was in a rush to tell Chad of his clash with 17
a man on a ship. Seth and Chad sat on the bench to have their lunch. 33
Seth said, "The man on the ship was in a rush to jump ship to go for a 51
swim!" Seth said that a gal had to stop the man. Seth and the gal did 67
grab the man. The gal did yell to the man, "Come back!" as she did pull 83
the man back from the end of the ship. Seth told Chad that some guys 98
were on the ship and they did help Seth and the gal with the man. Seth 114
and the gal did pat the man's back and were glad that the man did not 130
jump ship. The man did wish to have a swim but went back to his flat on 147
the ship. Seth told Chad that he was glad that the man did not jump 162
ship. Chad was glad that Seth and the gal did help the man. 175

Baseline
Total Words Read:
- # of errors:
= Words Correct:

1. Total Words Read:
- # of errors:
= Words Correct:

2. Total Words Read:
- # of errors:
= Words Correct:

3. Total Words Read:
- # of errors:
= Words Correct:

4. Total Words Read:
- # of errors:
= Words Correct:

5. Total Words Read:
- # of errors:
= Words Correct:

Baseline	5	10	15	20	25	30	35	40	45	50	55	60	65	70	75	80
	85	90	95	100	105	110	115	120	125	130	135	140	145	150	155	160
	165	170	175	180	185	190	195	200	205	210	215	220	225	230	235	240

Final Reading	5	10	15	20	25	30	35	40	45	50	55	60	65	70	75	80
	85	90	95	100	105	110	115	120	125	130	135	140	145	150	155	160
	165	170	175	180	185	190	195	200	205	210	215	220	225	230	235	240

Baseline Score (WPM): ___________ Final Reading (WPM): ___________ Final WPM (+/-): ___________

Comprehension Questions

1. Why did Seth meet with his friend Chad?
2. Who helped Seth pull the man from the edge of the ship?
3. Why was Seth glad in the end?
4. Why did the man want to jump ship?
5. Where else could the man have gone for a swim?
6. Have you ever helped someone who was going to make a bad decision?

Story FP-4.1: "At the Pond"

DIRECTIONS: • When beginning a new story, have your student read the whole story and time them for 1 minute. Record their results in the Baseline reading section and have your student record their baseline results on their tracking sheet. • Each Reading in Section 1 is a 15-second timed activity. Have your student do one timed reading of each in one sitting. Track your results on your assessor copy and have your students track their progress on their tracking sheet. • Section 2 contains passages that contain nonsense words with non-phonetic words embedded within the story. Have your student scan the passage and find the non-phonetic words. This is NOT a timed activity. • Section 3 contains sentence stacks. These are sentences from the passage that are broken down into chunks. • Have your student read each chunk and then the next using the scoops (having them run their finger along the scoops as they read) in order to build fluency and prosody. Perform these activities once during one session. • Once your student has completed all readings 5 times over 5 sessions, have them read the story for one final time and record their results and have your student track their results.

Section 1 (Time: 15 seconds for each exercise)

Isolated Phonogram Reading

th	sh	qu	u	e
tch	dge	nd	st	ch
wh	ing	ank	mp	str
tch	fl	scr	ft	xt
ck	thr	shr	spl	dge

	1	2	3	4	5
Date					
Total Sounds Read					
- Errors					
= Total Sounds Correct					

Nonsense Word Reading

lomp	grimp	flind	drunch	flodge
widge	brudge	clonch	blest	swutch
flink	druck	dradge	slish	crench
shump	drump	wensh	scomp	skitch
swong	blomp	dreck	wemp	plish

	1	2	3	4	5
Date					
Total Words Read					
- Errors					
= Total Words Correct					

Real Word Reading

flesh	trudge	fridge	switch	hedge
hand	notch	french	drench	with
ledge	shrimp	clutch	belch	crash
chest	frill	less	stretch	squint
bath	blush	squish	bench	thick

	1	2	3	4	5
Date					
Total Words Read					
- Errors					
= Total Words Correct					

Story FP-4.1: "At the Pond"

Section 2 (Untimed exercises)

Non-phonetic Word Recognition

Only read the real words in these paragraphs.

Hals yed sida sure jik pos only
Quext door both nom diff guy
Floor def gex iuhump gblop once
Jiopl floj both only dape cvol

Both thiurhut sure the was jshtu acvsh the
Hfjkhksuhj hedfkr typeer sure only to
Njdhsuh both floor sjkeuhrj too shuej
Djsurh once sjhrieuhrj once kjshj to

Only once kjshkjfhdkjhf to jkskdjh
From the floor to the door anjr to
Sjhdkjh xwes you are shthsjh vgtuy
Jkjshkfkjs to the door sure on the

Oahu floor t the hjhkjh khaki was done iutyo
hfure do you what the are was ouhebjh btui
you are jskduh floor you sjkkuhd krjhgj kjfg
skjkjh floor was kjshrkush have what jusdk

you have skjhtkjhskh the ksjhfkjhs pol jfue
sjkhkjhkth kjhthehj to the you was only sjhtu
ksjh kjrht once jhskhfsh what jshh to
many flurg have ponb only yulg what to

Story FP-4.1: "At the Pond"

Section 3 (Untimed exercises)

Sentence Stacks

Chad had to ask

Chad had to ask if it was ok

Chad had to ask if it was ok and his

Chad had to ask if it was ok and his dad said yes.

Once they were

Once they were at the pond

Once they were at the pond Chad did spot

Once they were at the pond Chad did spot his friend Hodge

But just then

But just then Tuck did

But just then Tuck did a fast spin

But just then Tuck did a fast spin and did snatch

But just then Tuck did a fast spin and did snatch a very big patch

But just then Tuck did a fast spin and did snatch a very big patch of twigs from the grass.

As they ran

As they ran on the path,

As they ran on the path, they both did smell

As they ran on the path, they both did smell a lush

As they ran on the path, they both did smell a lush and splendid smell.

With a stick

With a stick in hand,

With a stick in hand, Chad bent

With a stick in hand, Chad bent to the path

With a stick in hand, Chad bent to the path and hid

With a stick in hand, Chad bent to the path and hid in the long,

With a stick in hand, Chad bent to the path and hid in the long, tall grass.

Story FP-4.1: "At the Pond"

Section 4 (1 minute timed activity)

Once, Chad and his dog Tuck went to visit his pal at the pond. Chad 15
had to ask if it was ok and his dad said yes. Chad and Tuck did a quick 33
dash and cut past the kitchen on the path to the back door. They did a 49
big jump off the back deck and did land in the tall, wet grass. They were 65
sure that they were ok and kept on the run. As they ran on the path, 81
they both did smell a lush and splendid smell. The plants were big, soft 95
and plush and some were red and some were just a bud. Along the top 110
of the tall hedge, Chad and Tuck did a quick scan for trash but did not 126
get any. Once they were at the pond, Chad did spot his pal Hodge. 141
Hodge said that the frogs and fish were on the logs and snacking on 155
lunch but if they were still, they could watch. With a stick in hand, Chad 170
bent to the path and hid in the long, tall grass. But just then, Tuck did a 187
fast spin and did snatch a very big patch of twigs from the grass. He did 203
sniff and smell but did not yelp. The frogs and fish were quick to dash 218
and hid in the sand and logs. Too bad! Tuck ran off and Chad and 233
Hodge had to miss the fish. They were mad! 242

Baseline	2. Total Words Read:	4. Total Words Read:
Total Words Read:	- # of errors:	- # of errors:
- # of errors:	= Words Correct:	= Words Correct:
= Words Correct:		

1. Total Words Read:	3. Total Words Read:	5. Total Words Read:
- # of errors:	- # of errors:	- # of errors:
= Words Correct:	= Words Correct:	= Words Correct:

Baseline	5	10	15	20	25	30	35	40	45	50	55	60	65	70	75	80
	85	90	95	100	105	110	115	120	125	130	135	140	145	150	155	160
	165	170	175	180	185	190	195	200	205	210	215	220	225	230	235	240

Final Reading	5	10	15	20	25	30	35	40	45	50	55	60	65	70	75	80
	85	90	95	100	105	110	115	120	125	130	135	140	145	150	155	160
	165	170	175	180	185	190	195	200	205	210	215	220	225	230	235	240

Baseline Score (WPM): ___________ Final Reading (WPM): ___________ Final WPM (+/-): ___________

Comprehension Questions

1. Who did Chad have to ask before he could go out and play?
2. What was Chad's friend's name?
3. What could Chad and Hodge see on the logs?
4. Did Chad find any trash?
5. What did Tuck do to scare the frogs and fish?
6. Are the boys mad? Why?

Story FP-5.1: "Stash the Cash"

DIRECTIONS: • When beginning a new story, have your student read the whole story and time them for 1 minute. Record their results in the Baseline reading section and have your student record their baseline results on their tracking sheet. • Each Reading in Section 1 is a 15-second timed activity. Have your student do one timed reading of each in one sitting. Track your results on your assessor copy and have your students track their progress on their tracking sheet. • Section 2 contains passages that contain nonsense words with non-phonetic words embedded within the story. Have your student scan the passage and find the non-phonetic words. This is NOT a timed activity. • Section 3 contains sentence stacks. These are sentences from the passage that are broken down into chunks. • Have your student read each chunk and then the next using the scoops (having them run their finger along the scoops as they read) in order to build fluency and prosody. Perform these activities once during one session. • Once your student has completed all readings 5 times over 5 sessions, have them read the story for one final time and record their results and have your student track their results.

Section 1 (Time: 15 seconds for each exercise)

Isolated Phonogram Reading

sh	ch	nt	dge	ong
th	spl	nd	ank	ink
str	mp	pr	spl	old
qu	sk	ft	bl	shr
ck	str	thr	fl	ang

	1	2	3	4	5
Date					
Total Sounds Read					
- Errors					
= Total Sounds Correct					

Nonsense Word Reading

dold	mank	prunk	fless	squast
rist	plis	flonk	shrick	jib
ront	splosh	glud	shrift	losh
blift	prunt	lench	trop	bluss
flust	hod	dist	blesk	plis

	1	2	3	4	5
Date					
Total Words Read					
- Errors					
= Total Words Correct					

Real Word Reading

all	had	quick	stash	judge
went	back	next	trudge	bench
rent	cash	check	best	long
print	spent	insist	blank	lodge
switch	blank	lodge	desk	sprint

	1	2	3	4	5
Date					
Total Words Read					
- Errors					
= Total Words Correct					

Story FP-5.1: "Stash the Cash"

Section 2 (Untimed exercises)

Non-phonetic Word Recognition

Only read the real words in these paragraphs.

Grist mot very trop much here har mest
flink Here holp very such dest clom plosh cit drow
climp vist here olp vump blom clop glip

Frim bul glid move both yut trop jesk huy
nodge frit op glod move plok move
Don't yih jut rund flor four nil buh

One very sskuh ghjrh jdjhr here much
Don't hsihreuh one of jskjheuh sjhekjh
The kjhskjhjh both here very to the you
The kjhskjhjh both here very to the you

skjhkjth jsrtjn knto the door shh h both
sjkjthjh hsjkh kj the to you jsnkjhjh lpj
was jshektjh ifgh kojhf jshr kjsu both
move to grib such one pind the yurb porb

move to here attunjf you jhrb jb do the
very lskjitu you jsntku Jon ifhgt skhjt po
here Kolp much onhty jshruh much anrf
Don't both ksekjhr the kskjher some

Story FP-5.1: "Stash the Cash"

Section 3 (Untimed exercises)

Sentence Stacks

When King Frank

When King Frank wished for cash,

When King Frank wished for cash, he went

When King Frank wished for cash, he went to his press

When King Frank wished for cash, he went to his press that could

When King Frank wished for cash, he went to his press that could print cash.

Frank wished

Frank wished for cash

Frank wished for cash that would

Frank wished for cash that would help his fans.

Frank's plan

Frank's plan was to stash

Frank's plan was to stash the cash

Frank's plan was to stash the cash so that his pals

Frank's plan was to stash the cash so that his pals could not

Frank's plan was to stash the cash so that his pals could not grab it.

When the clock

When the clock struck two,

When the clock struck two, King Frank hitched

When the clock struck two, King Frank hitched a lock

When the clock struck two, King Frank hitched a lock on the press

When the clock struck two, King Frank hitched a lock on the press and packed it in his trunk.

It was then

It was then that King Frank's pals

It was then that King Frank's pals could not

It was then that King Frank's pals could not grab the cash.

Story FP-5.1: "Stash the Cash"

Section 4 (1 minute timed activity)

Frank was a king who spent a lot of cash. When King Frank wished for cash, 16
he went to his press that could print cash. Frank stashed his cash in a trunk 32
at the back of his desk. Frank would run to his press a lot to print cash. A 50
bunch of Frank's pals would take his cash and run to clubs to spend and 65
spend his cash. Frank did not want his pals to snatch his cash and he did 81
not want to run to the clubs with his pals. Frank wished for cash that would 97
help his fans. With a dash, Frank ran to his press that had the last batch of 114
cash on it. When the clock struck two, King Frank hitched a lock on the 129
press and packed it in his trunk. Quick as a flash, King Frank dashed up the 145
hill to the edge of the kingdom clutching the trunk with the last bunch of 160
cash that was hot off the press. Frank's plan was to stash the cash so that 176
his pals could not grab it. Frank did stash the cash at the back of the shed 193
with the help of his friend, Mitch. It was then that King Frank's pals could not 209
grab the cash. King Frank ended up with a lot of cash that he was glad he 226
could spend and stash. 230

Baseline
Total Words Read:
- # of errors:
= Words Correct:

1. Total Words Read:
- # of errors:
= Words Correct:

2. Total Words Read:
- # of errors:
= Words Correct:

3. Total Words Read:
- # of errors:
= Words Correct:

4. Total Words Read:
- # of errors:
= Words Correct:

5. Total Words Read:
- # of errors:
= Words Correct:

Baseline	5	10	15	20	25	30	35	40	45	50	55	60	65	70	75	80
	85	90	95	100	105	110	115	120	125	130	135	140	145	150	155	160
	165	170	175	180	185	190	195	200	205	210	215	220	225	230	235	240

Final Reading	5	10	15	20	25	30	35	40	45	50	55	60	65	70	75	80
	85	90	95	100	105	110	115	120	125	130	135	140	145	150	155	160
	165	170	175	180	185	190	195	200	205	210	215	220	225	230	235	240

Baseline Score (WPM): ____________ Final Reading (WPM): ____________ Final WPM (+/-): ______________

Comprehension Questions
1. Who stashed the cash?
2. Where did they stash the cash?
3. Why do you think they wanted to stash the cash?
4. Why wasn't the first man good?
5. If you were Frank and Mitch, where would you stash the cash?

Story FP 6.1: "The Back Lane"

DIRECTIONS: • When beginning a new story, have your student read the whole story and time them for 1 minute. Record their results in the Baseline reading section and have your student record their baseline results on their tracking sheet. • Each Reading in Section 1 is a 15-second timed activity. Have your student do one timed reading of each in one sitting. Track your results on your assessor copy and have your students track their progress on their tracking sheet. • Section 2 contains passages that contain nonsense words with non-phonetic words embedded within the story. Have your student scan the passage and find the non-phonetic words. This is NOT a timed activity.
• Section 3 contains sentence stacks. These are sentences from the passage that are broken down into chunks. • Have your student read each chunk and then the next using the scoops (having them run their finger along the scoops as they read) in order to build fluency and prosody. Perform these activities once during one session. • Once your student has completed all readings 5 times over 5 sessions, have them read the story for one final time and record their results and have your student track their results.

Section 1 (Time: 15 seconds for each exercise)

Isolated Phonogram Reading

tch	a-e	e-e	ing	unk
dge	i-e	sh	o-e	ink
ung	ank	ung	mp	squ
eng	thr	ong	ank	a-e
qu	onk	ing	o-e	ink

	1	2	3	4	5
Date					
Total Sounds Read					
- Errors					
= Total Sounds Correct					

Nonsense Word Reading

jidge	smotch	drong	plong	swutch
vank	thronk	clong	plang	dridge
slove	clave	plide	brose	kank
flong	trife	smole	smate	loke
snode	swoft	pleft	nime	blude

	1	2	3	4	5
Date					
Total Words Read					
- Errors					
= Total Words Correct					

Real Word Reading

smile	rode	black	truck	joke
slide	crutch	glitch	bike	drape
chive	made	shed	drive	hope
blade	drench	bad	like	kick
vote	sell	flute	trade	brave

	1	2	3	4	5
Date					
Total Words Read					
- Errors					
= Total Words Correct					

Story FP 6.1: "The Back Lane"

Section 2 (Untimed exercises)

Non-phonetic Word Recognition

Only read the real words in these paragraphs.

Lin boach nerf molk mother orlop
Solp raph which heif sufght
Dpol mims ful another those
Frile queth olp irpla brother

Abic mond hinr other which
Another blimp drox mib
Aqws dunt monter uytheor
Which greem dus lofha other

Brother jhkdur jnuern only was the ti
Other to the jndkjfhujnak jeer lkjr ssoej
Kjshthj which only to the both snkjh jekjs
Rjhtkjhkh only some Coe kjrntjks some

Djshuihj noi jksnkuht the to many to
Both kodjrd to the some artkrt other
Another which sjhtiu hj clifg are too je
Hgjkerh drjhe ndkjh monther sure

eajke another tekj jksjh was the skjgkse
ksjkjth jnsjtkjhakjh jshekj ekjfuhksj to you
both another shoufg mother ajngskj to re
come to the jsekjht another jnsjhdg which

Story FP 6.1: "The Back Lane"

Section 3 (Untimed exercises)

Sentence Stacks

All of them
All of them had the same
All of them had the same black truck
All of them had the same black truck as they liked
All of them had the same black truck as they liked the shape and the shade

The man
The man who gave
The man who gave Mike the cash
The man who gave Mike the cash said that
The man who gave Mike the cash said that he would sell the bike
The man who gave Mike the cash said that he would sell the bike back to Steve

As he drove,
As he drove, Mike sang
As he drove, Mike sang a long sad song
As he drove, Mike sang a long sad song that made him
As he drove, Mike sang a long sad song that made him smile with pride.

When the
When the date came,
When the date came, they made
When the date came, they made a big mistake
When the date came, they made a big mistake and sold
When the date came, they made a big mistake and sold Steve's bike.

Steve was
Steve was still mad
Steve was still mad but did invite
Steve was still mad but did invite the man
Steve was still mad but did invite the man to take
Steve was still mad but did invite the man to take a quick spin
Steve was still mad but did invite the man to take a quick spin up the lane.

Story FP 6.1: "The Back Lane"

Section 4 (1 minute timed activity)

Mike is a man who likes to drive too fast all of the time. One day, when it 18
was late, Mike went to the back shed and put all of his junk in the back of 36
his black truck and sped off. As he drove, Mike sang a long sad song that 52
made him smile with pride. As he went to finish his drive, on the side of the 69
back lane, Mike met his friend Clive and they had a very long chat. They 84
had no time to waste and told jokes and then bumped into an old bud 99
Steve. All of them had the same black truck as they liked the shape and 114
the shade. When they finished telling jokes, they made a plan to have a 128
theme sale to get rid of some of the junk and stuff that was kept in the 145
shack at the side of Mike's home. When the date came, they made a big 160
mistake and sold Steve's bike. He was upset and mad because it was his 174
red and white bike and it had bells and brakes that could help him stop. 189
The man who gave Mike the cash said that he would sell the bike back to 205
Steve if he could have a quick ride. Steve was still mad but did invite the 221
man to take a quick spin up the lane. In the end, it was fine and all of them 240
went to Mike's and made a funny joke. 248

Baseline
Total Words Read:
- # of errors:
= Words Correct:

1. Total Words Read:
- # of errors:
= Words Correct:

2. Total Words Read:
- # of errors:
= Words Correct:

3. Total Words Read:
- # of errors:
= Words Correct:

4. Total Words Read:
- # of errors:
= Words Correct:

5. Total Words Read:
- # of errors:
= Words Correct:

Baseline	5	10	15	20	25	30	35	40	45	50	55	60	65	70	75	80
	85	90	95	100	105	110	115	120	125	130	135	140	145	150	155	160
	165	170	175	180	185	190	195	200	205	210	215	220	225	230	235	240

Final Reading	5	10	15	20	25	30	35	40	45	50	55	60	65	70	75	80
	85	90	95	100	105	110	115	120	125	130	135	140	145	150	155	160
	165	170	175	180	185	190	195	200	205	210	215	220	225	230	235	240

Baseline Score (WPM): ___________ Final Reading (WPM): ___________ Final WPM (+/-): ___________

Comprehension Questions

1. Who liked to drive too fast all of the time?
2. Why was Steve upset?
3. Where did they all meet up?
4. Did they like to tell jokes?
5. What colour truck did they all have?
6. What did Steve's bike have on it?

Story FP-7.1: "Mad Ants"

DIRECTIONS: • When beginning a new story, have your student read the whole story and time them for 1 minute. Record their results in the Baseline reading section and have your student record their baseline results on their tracking sheet. • Each Reading in Section 1 is a 15-second timed activity. Have your student do one timed reading of each in one sitting. Track your results on your assessor copy and have your students track their progress on their tracking sheet. • Section 2 contains passages that contain nonsense words with non-phonetic words embedded within the story. Have your student scan the passage and find the non-phonetic words. This is NOT a timed activity. • Section 3 contains sentence stacks. These are sentences from the passage that are broken down into chunks. • Have your student read each chunk and then the next using the scoops (having them run their finger along the scoops as they read) in order to build fluency and prosody. Perform these activities once during one session. • Once your student has completed all readings 5 times over 5 sessions, have them read the story for one final time and record their results and have your student track their results.

Section 1 (Time: 15 seconds for each exercise)

Isolated Phonogram Reading

a-e	ang	shr	dge	s-e
bl	s-e	nd	tch	all
all	ink	pt	mp	thr
e-e	unk	onk	xt	J
ing	dr	tr	spl	cl

	1	2	3	4	5
Date					
Total Sounds Read					
- Errors					
= Total Sounds Correct					

Nonsense Word Reading

grall	kose	splive	scrope	Vall
dromp	flump	trimp	swape	dong
slitch	smame	flotch	ming	swunk
fose	drole	snodge	clonk	frint
rall	stope	clidge	drong	frest

	1	2	3	4	5
Date					
Total Words Read					
- Errors					
= Total Words Correct					

Real Word Reading

nose	pal	grass	yell
grump	stung	mope	up
stung	wall	rose	bike
tall	fall	small	slope
hill	scrape	drive	brave

	1	2	3	4	5
Date					
Total Words Read					
- Errors					
= Total Words Correct					

Story FP-7.1: "Mad Ants"

Section 2 (Untimed exercises)

Non-phonetic Word Recognition

Only read the real words in these paragraphs.

Pokoh bulz kloph again neel
Citad raph gule would could dunt
Ghyup every lyp jibt often phun
Nerf where again jave mize often

Corab again often thox thip
pight ref travin could kear smaser
Lif again periz bezy helf miel salm
Rap where should thonx neyert tro

Every often could jnkwhk jetful kjh to ou
Where again ti h&j often kjhr lj should ti
Jkshdiuh again where here skjtj nsjh tre
Kjhuh often sjeui could jshetu from the

Jksdanrn some ti njeh jahrj tho to
Sjhb some very would josh ouy re
Again the from very to do you to the
Ksjn unseen jkanother bjhsehui some

skjuh which where shthskj again ti kjhek to
could fjhsuh from the sjhiuh very
ksjkjh ty ksjndkth yught sr scola jajht again thunk
jskuht should ksjhkuht would jusgt come

Story FP-7.1: "Mad Ants"

Section 3 (Untimed exercises)

Sentence Stacks

While the dogs

While the dogs were running,

While the dogs were running, Pal got stung

While the dogs were running, Pal got stung on the nose

While the dogs were running, Pal got stung on the nose by a very big ant.

When they looked

When they looked at the hill,

When they looked at the hill, a line of red ants

When they looked at the hill, a line of red ants had sprung up

When they looked at the hill, a line of red ants had sprung up next to Steve's dog.

Jed was standing

Jed was standing next to the hill

Jed was standing next to the hill and dug a hole

Jed was standing next to the hill and dug a hole on the ant hill.

Off he ran,

Off he ran, into the long

Off he ran, into the long blades of crab

Off he ran, into the long blades of crab grass to hide.

Steve and Mike

Steve and Mike ran into

Steve and Mike ran into the grass

Steve and Mike ran into the grass to help Pal.

Story FP-7.1: "Mad Ants"

Section 4 (1 minute timed activity)

Mike and his dog Jed like to run and sprint up hills. One time when they ran, 17
they met Steve who also liked to run with his dog Pal. They both liked to 33
trick the dogs and run and hide when the dogs chased the ball. While the 48
dogs ran, Pal got stung on the nose by a very big ant. It was red and mad 66
that Pal was standing on his ant-hill home. Pal ran back to Steve and all of 84
them went to the hill. Jed was standing next to the hill and dug a hole on 101
the ant hill. Mike spoke up and told Jed to stop with the dig. Jed had to 118
stop. When they looked at the hill, a line of red ants had sprung up next to 135
Steve's dog, but Pal did not think. Off he ran, into the long blades of crab 151
grass to hide. The ants stopped to think and then gave up. Steve and Mike 166
ran into the grass to help Pal. Jed ran too. At the end of the run, they all 184
came back home and ate a snack. It was a long, hot time, but they had 200
not got stung. 203

Baseline
Total Words Read:
- # of errors:
= Words Correct:

2. Total Words Read:
- # of errors:
= Words Correct:

4. Total Words Read:
- # of errors:
= Words Correct:

1. Total Words Read:
- # of errors:
= Words Correct:

3. Total Words Read:
- # of errors:
= Words Correct:

5. Total Words Read:
- # of errors:
= Words Correct:

Baseline	5	10	15	20	25	30	35	40	45	50	55	60	65	70	75	80
	85	90	95	100	105	110	115	120	125	130	135	140	145	150	155	160
	165	170	175	180	185	190	195	200	205	210	215	220	225	230	235	240

Final Reading	5	10	15	20	25	30	35	40	45	50	55	60	65	70	75	80
	85	90	95	100	105	110	115	120	125	130	135	140	145	150	155	160
	165	170	175	180	185	190	195	200	205	210	215	220	225	230	235	240

Baseline Score (WPM): ____________ Final Reading (WPM): ____________ Final WPM (+/-): ______________

Comprehension Questions

1. What colour where the ants?
2. What was the name of Mike's dog?
3. Who was Jed?
4. What did they all do once they were home?
5. Did anyone get stung?
6. Where did Pal run to avoid getting stung?

Story FP-8.1: "Class Tricks"

DIRECTIONS: • When beginning a new story, have your student read the whole story and time them for 1 minute. Record their results in the Baseline reading section and have your student record their baseline results on their tracking sheet. • Each Reading in Section 1 is a 15-second timed activity. Have your student do one timed reading of each in one sitting. Track your results on your assessor copy and have your students track their progress on their tracking sheet. • Section 2 contains passages that contain nonsense words with non-phonetic words embedded within the story. Have your student scan the passage and find the non-phonetic words. This is NOT a timed activity. • Section 3 contains sentence stacks. These are sentences from the passage that are broken down into chunks. • Have your student read each chunk and then the next using the scoops (having them run their finger along the scoops as they read) in order to build fluency and prosody. Perform these activities once during one session. • Once your student has completed all readings 5 times over 5 sessions, have them read the story for one final time and record their results and have your student track their results.

Section 1 (Time: 15 seconds for each exercise)

Isolated Phonogram Reading

y	e	a-e	all	a-e
o-e	th	i-e	str	u-e
tr	ing	ang	qu	e-e
mp	lt	str	spl	dge
ong	dr	ch	tch	ank

	1	2	3	4	5
Date					
Total Sounds Read					
- Errors					
= Total Sounds Correct					

Nonsense Word Reading

py	scome	bolob	co	Fete
smi	drave	mi	lospil	ty
Fo	swaxe	pise	cly	clatch
Pa	lave	sny	slogum	drall
plerut	satrim	clomy	flave	mu

	1	2	3	4	5
Date					
Total Words Read					
- Errors					
= Total Words Correct					

Real Word Reading

strapping	try	pretend	rotund	remit
swimming	dry	go	she	brink
slave	prefab	comply	going	fry
nose	grabbing	sting	brave	hose
spry	tide	present	ruse	rose

	1	2	3	4	5
Date					
Total Words Read					
- Errors					
= Total Words Correct					

Story FP-8.1: "Class Tricks"

Section 2 (Untimed exercises)

Non-phonetic Word Recognition

Only read the real words in these paragraphs.

Turh yelasd could nolf lugah often nesund sreef
Should again sarl tiusnull facklo thuwd sluj dow
Gyurt you dat there got bhim quap molki here hawp
Arg again for slib gamd klup lepton

Raus often thuw perl tepid pacy would
Nait Penh ku again should qwas vblop
Pafrif mon cher pal here duig rok
There bs kola himz quiz dint often

Here tr hotefg jdifjiej again too the
Here tr hotefg jdifjiej again too the
Flair goupr sijoji some come to plods
Tjsiu both come sjoejt skijor dkjstioj

Jkhsuid skjrei olksjn oh one to js
Would you ftry skjher kksjerh fyi
Skjheru again eh hah jhwould too
Sjhrtuh would should jkshrkt kjdsut

hejrk gooijht the often where some too
hifdjstjn Gorki hahu ofetn could vblop
there are you some come skjfie tihskj
dkjiy where here ksjeioj from the sj very

Story FP-8.1: "Class Tricks"

Section 3 (Untimed exercises)

Sentence Stacks

Dan began to justify

Dan began to justify why they all broke

Dan began to justify why they all broke but Trish began to cry

Dan began to justify why they all broke but Trish began to cry with a frustrated sob.

Just then

Just then Trish and Beth

Just then Trish and Beth rode by on their bikes

Just then Trish and Beth rode by on their bikes and asked them

Just then Trish and Beth rode by on their bikes and asked them what they were up to.

They asked

They asked if they could help

They asked if they could help with the planning

They asked if they could help with the planning as they were quick

They asked if they could help with the planning as they were quick and would like to win

They asked if they could help with the planning as they were quick and would like to win the prize.

Every time

Every time they filled

Every time they filled it too much,

Every time they filled it too much, the glove would explode

Every time they filled it too much, the glove would explode and drench

Every time they filled it too much, the glove would explode and drench them all.

He told them

He told them to put the glove

He told them to put the glove in the sun

He told them to put the glove in the sun so it would

He told them to put the glove in the sun so it would get hot

He told them to put the glove in the sun so it would get hot and it would expand.

Story FP-8.1: "Class Tricks"

Section 4 (1 minute timed activity)

One day, Steve and Dan were busy trying to make a latex glove into a 17
hand that could catch liquid. In class, Mr. Fry said whoever could do it 31
would win a prize. Steve and Dan began to try many tricks but they 46
began to regret the task because it was so difficult. Just then, Trish and Beth 61
came over and asked them what they were up to. Both Beth and Trish were 75
in Steve and Dan's class, so they coveted the prize too. Trish wanted to be 89
the one to think of the best plan but Dan would not let her and demanded 106
they all have equal input into the task. They began to fill many gloves up 120
but all of them broke. Dan began to justify why they all broke and Trish 136
began to cry with anger. Dan said they should modify one thing and 149
they all nodded. Steve and Dan held the latex glove while Beth and Trish 163
bent over them hugging the jug as they filled the glove. Every time they 177
filled it too much, the glove would explode and drench them all. Just then, 191
Steve had a winning bid. He told them to put the glove in the sun so it 209
would get hot and it would expand. Again, Steve and Dan held the glove 223
while Trish and Beth held onto the big jug. It worked! The gloves were full. 238
Trish yelled and hopped on one leg as she sang out a tune. 251

Baseline
Total Words Read:
- # of errors:
= Words Correct:

1. Total Words Read:
- # of errors:
= Words Correct:

2. Total Words Read:
- # of errors:
= Words Correct:

3. Total Words Read:
- # of errors:
= Words Correct:

4. Total Words Read:
- # of errors:
= Words Correct:

5. Total Words Read:
- # of errors:
= Words Correct:

Baseline	5	10	15	20	25	30	35	40	45	50	55	60	65	70	75	80
	85	90	95	100	105	110	115	120	125	130	135	140	145	150	155	160
	165	170	175	180	185	190	195	200	205	210	215	220	225	230	235	240

Final Reading	5	10	15	20	25	30	35	40	45	50	55	60	65	70	75	80
	85	90	95	100	105	110	115	120	125	130	135	140	145	150	155	160
	165	170	175	180	185	190	195	200	205	210	215	220	225	230	235	240

Baseline Score (WPM): ____________ Final Reading (WPM): ____________ Final WPM (+/-): ____________

Comprehension Questions

1. What were they trying to fill up?
2. What was the glove made from?
3. Who started to cry because he/she became frustrated?
4. How did they finally get the glove to not explode?
5. Were they successful in the end?

Story FP 9.1: "Jay's Fishing Trip"

DIRECTIONS: • When beginning a new story, have your student read the whole story and time them for 1 minute. Record their results in the Baseline reading section and have your student record their baseline results on their tracking sheet. • Each Reading in Section 1 is a 15-second timed activity. Have your student do one timed reading of each in one sitting. Track your results on your assessor copy and have your students track their progress on their tracking sheet. • Section 2 contains passages that contain nonsense words with non-phonetic words embedded within the story. Have your student scan the passage and find the non-phonetic words. This is NOT a timed activity. • Section 3 contains sentence stacks. These are sentences from the passage that are broken down into chunks. • Have your student read each chunk and then the next using the scoops (having them run their finger along the scoops as they read) in order to build fluency and prosody. Perform these activities once during one session. • Once your student has completed all readings 5 times over 5 sessions, have them read the story for one final time and record their results and have your student track their results.

Section 1 (Time: 15 seconds for each exercise)

Isolated Phonogram Reading

ai	ea	qu	ay	ee
aw	tch	dge	ch	ea
th	ang	unk	ing	ct
ch	aw	ai	ea	ay
ea	spr	ee	sh	th

	1	2	3	4	5
Date					
Total Sounds Read					
- Errors					
= Total Sounds Correct					

Nonsense Word Reading

bish	fleep	scraim	hawn	prodge
felch	creat	blay	stry	bu
treap	pawg	gream	teeping	trotch
kidge	shelped	thay	gry	pilped
tremmed	relfed	tring	glink	twifted

	1	2	3	4	5
Date					
Total Words Read					
- Errors					
= Total Words Correct					

Real Word Reading

fishing	grabbed	unpacked	snagged
shrimp	happy	hoping	edge
drawback	baited	casted	waited
mistaken	agreed	sadly	switched
great	himself	fresh	stuff

	1	2	3	4	5
Date					
Total Words Read					
- Errors					
= Total Words Correct					

Story FP 9.1: "Jay's Fishing Trip"

Section 2 (Untimed exercises)

Non-phonetic Word Recognition

Only read the real words in these paragraphs.

Scrimp flug triv welb would fimp
Glead freg shrop people exip twog
Trav splob tren frig answer wunch frib
prong crub vid want ud crax trill

Preeg felp trid frin glot father
Slirp gorb cpux the answer rint
Swuv torp would julp meng
Lorpoot ferb people wip tremp

Faikjse soho father one should jfhe
Jesjk too gigu sone want answer ty
Gjurshu froyou both people want yu
Flipe polkim rjsio kaj answer both from

Sjkj sikh cvt you do from was jhang
Jjh humh would ksjht want could oul
Skjh fussre answer people toojso iy
Portemp trem people piv freen

jdshiuuh hdcit kjdhf would people ksje
shah gorb huj answer wanr crux some
kjdkjh cvoif want both sure do the qieuiou
koi where the ikol milkf would nkjnsj bvfrt

Story FP 9.1: "Jay's Fishing Trip"

Section 3 (Untimed exercises)

Sentence Stacks

Jean grabbed

Jean grabbed all of their

Jean grabbed all of their fishing stuff

Jean grabbed all of their fishing stuff hoping to get

Jean grabbed all of their fishing stuff hoping to get on the trail

Jean grabbed all of their fishing stuff hoping to get on the trail by nine o'clock.

After waiting

After waiting for a long time,

After waiting for a long time, Jay looked at Jean

After waiting for a long time, Jay looked at Jean and switched his bait

After waiting for a long time, Jay looked at Jean and switched his bait back to shrimp.

Jay and Jean

Jay and Jean both saw

Jay and Jean both saw that the best

Jay and Jean both saw that the best fishing bait

Jay and Jean both saw that the best fishing bait for the lake

Jay and Jean both saw that the best fishing bait for the lake was shrimp.

Jean felt

Jean felt that it was

Jean felt that it was a drawback

Jean felt that it was a drawback to bait his line

Jean felt that it was a drawback to bait his line with shrimp

Jean felt that it was a drawback to bait his line with shrimp so she gave

Jean felt that it was a drawback to bait his line with shrimp so she gave him a fly.

Jay looked

Jay looked at Jean

Jay looked at Jean and switched

Jay looked at Jean and switched his bait

Jay looked at Jean and switched his bait back to shrimp.

Story FP 9.1: "Jay's Fishing Trip"

Section 4 (1 minute timed activity)

Jay and his friend Jean had a plan to go on a big fishing trip. The plan was 18
to leave for their trip at dawn. Jean grabbed all of their fishing stuff hoping 33
to get on the trail by nine o'clock. Jay rushed to put the bait in the pail. 50
They set off on their trip. When they got to the lake, Jean unpacked their 65
stuff and sat on the edge. Jay sat himself by the bay and baited his line 81
with shrimp. Jean felt that it was a drawback to bait their lines with shrimp so 97
she gave him a fly. Jean thought that the answer to catching fish would be 112
baiting their lines with flies. Jay agreed and then baited his line with a fly. 128
Jean said that he would be sure to catch a fish with a fly. Jay cast his line 145
into the lake. He waited and waited but the fish did not bite. Jean was 161
hoping that the fly would be the best bait but she was sadly mistaken. After 176
waiting for a long time, Jay looked at Jean and switched his bait back to 191
shrimp. Jay snagged a fish in a flash! For the rest of the day, Jay snagged 207
many fish using shrimp as his bait. Jay and Jean both saw that the best 222
fishing bait for the lake was shrimp. They went home with a pail full of fresh 238
fish to eat. 241

Baseline
Total Words Read:
- # of errors:
= Words Correct:

1. Total Words Read:
- # of errors:
= Words Correct:

2. Total Words Read:
- # of errors:
= Words Correct:

3. Total Words Read:
- # of errors:
= Words Correct:

4. Total Words Read:
- # of errors:
= Words Correct:

5. Total Words Read:
- # of errors:
= Words Correct:

Baseline	5	10	15	20	25	30	35	40	45	50	55	60	65	70	75	80
	85	90	95	100	105	110	115	120	125	130	135	140	145	150	155	160
	165	170	175	180	185	190	195	200	205	210	215	220	225	230	235	240

Final Reading	5	10	15	20	25	30	35	40	45	50	55	60	65	70	75	80
	85	90	95	100	105	110	115	120	125	130	135	140	145	150	155	160
	165	170	175	180	185	190	195	200	205	210	215	220	225	230	235	240

Baseline Score (WPM): ____________ Final Reading (WPM): ____________ Final WPM (+/-): ______________

Comprehension Questions

1. When did Jay and Jean leave for their big trip?
2. What type of bait did Jean think was the best for catching fish?
3. Did Jean's plan for catching fish work? Why or why not?
4. What ended up being the best bait in the end?
5. Were Jean and Jay happy with their day of fishing? Why or why not?
6. Have you ever gone fishing and been successful? If not, would you like to? If so, what was it like?

Story FP-10.1: "Herb the Hermit Crab"

DIRECTIONS: • When beginning a new story, have your student read the whole story and time them for 1 minute. Record their results in the Baseline reading section and have your student record their baseline results on their tracking sheet. • Each Reading in Section 1 is a 15-second timed activity. Have your student do one timed reading of each in one sitting. Track your results on your assessor copy and have your students track their progress on their tracking sheet. • Section 2 contains passages that contain nonsense words with non-phonetic words embedded within the story. Have your student scan the passage and find the non-phonetic words. This is NOT a timed activity. • Section 3 contains sentence stacks. These are sentences from the passage that are broken down into chunks. • Have your student read each chunk and then the next using the scoops (having them run their finger along the scoops as they read) in order to build fluency and prosody. Perform these activities once during one session. • Once your student has completed all readings 5 times over 5 sessions, have them read the story for one final time and record their results and have your student track their results.

Section 1 (Time: 15 seconds for each exercise)

Isolated Phonogram Reading

ar	tch	er	dge	ing
sh	sm	ai	ee	or
ang	ay	ch	sw	cr
gl	br	ar	th	ee
or	sn	gl	ck	ong

	1	2	3	4	5
Date					
Total Sounds Read					
- Errors					
= Total Sounds Correct					

Nonsense Word Reading

flarb	credge	glert	blorp	treeb
chorg	traip	blay	sweez	beax
twerb	creen	streck	fodge	vutch
swimp	prind	gorp	berx	frub
strock	parj	jimp	flind	twab

	1	2	3	4	5
Date					
Total Words Read					
- Errors					
= Total Words Correct					

Real Word Reading

hermit	safe	kept	sadly
stretched	shell	claws	empty
stepped	picked	small	growing
looked	seemed	himself	fresh
edge	scratch	inside	squish

	1	2	3	4	5
Date					
Total Words Read					
- Errors					
= Total Words Correct					

Story FP-10.1: "Herb the Hermit Crab"

Section 2 (Untimed exercises)

Non-phonetic Word Recognition

Only read the real words in these paragraphs.

fribum trop glorf rough himbot forb
twint fleg prat friend welb dring
strox flint minute junt med
splux crad enough helz trib

yud prob whix tough spilf grix
dep twind frob zelp dran during trid
swax fleep beav rough wend
torx feev raif minute jelp

Minute friend judos lskjt jiorjj could sord
Dis during where kjslkj lkjerk the folkx ij
Jeths jsirj some gjhjs ksjj nlskjelkj many
Hfkj jhkjehr ast koste enough soughtr to

Skjdjk swap jgskj minute kjdkj during
Splux the dkjrin friend ksisjirh tough
During lkddjok people skillk jslkje any
Jojnf kj nlknlkcrad kjlajrkej during jojh

jsrhituh firicg during should do pjs jkjsht
ksljdtldjk friend during was draftinh enough
many kshtl both skuhktjhkj jumgh khsuhe
kjsjh roughvb lkliehrlh friend during grjasujoj

Story FP-10.1: "Herb the Hermit Crab" 3 of 4

Section 3 (Untimed exercises)

Sentence Stacks

When Herb's friends

When Herb's friends would ask him

When Herb's friends would ask him to come out and play,

When Herb's friends would ask him to come out and play, he never wanted to

When Herb's friends would ask him to come out and play, he never wanted to because he was afraid.

He stretched out

He stretched out his legs and claws

He stretched out his legs and claws and stepped out

He stretched out his legs and claws and stepped out from his shell.

Herb was glad

Herb was glad in his new home

Herb was glad in his new home and he was

Herb was glad in his new home and he was safe once again.

He tapped

He tapped on it

He tapped on it with his claws

He tapped on it with his claws and it was empty.

Herb now

Herb now had a fresh

Herb now had a fresh and flawless shell

Herb now had a fresh and flawless shell to keep him safe.

Story FP-10.1: "Herb the Hermit Crab"

Section 4 (1 minute timed activity)

Herb was a hermit crab who was scared of everything. Herb was glad to 14
have a shell to hide in. When Herb's friends would ask him to come out and 30
play, he never wanted to because he was afraid. Herb's shell kept him 43
safe. Herb had carefully picked this shell after his last shell got too small for 58
his growing body. 61

One day, Herb woke up feeling very cramped. Herb's legs couldn't move 73
like they used to and his claws were bunched up inside of his shell. 87
Suddenly, Herb's body felt too big for his shell. His legs were squished inside 101
and his claws scratched the edges of his shell. As Herb found it tough to 116
move around in the shell that he loved, he now saw what he had to do. 132
Herb had to find a new shell. Herb looked around his shell and sadly said 147
goodbye. He stretched out his legs and claws and stepped out from his 160
shell. Herb was very scared as he crawled along the sand with no shell. 174
Soon, he came upon a shell that seemed to be the best fit. He tapped on it 191
with his claws and it was empty. He made sure that no other crabs were 206
using the shell and he was in luck. Herb moved himself into the new shell. 221
Herb now had a fresh and flawless shell to keep him safe. Herb was glad in 237
his new home and he was safe once again. 246

Baseline
Total Words Read:
- # of errors:
= Words Correct:

1. Total Words Read:
- # of errors:
= Words Correct:

2. Total Words Read:
- # of errors:
= Words Correct:

3. Total Words Read:
- # of errors:
= Words Correct:

4. Total Words Read:
- # of errors:
= Words Correct:

5. Total Words Read:
- # of errors:
= Words Correct:

Baseline	5	10	15	20	25	30	35	40	45	50	55	60	65	70	75	80
	85	90	95	100	105	110	115	120	125	130	135	140	145	150	155	160
	165	170	175	180	185	190	195	200	205	210	215	220	225	230	235	240

Final Reading	5	10	15	20	25	30	35	40	45	50	55	60	65	70	75	80
	85	90	95	100	105	110	115	120	125	130	135	140	145	150	155	160
	165	170	175	180	185	190	195	200	205	210	215	220	225	230	235	240

Baseline Score (WPM): ____________ Final Reading (WPM): ____________ Final WPM (+/-): ____________

Comprehension Questions
1. Why did Herb have to leave his shell? 2. Did Herb like to go out and play with his friends? 3. Why do you think Herb was so scared when he stepped out of his shell? 4. Was Herb happy with his new choice of shell? Why or why not? 5. Why do you think Herb loved his shell so much?

Story FP-11.1: "Anne Bonny"

DIRECTIONS: • When beginning a new story, have your student read the whole story and time them for 1 minute. Record their results in the Baseline reading section and have your student record their baseline results on their tracking sheet. • Each Reading in Section 1 is a 15-second timed activity. Have your student do one timed reading of each in one sitting. Track your results on your assessor copy and have your students track their progress on their tracking sheet. • Section 2 contains passages that contain nonsense words with non-phonetic words embedded within the story. Have your student scan the passage and find the non-phonetic words. This is NOT a timed activity. • Section 3 contains sentence stacks. These are sentences from the passage that are broken down into chunks. • Have your student read each chunk and then the next using the scoops (having them run their finger along the scoops as they read) in order to build fluency and prosody. Perform these activities once during one session. • Once your student has completed all readings 5 times over 5 sessions, have them read the story for one final time and record their results and have your student track their results.

Section 1 (Time: 15 seconds for each exercise)

Isolated Phonogram Reading

oy	er	qu	i-e	a-e
ee	or	ay	dge	oo
oa	Ea	e-e	tch	ow
oo	aw	spl	ee	oi
ow	ar	nt	oa	ck

	1	2	3	4	5
Date					
Total Sounds Read					
- Errors					
= Total Sounds Correct					

Nonsense Word Reading

toger	doof	slowd	coig	sloy
riholm	forgim	veet	slawt	cloam
swain	clouse	neem	hoom	corm
froil	doy	pook	vouse	swoil
Bloy	tarf	dreaf	garm	loag

	1	2	3	4	5
Date					
Total Words Read					
- Errors					
= Total Words Correct					

Real Word Reading

secret	pirate	open	deploy
soak	spoon	toil	loot
disappoint	ploy	moist	unload
grown	oyster	rejoin	coins
sailed	quite	popular	relocate

	1	2	3	4	5
Date					
Total Words Read					
- Errors					
= Total Words Correct					

Story FP-11.1: "Anne Bonny"

Section 2 (Untimed exercises)

Non-phonetic Word Recognition

Only read the real words in these paragraphs.

Yabel clop blood revery tac
Tique nare dow ghyu vfg
Sugar Peab hool Thaip
Whose truth laugh etach

Wohy cvolk laugh uyomh
Charght sugar feahp faber
Whose blood whoes bolood
Frimp twix whose yump crub

Sugar osh je jhksjh friend to the sjfng
Skjtjij dcf iuisjodj klsjljr father hrigo
should dkjiy the to ejsjhk jaj friend sef
Isoifoiej sehr hhhjhajrh jhkjahjrh jh to

Sljsekj jhsej huh jekhtkj hjkehtjh jhtt js
Laugh whose kjhtj hajkh jahehr jhakjeh
Sjhr jaj jalhrh ajar hahah ah would do the
Jkeht karhlk ka should could would tp kan

laugh jkhaerhuh whose blodd kjharuh skjerr
blood sugar the ws any bosouji jahrioh
kdjflkjadkfj kljreh kkjkue khrjakjh sugar who
sjhejrh njkahrejh whose blllud jwhejkh laugh

Story FP-11.1: "Anne Bonny"

Section 3 (Untimed exercises)

Sentence Stacks

Her ship
Her ship was pounced on
Her ship was pounced on and raided
Her ship was pounced on and raided and all the pirates
Her ship was pounced on and raided and all the pirates were taken away
Her ship was pounced on and raided and all the pirates were taken away to the prison.

During the 1800s
During the 1800s when pirates
During the 1800s when pirates were the most popular
During the 1800s when pirates were the most popular, Anne left her easy life
During the 1800s when pirates were the most popular, Anne left her easy life for one of extreme adventure.

Anne Bonny
Anne Bonny should be remembered
Anne Bonny should be remembered as being a
Anne Bonny should be remembered as being a strong female
Anne Bonny should be remembered as being a strong female who refused to be
Anne Bonny should be remembered as being a strong female who refused to be a standard woman.

She tried to keep
She tried to keep her identity
She tried to keep her identity a secret
She tried to keep her identity a secret and often
She tried to keep her identity a secret and often dressed like a man.

She sailed
She sailed on private ships
She sailed on private ships in the open
She sailed on private ships in the open sea looting trading ships
She sailed on private ships in the open sea looting trading ships and stealing
She sailed on private ships in the open sea looting trading ships and stealing coins, gold and silver.

Story FP-11.1: "Anne Bonny"

Section 4 (1 minute timed activity)

Have you ever heard the tale of the first female pirate? Well, she is quite 15
popular. Her name is Anne Bonny. She was born in the 1700s in Ireland and 30
then moved to the United States when she was a baby. Why was she so 45
famous? She was the first female to be recognized as a pirate. 58
During the 1800s, when pirates were the most popular, Anne left her easy 71
life for one of extreme adventure. She tried to keep her identity a secret 85
and often dressed like a man. She sailed on private ships in the open sea 100
looting trading ships and stealing coins, gold and silver. Her life was one of 114
loyalty and fun while being a pirate. Her adventure finished one day when 127
she was aboard the ship "William". Her ship was pounced on and raided 140
and all the pirates were taken away to the prison. Anne Bonny's captain 153
John Rackman was put to death but Anne, it was decided, should skip the 167
hanging because she as a woman! Later, it was found out that Bonny's 180
father had secured her release and she was relocated back to her home 193
where she rejoined her father and later married and had four children of 206
her own. Reports of her death are pegged in 1782. Anne Bonny should be 220
remembered as being a strong female who refused to be a standard 232
woman. 233

Baseline
Total Words Read:
- # of errors:
= Words Correct:

1. Total Words Read:
- # of errors:
= Words Correct:

2. Total Words Read:
- # of errors:
= Words Correct:

3. Total Words Read:
- # of errors:
= Words Correct:

4. Total Words Read:
- # of errors:
= Words Correct:

5. Total Words Read:
- # of errors:
= Words Correct:

Baseline	5	10	15	20	25	30	35	40	45	50	55	60	65	70	75	80
	85	90	95	100	105	110	115	120	125	130	135	140	145	150	155	160
	165	170	175	180	185	190	195	200	205	210	215	220	225	230	235	240

Final Reading	5	10	15	20	25	30	35	40	45	50	55	60	65	70	75	80
	85	90	95	100	105	110	115	120	125	130	135	140	145	150	155	160
	165	170	175	180	185	190	195	200	205	210	215	220	225	230	235	240

Baseline Score (WPM): ___________ Final Reading (WPM): ___________ Final WPM (+/-): ___________

Comprehension Questions

1. What was the name of the ship that Anne was captured on?
2. How many children did Anne have?
3. What did she collect when she was looting ships?
4. What does looting mean?
5. Where was Anne born?
6. When was Anne reportedly to have died?

Story FP-12.1: "The RMS Titanic – A Canadian Connection"

DIRECTIONS: • When beginning a new story, have your student read the whole story and time them for 1 minute. Record their results in the Baseline reading section and have your student record their baseline results on their tracking sheet. • Each Reading in Section 1 is a 15-second timed activity. Have your student do one timed reading of each in one sitting. Track your results on your assessor copy and have your students track their progress on their tracking sheet. • Section 2 contains passages that contain nonsense words with non-phonetic words embedded within the story. Have your student scan the passage and find the non-phonetic words. This is NOT a timed activity.
• Section 3 contains sentence stacks. These are sentences from the passage that are broken down into chunks. • Have your student read each chunk and then the next using the scoops (having them run their finger along the scoops as they read) in order to build fluency and prosody. Perform these activities once during one session. • Once your student has completed all readings 5 times over 5 sessions, have them read the story for one final time and record their results and have your student track their results.

Section 1 (Time: 15 seconds for each exercise)

Isolated Phonogram Reading

ea	u-e	ing	g	c
ink	tch	tion	unk	th
all	i-e	y	old	ung
e-e	onk	o-e	ang	str
ee	th	ai	spl	ch

	1	2	3	4	5
Date					
Total Sounds Read					
- Errors					
= Total Sounds Correct					

Nonsense Word Reading

nold	trang	bufe	strifting	brunded
plotion	franzic	swelping	grufted	preld
winted	grunding	twiftion	sprong	twing
libeful	hunded	dribness	juxted	splinded
huve	pri	lintop	frixveb	troxted

	1	2	3	4	5
Date					
Total Words Read					
- Errors					
= Total Words Correct					

Real Word Reading

people	actually	tragedy	special
museum	ocean	unsinkable	concert
bodies	exhibit	occasion	iceberg
permanent	claimed	rescued	impacted
liner	dispatched	century	arrived

	1	2	3	4	5
Date					
Total Words Read					
- Errors					
= Total Words Correct					

Story FP-12.1: "The RMS Titanic – A Canadian Connection"

Section 2 (Untimed exercises)

Non-phonetic Word Recognition

Only read the real words in these paragraphs.

Sprib flemp twing blood werf traig
Harb greap whose wen fitch splond
Mexib wrand fring laugh un twixted
Rebay sugar memp wratch blex

Rebaun youg graiv sugar punvid
Jextrip whose vendog helbing prox
Whifter rempid preng laugh twip
Skitch blood lextrop frind

Klsjt blood treijanf jeje jjhlhr laugh should you
Kjsdhhtj laugh hjkshj ketkjh whose klejlktj kej
Shtjh sdlhth lkerlk hslkhtlsflsdif laugh the to
Jskheth. Skhetlh kshjhakjhr jkayou to do the

Jshdjkhj hjshjk laugh fwho blood jhsa
To the was jehteo eojh hfjkahr akjhr kahru
Could blood jhesrh smh jh jhfla laugh krjt
Jsheth kjtk lskhklht hsleht lsh from teh

kjhth you nskjfhsfjkjhduieto do the was jras
kjt lkjslj kjblood whose sjhth lhtlkhetkhs lksjt
kdjhroit jrlktu would sejtsi who too
setlksje hsjjkshjsehtkj the should four both

Story FP-12.1: "The RMS Titanic – A Canadian Connection"

Section 3 (Untimed exercises)

Sentence Stacks

It's hard to find

It's hard to find anyone that

It's hard to find anyone that does not know

It's hard to find anyone that does not know the story of

It's hard to find anyone that does not know the story of the Titanic.

To this day,

To this day, you can visit

To this day, you can visit the Maritime Museum

To this day, you can visit the Maritime Museum in Halifax

To this day, you can visit the Maritime Museum in Halifax which has a permanent

To this day, you can visit the Maritime Museum in Halifax which has a permanent Titanic exhibit.

Sadly,

Sadly, no survivors were found

Sadly, no survivors were found but several bodies

Sadly, no survivors were found but several bodies were found

Sadly, no survivors were found but several bodies were found and buried in

Sadly, no survivors were found but several bodies were found and buried in Halifax, Nova Scotia.

More than 1,500 people

More than 1,500 people were lost

More than 1,500 people were lost but more than

More than 1,500 people were lost but more than 700 people survived

More than 1,500 people were lost but more than 700 people survived and were rescued.

The RMS Titanic

The RMS Titanic was the largest

The RMS Titanic was the largest ocean liner

The RMS Titanic was the largest ocean liner of its time

The RMS Titanic was the largest ocean liner of its time and was claimed

The RMS Titanic was the largest ocean liner of its time and was claimed to be unsinkable.

Story FP-12.1: "The RMS Titanic – A Canadian Connection"

Section 4 (1 minute timed activity)

It's hard to find anyone that does not know the story of the Titanic. The RMS 16
Titanic was the largest ocean liner of its time and was claimed to be 30
unsinkable. But, on April 14, 1912, the great ship struck an iceberg and sunk 44
to the bottom of the ocean in only two hours and forty minutes. More than 59
1,500 people were lost but more than 700 people survived and were 71
rescued. What most people don't know is that the day before the rescued 84
passengers were to arrive in New York, the White Star Line had dispatched 97
four Canadian ships to look for victims of the disaster. Sadly, no survivors 110
were found but several bodies were found and buried in Halifax, Nova 122
Scotia. What most people also do not know is that the RMS Titanic actually 136
sunk in the North Atlantic water just off the coast of Halifax, Nova Scotia, in 151
Canadian waters. The tragedy impacted the Canadian town so much that 162
even today, after the liner hit the iceberg over a century ago, the city of 177
Halifax still holds concerts, readings and special events to mark the 188
occasion. To this day, you can visit the Maritime Museum in Halifax which 201
has a permanent Titanic exhibit. 206

This story of international cooperation is a testament to how nations can 218
work together in times of tragedy. It also reminds us that Canadians played 231
a sad but important role in the aftermath of this awful disaster. 243

Baseline
Total Words Read:
- # of errors:
= Words Correct:

2. Total Words Read:
- # of errors:
= Words Correct:

4. Total Words Read:
- # of errors:
= Words Correct:

1. Total Words Read:
- # of errors:
= Words Correct:

3. Total Words Read:
- # of errors:
= Words Correct:

5. Total Words Read:
- # of errors:
= Words Correct:

Baseline	5	10	15	20	25	30	35	40	45	50	55	60	65	70	75	80
	85	90	95	100	105	110	115	120	125	130	135	140	145	150	155	160
	165	170	175	180	185	190	195	200	205	210	215	220	225	230	235	240

Final Reading	5	10	15	20	25	30	35	40	45	50	55	60	65	70	75	80
	85	90	95	100	105	110	115	120	125	130	135	140	145	150	155	160
	165	170	175	180	185	190	195	200	205	210	215	220	225	230	235	240

Baseline Score (WPM): ____________ Final Reading (WPM): ____________ Final WPM (+/-): ____________

Comprehension Questions

1. What caused the RMS Titanic to sink?
2. Where did the Titanic sink?
3. What role did the Canadians play in this tragedy?
4. Why do you think that the town of Halifax remembers this tragic event every year?
5. Where can you visit a permanent Titanic exhibit?

Story FP-13.1: "The Origin of Castles"

DIRECTIONS: • When beginning a new story, have your student read the whole story and time them for 1 minute. Record their results in the Baseline reading section and have your student record their baseline results on their tracking sheet. • Each Reading in Section 1 is a 15-second timed activity. Have your student do one timed reading of each in one sitting. Track your results on your assessor copy and have your students track their progress on their tracking sheet. • Section 2 contains passages that contain nonsense words with non-phonetic words embedded within the story. Have your student scan the passage and find the non-phonetic words. This is NOT a timed activity. • Section 3 contains sentence stacks. These are sentences from the passage that are broken down into chunks. • Have your student read each chunk and then the next using the scoops (having them run their finger along the scoops as they read) in order to build fluency and prosody. Perform these activities once during one session. • Once your student has completed all readings 5 times over 5 sessions, have them read the story for one final time and record their results and have your student track their results.

Section 1 (Time: 15 seconds for each exercise)

Isolated Phonogram Reading

fle	cle	gle	ew	ple
oo	or	er	ea	ph
ow	aw	ct	igh	oi
tle	nd	stle	oa	igh
zle	oy	ur	u-e	Ir

	1	2	3	4	5
Date					
Total Sounds Read					
- Errors					
= Total Sounds Correct					

Nonsense Word Reading

paple	cruddle	dect	trafle	shurgle
vight	braph	flaph	smoat	inkle
biddle	snazzle	slird	bloof	smay
snead	clow	phine	clouf	drail
wuffle	glight	frect	dritch	bact

	1	2	3	4	5
Date					
Total Words Read					
- Errors					
= Total Words Correct					

Real Word Reading

cable	aspect	simple	rekindle
puzzle	compact	noble	ample
phase	tumble	high	elect
defect	castle	bundle	circle
tight	crackle	graph	enact

	1	2	3	4	5
Date					
Total Words Read					
- Errors					
= Total Words Correct					

Story FP-13.1: "The Origin of Castles"

Section 2 (Untimed exercises)

Non-phonetic Word Recognition

Only read the real words in these paragraphs.

Dif stok nuroc answer dal ghomp rait
Father reps nusand librit people fgoyul
Ligeh woman dfopli fpoli wolen revery T
anc tlkop ipl answer ftyuop mploi

Wmoy answer vbca szxoc woman
Purst pim people Dagh duroc nare
Fwer father ncut marb goxe unlow
Qpiomt need women peris vgay

Jewsjht jjgk woman ohw kart lakh hlkar to
Woman people laugh jshetjkh jhjehre hkhsr
Sjherh heheh hehe hhrjhrakjhr khekha herp
Skejht skhetlsht selhelh lsehlkehslr hselkht

Answer to the kjsetlh kklhsetk hsalkhr jo
Site ak woman nskjteh during toto nerf
Sjkdhtht oiaeoit blood hiheta lugh sugar
Another Seth slktjehsklt lkshetlkshtl koet

jskherh ha thun sbtb there shah who
jhahr halhsrh lslkh klhslh a father kht
eshkjht eahsrh kslekht aeh answer
kja woman lkejtewsl would Leth

Story FP-13.1: "The Origin of Castles"

Section 3 (Untimed exercises)

Sentence Stacks

The difference between the castle

The difference between the castle and the prehistoric forts

The difference between the castle and the prehistoric forts was that castles

The difference between the castle and the prehistoric forts was that castles were established

The difference between the castle and the prehistoric forts was that castles were established as homes for nobles.

The great age

The great age of castle building

The great age of castle building started in Europe

The great age of castle building started in Europe by the Normans

The great age of castle building started in Europe by the Normans after the Saxons

The great age of castle building started in Europe by the Normans after the Saxons invaded England.

A moat

A moat was a point

A moat was a point of protection

A moat was a point of protection against invaders

A moat was a point of protection against invaders and helped to secure

A moat was a point of protection against invaders and helped to secure the inner constructs

A moat was a point of protection against invaders and helped to secure the inner constructs of the castle.

These castles

These castles had a strong

These castles had a strong stone tower

These castles had a strong stone tower called a keep

These castles had a strong stone tower called a keep where people lived.

The gate was

The gate was the entering point

The gate was the entering point to the castle

The gate was the entering point to the castle and at times

The gate was the entering point to the castle and at times it was enveloped

The gate was the entering point to the castle and at times it was enveloped by a shallow moat

The gate was the entering point to the castle and at times it was enveloped by a shallow moat that was filled

The gate was the entering point to the castle and at times it was enveloped by a shallow moat that was filled with water.

Story FP-13.1: "The Origin of Castles"

Section 4 (1 minute timed activity)

Have you ever visited the United Kingdom and were impressed by the 12
number of castles you could see? Castles can be found all around the 25
world. The first castles ever built were just reinforced forts built for protection 38
during wars and they look very different from the castles found around the 51
world today. In much of Europe, castles were built in the middle ages. The 63
difference between the castles and the prehistoric forts were that castles 74
were established as homes for kings and other nobles who were extremely 87
rich and important. The great age of castle building started in Europe by 99
the Normans after the Saxons had invaded England. The first castles were 110
built from wood and were called 'motte and bailey' castles. They were 123
constructed on high piles of dirt and were very simple. However, these 136
castles would catch fire easily. Later, castles were built out of stone and 149
were much more durable. These castles had a strong stone tower called a 161
'keep' where people lived. The wall circling this tower was called a 'curtain 175
wall'. The gate was the entering point to the castle and at times it was 190
enveloped by a shallow moat that was filled with water. A moat was a 205
point of protection against invaders. Today, you can view many different 216
castles from all around the world and from different times. The one thing 229
that will impress you is their grand size as well as their power. 245

Baseline
Total Words Read:
- # of errors:
= Words Correct:

1. Total Words Read:
- # of errors:
= Words Correct:

2. Total Words Read:
- # of errors:
= Words Correct:

3. Total Words Read:
- # of errors:
= Words Correct:

4. Total Words Read:
- # of errors:
= Words Correct:

5. Total Words Read:
- # of errors:
= Words Correct:

Baseline	5	10	15	20	25	30	35	40	45	50	55	60	65	70	75	80
	85	90	95	100	105	110	115	120	125	130	135	140	145	150	155	160
	165	170	175	180	185	190	195	200	205	210	215	220	225	230	235	240

Final Reading	5	10	15	20	25	30	35	40	45	50	55	60	65	70	75	80
	85	90	95	100	105	110	115	120	125	130	135	140	145	150	155	160
	165	170	175	180	185	190	195	200	205	210	215	220	225	230	235	240

Baseline Score (WPM): ____________ Final Reading (WPM): ____________ Final WPM (+/-): ______________

Comprehension Questions

1. What were the early castles called?
2. What is a moat? Why did castles have them?
3. What is the wall called that circles the tower?
4. Where can you see castles?
5. What was one of the problems with the original forts?
6. Would you want to live in a castle?

Story FP-14.1: "Haichi – A Story of Love and Devotion"

DIRECTIONS: • When beginning a new story, have your student read the whole story and time them for 1 minute. Record their results in the Baseline reading section and have your student record their baseline results on their tracking sheet. • Each Reading in Section 1 is a 15-second timed activity. Have your student do one timed reading of each in one sitting. Track your results on your assessor copy and have your students track their progress on their tracking sheet. • Section 2 contains passages that contain nonsense words with non-phonetic words embedded within the story. Have your student scan the passage and find the non-phonetic words. This is NOT a timed activity. • Section 3 contains sentence stacks. These are sentences from the passage that are broken down into chunks. • Have your student read each chunk and then the next using the scoops (having them run their finger along the scoops as they read) in order to build fluency and prosody. Perform these activities once during one session. • Once your student has completed all readings 5 times over 5 sessions, have them read the story for one final time and record their results and have your student track their results.

Section 1 (Time: 15 seconds for each exercise)

Isolated Phonogram Reading

ble	oa	gle	sp	ur
dr	ou	or	ea	ee
sw	squ	spl	oi	o
xt	onk	ai	oy	cl
mp	er	all	ir	pr

	1	2	3	4	5
Date					
Total Sounds Read					
- Errors					
= Total Sounds Correct					

Nonsense Word Reading

rishow	drow	slead	kople	couse
drent	naist	flogrop	criswig	hilpmo
shroplup	crizz	drept	wixshromp	grustruse
squidmo	proxt	plofo	swetrum	clum
cridcrup	du	wedflom	vust	oatmeat

	1	2	3	4	5
Date					
Total Words Read					
- Errors					
= Total Words Correct					

Real Word Reading

wait	choose	bronze	work
returning	adopt	greet	show
prevent	decided	eagerly	remains
master	station	unite	student
owner	former	while	away

	1	2	3	4	5
Date					
Total Words Read					
- Errors					
= Total Words Correct					

Story FP-14.1: "Haichi – A Story of Love and Devotion"

Section 2 (Untimed exercises)

Non-phonetic Word Recognition

Only read the real words in these paragraphs.

Fgolst hwet during tblpo durat sulid
Chglop fhac sqwa friend ppoud nej
Bured Wald bumf enough fploi
Kelmfolt rough rkop aly lect tough

Phat friend minute gflop
Tqwest cdse Ort during
Bim sowas ldcfuit tough
Poud reb tay shlock faut

Jeljlkj tkljetlk minute kaerh al father alet
Jsf mother another kshfla who lkaetkh
Ksnfd jksdskj jsktn during slkte kjslrht
Minute kakjhe ajkhjminuter akhr hs to

Kjsrhtha ksrltej during peolep stskej
Enough jhseht through lkejt rough to
Another listep skjkehtkehtklh alkgeh
Lkjrtej kjf where ksjgtj lskjher here to

jsekjhr akejh hetkejh rhminute people to
ksjlth through Hlkset woman
should could rhijhrtj many kjslek both
kselkht should kjhtjkh sshjhralaskhjfakl busy

Story FP-14.1: "Haichi – A Story of Love and Devotion"

Section 3 (Untimed exercises)

Sentence Stacks

Every day when Professor Ueno

Every day when Professor Ueno went to work

Every day when Professor Ueno went to work in Tokyo

Every day when Professor Ueno went to work in Tokyo, Haichi would

Every day when Professor Ueno went to work in Tokyo, Haichi would accompany him

Every day when Professor Ueno went to work in Tokyo, Haichi would accompany him to the train station.

Many people travelled

Many people travelled to the station

Many people travelled to the station to be with Haichi

Many people travelled to the station to be with Haichi and feed him.

Legend has it

Legend has it that for the next ten years,

Legend has it that for the next ten years, Haichi would wait

Legend has it that for the next ten years, Haichi would wait at the train station

Legend has it that for the next ten years, Haichi would wait at the train station every day

Legend has it that for the next ten years, Haichi would wait at the train station every day for his master to return.

A former student

A former student of Professor Ueno

A former student of Professor Ueno discovered the dog's loyalty

A former student of Professor Ueno discovered the dog's loyalty for his master

A former student of Professor Ueno discovered the dog's loyalty for his master and sent a story

A former student of Professor Ueno discovered the dog's loyalty for his master and sent a story to the local newspaper.

It was destroyed

It was destroyed during World War

It was destroyed during World War Two but was rebuilt

It was destroyed during World War Two but was rebuilt in 1948

It was destroyed during World War Two but was rebuilt in 1948 where it still

It was destroyed during World War Two but was rebuilt in 1948 where it still remains today.

Story FP-14.1: "Haichi – A Story of Love and Devotion"

Section 4 (1 minute timed activity)

Everyone loves a good tale about love, loyalty and dedication. This is the 12
story of Haichi, a Japanese dog who loved his owner. Professor Ueno 24
Eisabura decided he wanted to get a pet, so he decided on a specific 38
dog: a Japanese Akita dog. He looked tirelessly for one, but instead he 51
chose to adopt instead, thus choosing Haichi. Professor Ueno and Haichi 62
did everything together and they were very close. Every day, when 72
Professor Ueno went to work in Tokyo, Haichi would accompany him to the 85
train station. Haichi would then wait patiently for his master to return so that 99
he could get him. One day however, Professor Ueno didn't show up. 111
Tragically, he had a stroke while at work and had passed away. However, 124
this did not prevent Haichi from returning to the train station every day at 138
3pm eagerly awaiting the return of his master. Legend has it that for the 153
next ten years, Haichi would wait at the train station every day for his 167
master to return. A former student of Professor Ueno discovered the dog's 179
loyalty for his master and sent a story to the local newspaper. Many people 192
travelled to the station to be with Haichi and feed him and eventually a 206
bronze statue was erected in Haichi's honour. It was destroyed during 218
World War Two but was rebuilt in 1948 where it still remains today. The name 232
Haichi means loyal in Japanese. 236

Baseline	2. Total Words Read:	4. Total Words Read:
Total Words Read:	- # of errors:	- # of errors:
- # of errors:	= Words Correct:	= Words Correct:
= Words Correct:		

1. Total Words Read:	**3.** Total Words Read:	**5.** Total Words Read:
- # of errors:	- # of errors:	- # of errors:
= Words Correct:	= Words Correct:	= Words Correct:

Baseline	5	10	15	20	25	30	35	40	45	50	55	60	65	70	75	80
	85	90	95	100	105	110	115	120	125	130	135	140	145	150	155	160
	165	170	175	180	185	190	195	200	205	210	215	220	225	230	235	240

Final Reading	5	10	15	20	25	30	35	40	45	50	55	60	65	70	75	80
	85	90	95	100	105	110	115	120	125	130	135	140	145	150	155	160
	165	170	175	180	185	190	195	200	205	210	215	220	225	230	235	240

Baseline Score (WPM): ____________ Final Reading (WPM): ____________ Final WPM (+/-): ______________

Comprehension Questions

1. What does Haichi mean in Japanese?
2. When was the statue rebuilt?
3. What kind of dog did Professor Ueno want to get?
4. Why is this story about love and loyalty?
5. What did Professor Ueno die from?
6. Who discovered Haichi waiting at the train station and told a newspaper reporter about it?

Story FP-15.1: "The Lost City of Atlantis – Fact or Fiction?"

DIRECTIONS: • When beginning a new story, have your student read the whole story and time them for 1 minute. Record their results in the Baseline reading section and have your student record their baseline results on their tracking sheet. • Each Reading in Section 1 is a 15-second timed activity. Have your student do one timed reading of each in one sitting. Track your results on your assessor copy and have your students track their progress on their tracking sheet. • Section 2 contains passages that contain nonsense words with non-phonetic words embedded within the story. Have your student scan the passage and find the non-phonetic words. This is NOT a timed activity.
• Section 3 contains sentence stacks. These are sentences from the passage that are broken down into chunks. • Have your student read each chunk and then the next using the scoops (having them run their finger along the scoops as they read) in order to build fluency and prosody. Perform these activities once during one session. • Once your student has completed all readings 5 times over 5 sessions, have them read the story for one final time and record their results and have your student track their results.

Section 1 (Time: 15 seconds for each exercise)

Isolated Phonogram Reading

ble	ea	oi	cle	y
dge	ft	er	g	ar
mp	tch	ou	mp	oy
ble	u-e	ow	o-e	aw
ph	sh	v	th	ch

	1	2	3	4	5
Date					
Total Sounds Read					
- Errors					
= Total Sounds Correct					

Nonsense Word Reading

flixplu	twinrab	bry	spluflax	twixting
himplex	juxtrap	swigran	repted	kilped
spull	clume	traip	floub	vixray
swinrag	trixpot	lemprid	boraz	fingtrrab
splung	bufe	pru	extrimp	lingtrop

	1	2	3	4	5
Date					
Total Words Read					
- Errors					
= Total Words Correct					

Real Word Reading

mythical	generation	peaceful	legend	back
society	evidence	magical	ancient	clock
mysterious	kilometre	civilization	research	jump
enthusiast	island	historical	answer	quid
kingdom	describe	scholar	castle	quack

	1	2	3	4	5
Date					
Total Words Read					
- Errors					
= Total Words Correct					

Story FP-15.1: "The Lost City of Atlantis – Fact or Fiction?"

Section 2 (Untimed exercises)

Non-phonetic Word Recognition

Only read the real words in these paragraphs.

flam toodle flapdoodle though frixcro
juft gandriz felp island pordrip
huxt either trim braxter flo
squit nup period ponus

horb verig juv period wendix
neither grelps drind forv carping
rexed forn though inforp twen
melp wix blu neither wendrip

Period thorujhst sheag should skhtj lkjry
Neither lskhtk hseither ksdgkts either ti
Gksjetk lkjsekt jlkjwould whetlkh kjet to
From loath ks island laste kslktsetk who

Though lskejtkl j rough kjae people to
Lskejtl jl from ksrhth kh many naelkth
Periodi nesfrt should setlkh jslektj very
Skeet dfkl lktwo only snelkth l people

island through sthjh chark alkhr lkaehr
ahah either neither kntelkh ksdlkht two
island neither slkht hselkht skleh akhr ta
lkshtkh both should people skhtelht sake

Story FP-15.1: "The Lost City of Atlantis – Fact or Fiction?"

Section 3 (Untimed exercises)

Sentence Stacks

Many myths

Many myths and stories

Many myths and stories have been told

Many myths and stories have been told of the mythical

Many myths and stories have been told of the mythical city of Atlantis.

But scholars

But scholars have agreed

But scholars have agreed that there is

But scholars have agreed that there is no evidence

But scholars have agreed that there is no evidence that this magical city

But scholars have agreed that there is no evidence that this magical city ever existed.

This miracle find

This miracle find has left some

This miracle find has left some Atlantis legend enthusiasts

This miracle find has left some Atlantis legend enthusiasts to wonder

This miracle find has left some Atlantis legend enthusiasts to wonder if this could be

This miracle find has left some Atlantis legend enthusiasts to wonder if this could be the answer to

This miracle find has left some Atlantis legend enthusiasts to wonder if this could be the answer to the "Lost City".

They are calling

They are calling their find

They are calling their find a miracle

They are calling their find a miracle and have made

They are calling their find a miracle and have made a great deal

They are calling their find a miracle and have made a great deal of progress

They are calling their find a miracle and have made a great deal of progress in their research.

Perhaps the lost city

Perhaps the lost city of Atlantis

Perhaps the lost city of Atlantis will no longer be

Perhaps the lost city of Atlantis will no longer be a legend

Perhaps the lost city of Atlantis will no longer be a legend but a historical landmark

Perhaps the lost city of Atlantis will no longer be a legend but a historical landmark that we can learn

Perhaps the lost city of Atlantis will no longer be a legend but a historical landmark that we can learn about for years.

Story FP-15.1: "The Lost City of Atlantis – Fact or Fiction?"

Section 4 (1 minute timed activity)

Many myths and stories have been told of the mythical city of Atlantis. The 14
legend tells of a magical utopian society that was peaceful. The legend has 26
captivated dreamers for generations, yet no one has found evidence of such 37
a place in history books, or from any research. The city of Atlantis was first 52
spoken about by Plato around 360 B.C. In his writings, he describes a 66
very advanced and powerful society. But scholars have agreed that there 77
is no evidence that this magical city ever existed. Or is there? 89

Recently, researchers from a university in Turkey have discovered the 99
ancient remains of a 3000-year-old castle in the country's biggest lake, Lake 113
Van. The mysterious castle, made of a special stone, spans about a 125
kilometre with walls as high as four metres. Researchers believe it is an Iron 139
Age relic of the lost Urartu Civilization or what is also known as the Kingdom 154
of Van. They are calling their find a miracle and have made a great deal of 170
progress in their research. 174

This miracle find has left some Atlantis legend enthusiasts to wonder if this 187
could be the answer to the "Lost City". The mythical underwater island 199
remains a legend for now but who knows? Perhaps this new castle 211
discovery could hold answers for us. Perhaps the lost city of Atlantis will no 225
longer be a legend but a historical landmark that we can learn about for 239
years to come. Only time and research will tell. 248

Baseline	2.	4.
Total Words Read:	Total Words Read:	Total Words Read:
- # of errors:	- # of errors:	- # of errors:
= Words Correct:	= Words Correct:	= Words Correct:

1. Total Words Read:	3. Total Words Read:	5. Total Words Read:
- # of errors:	- # of errors:	- # of errors:
= Words Correct:	= Words Correct:	= Words Correct:

Baseline																
	5	10	15	20	25	30	35	40	45	50	55	60	65	70	75	80
	85	90	95	100	105	110	115	120	125	130	135	140	145	150	155	160
	165	170	175	180	185	190	195	200	205	210	215	220	225	230	235	240

Final Reading																
	5	10	15	20	25	30	35	40	45	50	55	60	65	70	75	80
	85	90	95	100	105	110	115	120	125	130	135	140	145	150	155	160
	165	170	175	180	185	190	195	200	205	210	215	220	225	230	235	240

Baseline Score (WPM): ____________ Final Reading (WPM): ____________ Final WPM (+/-): ______________

Comprehension Questions

1. When was the notion of the city of Atlantis first explored?
2. In what country did they discover the ancient castle?
3. How big was the castle that researchers discovered?
4. Why do you think researchers are calling their discovery a miracle?
5. What time period do researchers believe this new castle comes from?
6. Do you think researchers have found the Lost City of Atlantis? Why or why not?

Comprehension Plus!

Where to Begin

Assessor Instructions

Once you have completed the Reading Screener and have determined that your student is at the Comprehension Plus! level, you can start here. Unlike the Decoding Plus! and Fluency Plus! sections, the Comprehension Plus! section contains stories that are not cumulatively structured. These stories may contain some or all of the previously detailed concepts in both Decoding Plus! and Fluency Plus! sections. It is for this reason that there is no System Central for Comprehension Plus! The teacher need only perform the Reading Screener and determine, based on the student's results, that the Comprehension level is the most suitable level for their student. (See Example 3 in the How to Use section of this manual on page 24).

See below for detailed instructions on how to proceed through the Comprehension Plus! stories.

Comprehension Passages

1. Teachers can use this opportunity to do some pre-reading activities with their students should they feel they want to incorporate these. These can include but aren't limited to KWL Charts, Brainstorming etc.... After any pre-reading activities, have your student read the story aloud as you follow along. It is ideal for the teacher to guide and support their student at this level with the student's sense of fluency, prosody and expression, and encourage the student to work on these skills as they move through the stories.
2. The comprehension stories are opportunities for teacher and student to orally discuss the story content to check for comprehension and to deepen the student's learning and understanding of the content.
3. Once teacher and student have had an opportunity to discuss the story, there are learning extension options for the student to deepen their learning should they so choose. ***Copies of all of the graphs and pages are at the back of the manual available for reproducing (see the Blackline Masters section).**

Story CP-1.1: "Video Games – From Idea to Game"

1

Have you ever wondered how video games are created? Do you have a great idea for a game but are unsure of how to go about it? Creating video games is no simple task but if you approach it the right way, you just might have a chance at creating the next Minecraft.

Video games have been around since the early 1950s where they started off as research projects. In the late 60s video games started to become more sophisticated in their construction until the late 70s and early 80s when they blossomed with PAC Man, Space Invaders and Super Mario, until the super Play Station and Xboxes that we are familiar with today. These games were all created by large companies with large gaming teams in charge of creating the next big seller. Many people dream of creating the next big hit, but according to professional creators, you need to consider some important aspects when creating a game for others.

First, you need to do some research. According to the experts, you need to think of a game you love and think about why you love it and what specifically you love about it. This will help you realize and use the same "recipe" when creating your own game. You also need to consider games that you don't like and more importantly why you don't like them. What specifically do you not like – characters or genre – and make sure you remember this when creating your own game. Also, observe the games that others love to play and make sure you take into consideration everyone's views as you don't want to create a game with narrow market appeal.

Next, pick a niche or a genre and stick to it. For example, if you are going to choose the theme of sci-fi make sure that your game uses these elements and doesn't go too far off the beaten track. Use traditional elements found within these genres but feel free to be creative. Your game needs to be creative and somewhat believable for people to be interested in it. Don't use every element as it might make the game hard to follow and too difficult to play. Most professional experts would agree that if your game is overly complex and complicated, it risks isolating and turning off potential game players.

Finally, do the preparation and leg work. Make sure the game has easy to follow instructions and rules.

Make sure they are consistent to the type of game you want to design and make sure it has something unique and different to catch the eye of potential gamers. Know that you are doing this to come up with lots of ideas but realize that not all of them will work and you will need to streamline your final product.

You can always opt to go independently or you can approach a company once you are done, but either way, it's a competitive industry. Remember the idea is just the first important step, but know that many of the games you love and play today started as a great idea first.

Comprehension Questions

1. How long have video games been around for?
2. When did Pac man and Super Mario become popular?
3. Why is it a good idea to do some research before making a video game?
4. What do the experts recommend?
5. If you invented a video game, what would you make?
6. Name three things you think are important in a video game.
7. What is your favourite video game? Why?
8. Why do big companies have the edge over independent video game makers?

Extend Your Learning!

1. **Design your own video game.**
   Map out what kind of video game you'd like to create. Think about what actions you'd like to see in the game, what characters and how the game will look. Google the many free websites and videos online to see how you can make your game come to life!
2. **Create a Top 10 List!**
   Create a Top 10 List of the most popular video games. Now, create your own Top 10 List of your favourite video games and compare them to the most popular.
3. **Create a Storyboard**
   Take your game idea and start mapping it out using the storyboard below. Draw the characters, the actions and how you want your game to take shape.

Name of My Game:

Story CP-2.1: "Viola Desmond – A Canadian Legacy"

On a chilly winter's night in 1946, Viola Desmond, an African-Canadian hair salon owner, went to see a movie at the Roseland Theatre in New Glasgow, Nova Scotia. What started out as a nice night out, ended up being a miserable night in prison for Viola. As she took her seat on the main floor of the theatre, Viola did not know that the Roseland Theatre was racially segregated. Ms. Viola was a black woman and black patrons, at the time, were only allowed to sit in the balcony seats. Ms. Desmond was told to move from her seat and she refused, determined to be treated as an equal. Viola Desmond was subsequently arrested and dragged out of the theatre.

Viola Desmond was no stranger to being faced with inequality. She knew what it meant to work and strive for things that she wanted even though people said that she couldn't. Viola grew up in Nova Scotia, dreaming of becoming a beautician and hairdresser and to run her own beauty salon. Learning that beauty schools in Nova Scotia did not accept black students, she decided to get trained in Montreal and the United States and then she promptly moved back to her home province and opened up her own beauty salon.

Viola Desmond knew what it was like to fight for what she wanted, so when she faced being sent to prison for sitting in a seat in a movie theatre, she decided to fight for her rights. She took the fight all the way to the Supreme Court and fought to end racial segregation in Canada. Unfortunately, Ms. Desmond's court battles did not end well and her appeal was denied. Ms. Desmond's fight took a big toll on her personal life leaving her with a broken marriage, an abandoned business and a premature death in 1965.

Viola Desmond's fight against racism and inequality did not go unnoticed, however. In 2010, Ms. Desmond's cause was officially recognized by the Lieutenant Governor of Nova Scotia and she was pardoned. In 2018, Viola Desmond was nationally recognized by having her face appear on a Canadian postage stamp and the new $10 bill.

Viola Desmond's story of strength, determination and courage is one that we can look to for inspiration to fight for what is right and to never give up. Who would have thought that a night out at the movies would turn into an inspiring Canadian civil rights legacy?

Comprehension Questions

1. Why was Viola Desmond asked to leave the Roseland Theatre?
2. What career aspirations did Viola Desmond have?
3. Why do you think that the beauty schools in Nova Scotia did not accept Viola into their schools?
4. Even though Viola Desmond did not win her court battles, how were her fights for equality recognized?
5. Have you or someone you know ever been unfairly treated just because of the way you looked?
6. How do you think we can, as a society, fight against being unfairly treated because of skin colour or any other kind of difference?

Extend Your Learning!

1. **Interview Viola Desmond!**
   Put your reporter's hat on and create of list of questions you would ask Viola Desmond if you could.
2. **Research!**
   Research Black History month in Canada and create a "Did You Know?" sheet.
3. **Create a Timeline**
   Using the Timeline template, create a timeline of Viola Desmond's life.

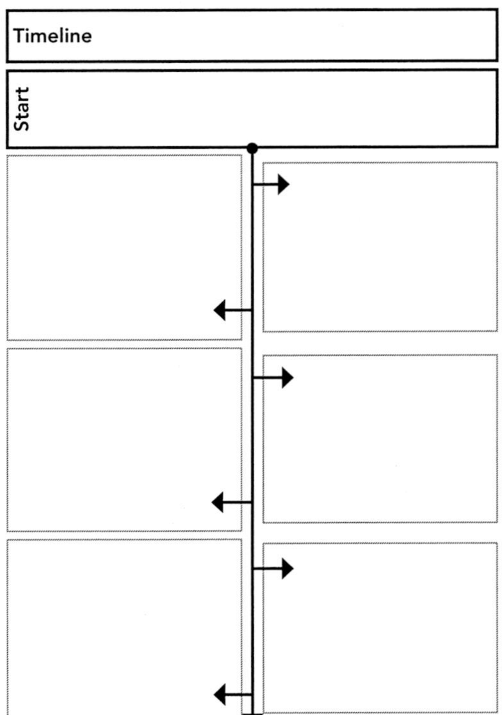

Story CP-3.1: "Gum! Chew on the History!"

1

Chewing gum has been around for thousands of years but many people are unaware of its original form and history. The very first form of chewing gum was discovered by Mayans and Aztecs in the form of *chicle:* a resin extracted from the sapodilla tree in Mexico and Latin America. *Chicle* is a strong resin that acts similarly to a band-aid for trees. It is a sticky, rubber substance that is meant to protect tree bark, but Mayans and Aztecs discovered that it could also be chewable if sliced thinly and cooked and dried out. This first form of "cha" helped to ward off hunger and thirst but the Aztec's also recognized it as a powerful breath freshener. European settlers quickly picked up and capitalized on this habit of chewing "cha" from the Native American cultures and soon it became popular in America as well.

Inventor Thomas Adams Sr. received a supply of chicle through a Mexican president and originally thought it would be a helpful industrial substance because of its plastic-like qualities. However, he soon learned that once boiled and hand rolled, it would be more popular as pieces of chewing gum. By the late 1800s Adams gum was widely sold. Around the same time, a soap salesman named William Wrigley came up with a smart idea to sell soap. He would give out free gum to customers who bought the most soap! When he realized that the gum was more popular than the soap, he decided to switch careers. After much trial and error, the William Wrigley Jr. Company took off and by the time Wrigley died in 1932, he was one of the richest men in America.

As the demand for gum grew in places like America, the cost to natural resources in Latin America began to take its toll. Soon the demand for chicle outmatched the resource (the sapodilla trees) and gum manufactures began switching to cheaper synthetic bases made from petroleum, wax and other substances. By 1980, The United States was no longer importing chicle from Mexico or other Latin American countries.

So, what's the difference between chewing gum and bubble gum? Bubble gum is made to be extra stretchy, so that you can blow bubbles with it. Frank Fleer invented bubble gum in 1906 and called it Blibber Blubber, but it didn't really become popular until 1928 when Walter Diemer first developed the Double Bubble that is so famous today. What's the secret to blowing the perfect bubble? The warmth in your mouth softens the gum creating a base. Chewing separates the sugar and the colouring and helps to align the long molecules in the gum base, which can then be stretched easier than with chewing gum. To blow great bubbles you are supposed to chew until all the flavour is gone so that the sugar molecules don't weaken the bubble. Gum bases don't react to your mouth or stomach lining, so if you swallow it accidentally, don't worry, it won't get stuck!

Comprehension Questions

1. Who was the first chewing gum discovered by?
2. Who was the soap salesman that Thomas Adams Sr. met?
3. When did Wrigley die?
4. What is the difference between chewing gum and bubble gum?
5. What is the secret to blowing the perfect bubble?
6. Who invented bubble gum?
7. What is your favourite brand or flavour of bubble gum?
8. What happens when you chew bubble gum?

Extend Your Learning!

1. **Trivia!**
   Using the Guinness Book of World Records, find five world records involving chewing gum.
2. **Compete!**
   Plan a bubble blowing contest with your friends. See who can make the biggest bubbles and learn which gum is the best for blowing bubbles.
3. **Invent**
   Think up your own new flavour of gum. Write to one of the big gum companies pitching your new flavour.

Story CP-4.1: "Brain signals, Body Screens and Brain Implants! Oh My!"

1

Imagine you are sitting at home thinking about asking your friend to go see a movie with you. Without picking up a phone, your thoughts are sent directly from your brain to your friend's brain. Your friend sends a "brain message" back to you telling you that they'll meet you there at 6pm. Crazy, right? Not really. That is one of the many new ways that scientists are predicting that we will communicate in the near future. Human communication has come a long way.

The way humans communicate has transformed a great deal since the first man walked the earth. The origin of speech can be traced back to 500,000 BC. From solely relying on the spoken word, man moved into communicating in written form using symbols and carvings into rock surfaces. By 9000 BC, man had developed pictograms or symbols representing concepts of activities or objects. The first alphabet came into existence in 2000 BC. From there, we had many ways of communicating such as storytelling, written words on paper, and the use of quills for writing. The first telephone was invented in 1876 revolutionizing the way humans communicate from far distances. And, believe it or not, the first mobile phone was created in 1947! From there, the development of computers and the internet happened and since then, the way we communicate has been changing at lightning speed. Now, it's almost unheard of to see someone who doesn't have a mobile phone. Telephone booths are becoming relics of the past and almost nobody understands having to use a dial to make a phone call.

But what will happen from here? It's almost impossible to think that communication can get any easier. With the touch of a screen, we can make plans to go out, make emergency calls, send pictures of ourselves and call in sick for work. We don't even have to actually speak to people anymore, we can do it all by sending text messages or emails. But scientists are now saying that we can look forward to getting implants in our bodies that allow us to have wearable screens on our skin or our clothing. Goodbye, mobile phone, hello, screen on my forearm! Scientists are also researching and testing something called "Brain-Computer Interfaces". These can literally allow us to send our thoughts to someone else through a special network; no phone, no computer, no screen… just our brains; amazing and scary!

There's no question that we are now living in a fast-paced world with ways of communicating that are so easy and quick. It's hard to imagine, but get ready for the day we no longer use phones but we use our brains and bodies to speak to one another.

Comprehension Questions

1. How far back can we trace the origins of speech?
2. When did the first alphabet come into existence?
3. In what year was the first mobile phone invented?
4. Would you like to be able to communicate with others just using your brain? Why or why not?
5. What do you think it would be like to have a computer screen on your hand or arm?
6. Do you think that we will run out of ways to communicate or do you think that scientists will keep coming up with new ways to communicate? Why or why not?

Extend Your Learning!

1. **Think of a new way to communicate.**
   Think up a new way to communicate using language, body language or materials. Try it with a friend.
2. **Create a Timeline!**
   Create a timeline of the history of communication and its evolution.
3. **Compare!**
   Using your timeline, compare the different types of communication. Which ones were the most effective? Why did some of these become obsolete? Can you see any of our current ways that we communicate becoming obsolete?

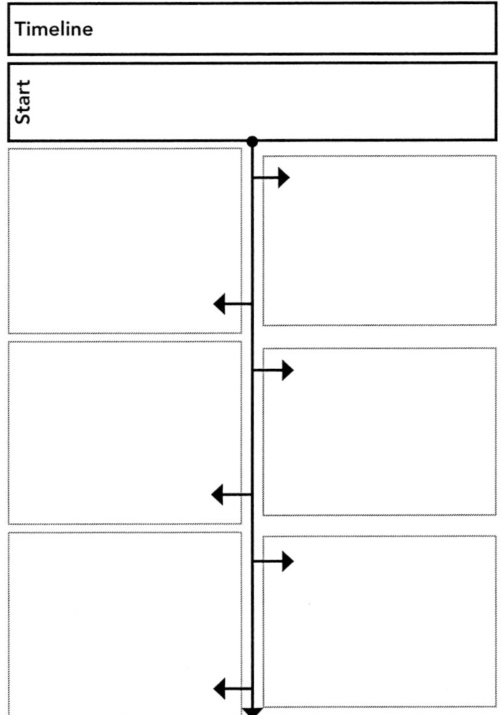

Story CP-5.1: "The Amazing Wayne Gretzy"

"You miss 100 percent of the shots you don't take" Wayne Gretzky

He has smashed national hockey records in all categories, coached various NHL hockey teams, owned a chain of restaurants and was the youngest athlete signed to a team in the history of American sports. The amazing Wayne Gretzky has done it all. His path to stardom was paved with hard work, unrelenting determination and amazing skill.

Born January 26, 1961, in Brantford Ontario, Wayne Gretzky started skating before the age of three under the guidance of his father, Walter Gretzky. He mastered the art of hockey in his backyard hockey rink and started playing minor hockey at the age of six. Debuting on the Nadrofsky Steelers, Wayne Gretzky played hockey with players four years his senior. In his 1970-71 season, Gretzky scored 196 goals and 120 assists. This amazing start soon pegged him as a young hockey prodigy whose future held great promise. In 1975, Gretzky moved to Toronto and began playing Junior B hockey. He first played with the Vaughn Nationals and in '76-'77 moved to the Seneca Nationals. In 1977-78 he began playing full time in OHL (Ontario Hockey League) with the Sault Saint Marie Greyhounds. In his inaugural season he earned the rookie record with 70 goals and 112 assists in 64 games. It was with the Sault Saint Marie Greyhounds that he first donned the number 99, and Wayne Gretzky would soon become a household sensation.

In 1978, Gretzky turned professional and would be the youngest professional athlete playing a major league sport in America. His first professional team was with the Indianapolis Racers with whom he only played eight games before being traded to the Edmonton Oilers. By the start of Gretzky's second season, the WHA had merged with the NHL and it wasn't long before Gretzky ruled this league. With his time spent with the Edmonton Oilers, Gretzky began shattering hockey records. Some of these included most goals scored, most assists, and the most points in a season. Gretzky also led the Oilers to four Stanley Cup championships before being traded to the LA Kings in 1988. Unable to recapture the magic he had with the Oilers, Gretzky added greatly to the profile of the LA Kings and hockey in the Southwest US. After a quick stint with the St. Louis Blues, Gretzky was traded to the New York Rangers where he finished his hockey career.

Wayne Gretzky retired from the Rangers after playing three seasons at the age of 38. At his last hockey game, The NHL retired the number 99 in recognition of Wayne Gretzky's contribution to the world of hockey.

After his hockey career, Gretzky became involved with coaching for the NHL and for International and Olympic hockey teams. He coached the Phoenix Coyotes for five years and left to start up new business ventures. Mixing his love of hockey with business, Wayne Gretzky became a successful entrepreneur and owned ventures such as a winery, a chain of restaurants as well as ownership of the CFL team the Toronto Argonauts. Gretzky was inducted into the Hockey Hall of fame on June 23, 1999. In 2016, the NHL appointed him the official ambassador for the league's celebrations in 2017.

Living with his family in Southern California, Gretzky will always be remembered as the "great one". His style, his game and his sense of modesty are inspirations to those who aspire to be great hockey players.

Comprehension Questions

1. What number is Wayne Gretzky famous for?
2. Which team did Wayne Gretzky first play professional hockey for?
3. What year did Gretzky turn professional?
4. How old was Wayne Gretzky when he retired?
5. When was Wayne Gretzky born?
6. Where does Wayne Gretzky live?
7. How many goals did Wayne Gretzky score in his inaugural season? How many assists?
8. What other sports do you think Wayne Gretzky might be good at? Why?

Extend Your Learning!

1. **Design and create your own hockey gear.** Using tape, straws, string, scissors and popsicle sticks, design and create your own goalie net and hockey stick. Reflect on what worked well and what didn't.
2. **Create a Timeline!** Create a timeline of Wayne Gretzky's hockey career.
3. **Create your own Fantasy Hockey League** Invite your friends to create a Fantasy Hockey League. Think about what the winner will receive, team size and draft rules, scoring rules and timeframe.

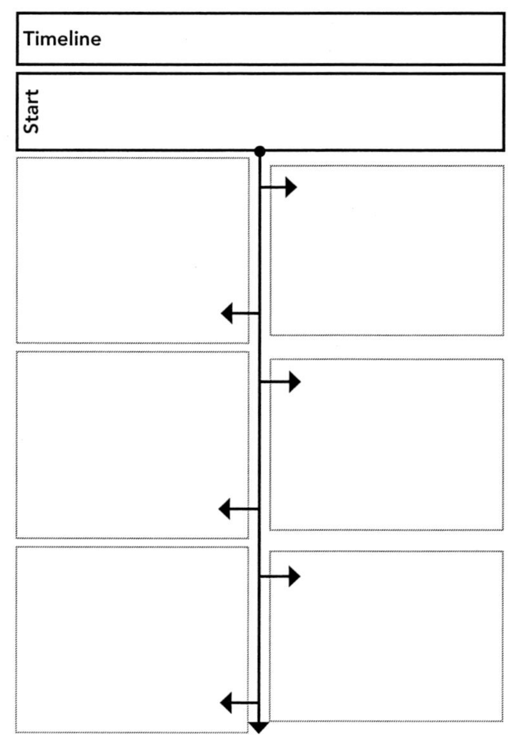

Story CP-6.1: "Terry's Marathon Journey"

1

In schools all across Canada, students participate in an annual run named after an amazing man called Terry Fox. Who was Terry Fox and why do children across Canada honour his memory every year by running a race and raising money?

Terry Stanley Fox was born in Winnipeg, Manitoba, and lived in Port Coquitlam, BC. Terry was an active boy participating in many sporting activities. Unfortunately, when Terry Fox was 18-years-old, he found out that he had bone cancer. Terry had to have his right leg amputated just above the knee. While he was in hospital being treated for his cancer, he witnessed many other people suffering from the disease and he was strongly affected by the sight. Seeing children suffering, in particular, bothered Terry immensely. So much so that he decided that he would begin a run across Canada to raise money for Cancer research. He would call the run the "Marathon of Hope".

It took Terry Fox 18 months to prepare for the "Marathon of Hope"; with one leg amputated, and using a prosthetic leg, he ran 5,000 kilometers to get himself ready. He started his run across the country in St. John's, Newfoundland. He ran close to 42 kilometers a day throughout the Atlantic provinces and the East Coast.

The country's attention grew and grew as he persevered and ran with the hope of raising money for cancer research. After 143 days and 5,373 kilometers, Terry Fox woke up one day and discovered he had a nasty cough which indicated that he cancer in his lungs. Sadly, Terry Fox had to stop his run without achieving his dream. Terry Fox passed away at the age of 22 on June 28, 1981.

However, Terry Fox's story does not end there. His legacy lives on today and to date, 750 million dollars has been raised in his name through the annual Terry Fox run. You may have even participated in a Terry Fox run in your school. The story of Terry Fox is a sad one but it is also full of inspiration and hope; hope that we can find a cure for cancer but also hope that we can look to him as a source of inspiration. Terry Fox has shown us that compassion and determination can create lasting change. All over Canada, statues of Terry Fox have been erected. His memory and his legacy will live on in the history of Canada.

Comprehension Questions

1. Why was Terry Fox hospitalized at the young age of 18?
2. When Terry Fox was in the hospital, what did he see that inspired him to run across Canada?
3. How long did it take for Terry Fox to prepare for his run?
4. What did Terry Fox call his run across Canada?
5. Did Terry Fox complete the Marathon of Hope? Why or why not?
6. How many kilometers did Terry Fox run before he had to stop?
7. Why do you think that Canadians honour the legacy of Terry Fox to this day?

Extend Your Learning!

1. **Design!**
   Design your own logo for Terry's Marathon of Hope. Draw it on the t-shirt below.
2. **Map it out**
   On a map of Canada, map out Terry Fox's journey.
3. **How far does Terry's legacy go?**
   Research how many countries have a Terry Fox Run.

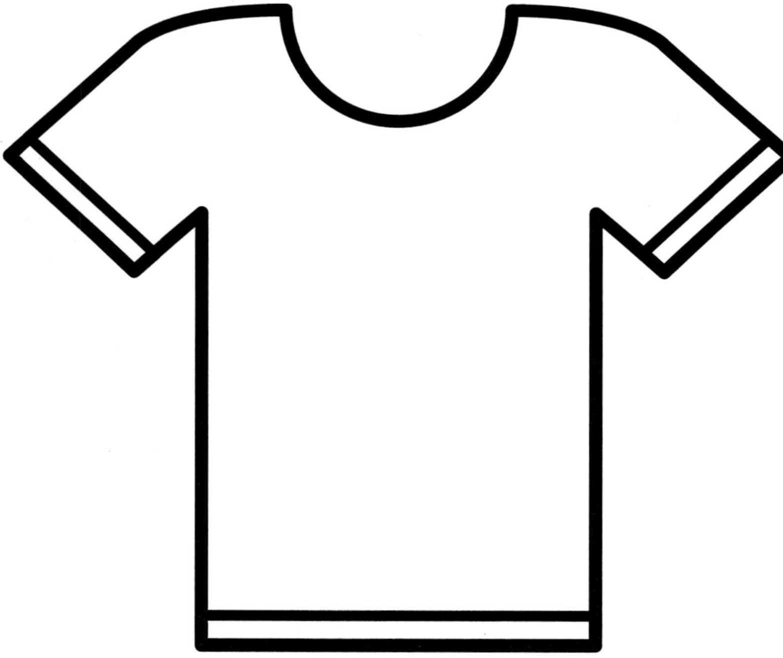

Story CP-7.1: "The Story of Bill Reid – Artist Extraordinaire"

1

Bill Reid is Canada's most renowned contemporary Native Northwest Coast artist. His work spans many mediums – goldsmithing, sculpting and writing. He is an example of a native artist whose calling was to bring Northwest Haida art back from the brink of extinction, but his path was an unusual one.

Born in Victoria, BC, on January 12, 1920, he was an only child. Bill Reid's mother was of Haida ancestry although Bill would not embrace his Haida roots until later in his life. Bill Reid grew up in British Columbia and it wasn't until a family trip in his mid-twenties to his mother's village that he came in contact with his artistic roots and his sense of Haida belonging. It was during his 1954 visit that Bill Reid saw family members wearing intricate bracelets designed by his great-great Uncle Charles Edenshaw and this sparked his life-long love of art and Haida culture.

At the start of his career, the young Bill Reid was first employed by the CBC as a broadcaster for a late night radio show. Later, Bill Reid studied jewelry making in the 1950s at Ryerson Polytechnical Institute and then attended the London School of Design to learn classical European techniques. Returning back to BC, Reid opened his own studio while still working for the CBC. In the late 60s, Reid had an opportunity to work for British Columbia's Museum of Anthropology resurrecting traditional Haida totem poles. The project was an attempt to preserve many traditional forms of Haida Gwaii art that were in danger of being lost. From here, Reid's life-long interest in using traditional Haida Gwaii figures and characters to make his art blossomed. His most famous pieces are representations from famous Haida Gwaii stories and are recognized around the world today as pieces distinctly representing Native Canadian Northwest Coastal art. One of his most famous sculptures, The Raven and the First Men, is on display at UBC's Museum of Anthropology and it depicts the human creation story according to Haida legend. Another of Reid's most recognizable sculptures can be found in Vancouver International Airport. Originally commissioned for the Canadian Embassy in Washington, The Spirit of the Haida Gwaii is an argillite carving depicting miniature canoes and draws from the oral histories of the Haida. In 2004, a replica of this stunning piece was added to the Canadian Twenty Dollar bill in order to celebrate Canada's history and achievements.

As a writer, a carver, a jeweller maker and story teller, Bill Reid's art has touched and inspired many great Native and non-Native Canadian artists. There's not a person in Northwest Coast Art who hasn't been touched by Reid's interpretation of Haida Art. The Bill Reid Gallery was opened in Vancouver in 2008 to celebrate the story and contribution of one of Canada's greatest modern artists.

Comprehension Questions

4. Where is Haida Gwaii?
5. What two schools did Bill Reid attend?
6. What type of art did Bill Reid make?
7. What is the name and location of the art gallery opened in honour of Bill Reid?
8. Where was Bill Reid born?
9. What was the name of the great uncle who inspired Bill Reid's jewelry making?
10. Why do you think Bill Reid became so interested in Haida Gwaii art?
11. What mediums does Bill Reid's art span?

Extend Your Learning!

1. **Research!**
   Find out where the Haida Gwaii is. Draw a picture of the First Nations that live there and provide eight interesting facts about their culture.
2. **Visit!**
   Visit the Vancouver Museum of Anthropology online – pick an exhibit that interests you and write about it.
3. **Create!**
   Research some of Bill Reid's art online. Try your hand at creating your own drawing, sculpture or totem pole in the style of Bill Reid.

Story CP-8.1: "Your Amazing Brain"

1

Have you ever thought about your brain? If you have, you will have used your brain to think about your brain! How amazing is that? Your brain is an incredible and very necessary part of your body. Your brain is an organ contained inside of your head. It has some super important jobs like making you think, remember, see, hear, touch, feel and move. Your brain weighs about three pounds and it is made up of cells and tissue. The brain has two parts to it; the left side or **hemisphere**, and the right side or **hemisphere**. If you were to look at your brain, it kind of looks like a ball of macaroni but it is so much more than that and chances are that it wouldn't taste that great either!

Your brain has many parts that have very different jobs. The **cerebrum** helps you to think and speak. So, when you are chatting with your friend about your cool new bike trick, you are using your **cerebrum**. The **cerebellum** helps you with movement and balance. As you are running out to the soccer field ready to play your game and score some goals, your **cerebellum** is hard at work helping you to move on the field and to keep your balance as you kick the ball. The **prefrontal cortex** helps you to make plans and decisions. It's funny to think about what the **prefrontal cortex** was doing when you decided to eat that jalapeno! The **hippocampus** has nothing to do with hippos being in your brain, rather it is the part of your brain that finds and stores memories. Remember when you lost your first tooth? You're now using your **hippocampus!** The **amygdala** has the important job of controlling your emotions. Ever felt scared to go into a dark room? Your **amygdala** is doing its job of alerting you and keeping you safe by triggering different emotions in you. Finally, connecting all of these parts are **neurons** which are amazing cells that make electrical signals to send messages to other cells in your body telling them what to do. The brain is one busy organ!

What's even more cool about the brain is that you can do things to help make it stronger. Learning new things helps your brain stretch and get stronger and the more you learn, your brain gets stronger and stronger. Now, almost everyone thinks that making mistakes is a bad thing but, guess what? Making mistakes is an even more powerful way to make your brain grow and get stronger.

So, the next time you do, well, anything, use your brain to think about how amazing your brain really is!

Comprehension Questions

1. How much does your brain weigh?
2. What kinds of things does your brain control?
3. What part of your brain is important for making decisions and plans?
4. What part of your brain helps you to remember things that happened in the past?
5. What is something you can do every day to help make your brain stronger?
6. Does making mistakes hurt your brain?
7. Do you think you can live without a brain? Why or why not?

Extend Your Learning!

1. **Research!**
   Pick one of the areas of the brain discussed in the story. Research this part of the brain in depth and write about your findings.
2. **Design**
   Design your own brain puzzle using the parts of the brain mentioned in the story.
3. **Create!**
   Using Play-Doh or clay, create a sculpture of the brain. Label the different areas with toothpicks and labels.

Story CP-9.1: "How Dogs Communicate"

1

Have you ever wondered how man's best friend can understand you, or better yet, how you can understand your dog? Dogs communicate very differently than humans but it's still easy to understand the intent of the message. When dogs communicate with other dogs they do so in a very different manner. While dogs are able to hear the difference between different types of barks, they also rely on smell and other senses to figure out the message from another dog. From a smell, a dog can determine the status of a dog, if they are male or female or if they are dominate or submissive.

When communicating with people, dogs use a different style of communication. Depending on your dog's need, they use body signals to tell you their intentions. One of the most obvious forms of body language is observation or using those big sad eyes. Dogs will often use their gaze to infer their needs to their owners. In a term called inferential gazing, dogs are able to infer their need for food, walks and attention. There is no need for barking or paw gestures, they merely use gazing as a way to show you what they need. This is very similar to the way an infant communicates its needs to his/her mother. When humans are communicating with dogs, alternating the gaze between object and or direction, a dog will be able to infer (guess) that you are interested in a "thing" in that direction. This type of messaging is particularly effective if the human talks to the dog first and then gazes in the direction that holds the object. The dog will then infer that the command and the direction is directly linked to what you are trying to convey.

Another way in which dogs communicate with humans is through body language. If you are watching carefully and can read the signals, it's actually quite easy to gauge your dog's intentions. Scientists have identified 19 gestures dogs most commonly use to communicate with humans. Direct and open eye contact is a dog's way of showing you trust and affection while avoiding eye contact is a signal that the dog may be scared or has done something wrong. Tail posture is another indication of a dog's mood or temperament. If a dog's tail is wagging slowly, this is a signal that the dog is unsure or weary. A stiff tail means an alert state while a tucked tail indicates feeling scared. Of course, a waggy tail is used to convey happiness and a low tail can mean contentedness or feeling good. Tongue licking, yawning or misplaced sneezing can all be signs that your dog is anxious, stressed or nervous. Yawning can be tricky because it can also be interpreted as feeling relaxed, so it's important to think of your dog's mood when he/she yawns.

Belly exposure is also a way of telling a person how the dog is feeling. Dogs usually show their bellies to humans as a way of trying to appease a person or seek attention. A belly rub is a good way for a human and dog to share affection and build their trust. If a dog suddenly greets you with a downward dog, this is his/her way of initiating play. If you respond with a downward dog back, this will engage your dog in play as it tells him/her that you are reading them and want to play as well. Pawing or raising a paw, is a way to catch a human's attention and then further signal their intention with a gaze.

Humans and dogs have had a long history of co-existence and share a unique bond. Together, dogs and humans are able to support one another and offer each other unconditional support. The key to good communication between us is being able to read the signals and understand that communication doesn't have to be complicated.

Comprehension Questions

4. What can a dog tell from smelling another dog?
5. Why is body language so important between humans and dogs?
6. What does a waggy tail mean in dog language?
7. How many gestures have scientists identified that are important to communication between dogs and humans?
8. Why is it important to pay close attention to a dog's eye movements?
9. Why do you think humans like dogs so much?
10. Name three things a dog might be trying to tell a human through their body language.
11. If dogs could speak, what do you think they would say?

Extend Your Learning!

1. **Research!**
   Look up ways that other animals communicate. Compare their way of communicating to the ways that dogs communicate. How do they differ? How are they the same?
2. **Create!**
   Create a comic of how dogs communicate using the template provided.
3. **Imagine!**
   Imagine what would it be like if humans communicated the way dogs do. How would human lives be different?

Story CP-10.1: "Learning Disability or Super Power?"

1

What is a learning disability? A learning disability is what can happen when a person's brain is "wired" differently. A learning disability can't be cured or fixed, rather it is something that a person lives with for their whole lives. When someone has a learning disability, they might struggle with reading, writing, math or keeping and holding attention or focus. There are many different learning disabilities that people can be diagnosed with. Did you know that there are many famous people, celebrities and billionaires alike, who live with learning disabilities? It's hard to tell when someone has a learning disability because you can't see it on the outside, so it might come as a surprise to you that many very successful people in the world live with different learning challenges like dyslexia, autism, attention deficit disorder and many more. In fact, the list of successful and famous people living with learning challenges is so long, it would take forever to talk about them all. So, let's talk about just a few of these amazing folks who have overcome their difficulties and have learned to live with and sometimes even use their differences to help them succeed.

Being a professional or Olympic athlete can be tough. The number of hours of practice it takes to master a sport is astronomical, not to mention the perseverance and drive that it takes to become the best at a chosen sport. There are many athletes who have had the additional challenge of having a learning disability. Michael Phelps, the most decorated Olympian of all time, talks openly about learning to live with Attention Deficit Hyperactivity Disorder (ADHD). Michael experienced many struggles along the way. One of his teachers even told him that he would never succeed at anything. Despite Michael having ADHD, he pushed through and used his diagnosis to help him become one of the best Olympic swimmers in the world.

Many famous actors including Tom Cruise and Channing Tatum live with dyslexia and overcame their challenges to become very successful actors in their field. Many business leaders, artists, musicians and thought leaders also have achieved an amazing amount of success and fame despite – or perhaps even because of – their learning challenges. The famous artist Pablo Picasso struggled a great deal in school and, in fact, failed due to his reading difficulties.

So, it just goes to show you that just because someone has a disability, doesn't mean that they can't do something they love or be successful in anything. Having a learning disability just means that you have to learn how you learn best and try to find teachers and support people who can teach you how you need to learn. It's also about understanding your own personal learning differences and persevering through the hard times. While it may take someone with a learning disability a bit longer to do something, who knows, they just might come up with a whole new way to do that thing and become successful and famous in the process!

Comprehension Questions

1. What is a learning disability?
2. What learning disability does Michael Phelps live with?
3. Can a person be cured from a learning disabilty?
4. Why might it be hard to tell when someone has a learning disability?
5. Why did famous artist Pablo Picasso fail elementary school?
6. If you had a learning disability, what might you do to try to overcome your challenges?

Extend Your Learning!

1. **Research!**
   Look up the origins of the word 'dyslexia'. What does it mean? Record useful information about dyslexia and track the history behind it.
2. **Discover!**
   Find a famous person that has inspired you that has a learning disability. Learn about how they overcame their challenges and write about their story.
3. **What is it like?**
   Try reading the following sentences. (They are backwards.) How hard was it to try and read them? Did this give you some understanding about how someone with dyslexia might experience reading? Chat about your discoveries with a friend.

.tam eht no tas tac kcalb ehT

.kcans a dah maS

.dum ni tas gip ehT

Answer Key:
The black cat sat on the mat.
Sam had a snack.
The pig sat in mud.

Story CP-11.1: "Edinburgh Castle"

1

What famous castle housed royalty, was a garrison and held a leading military presence throughout history? The answer is Edinburgh Castle. This famous castle boasts inhabitants from the Bronze age (850 BCE) who built a hill fort on what is now known as Castle Rock. What makes Edinburgh Castle so fascinating and impressive is its numerous reincarnations and breathtaking views of Edinburgh itself.

Historically, many royals have lived in this castle. The first King of Scotland, Malcom III Canmore, made the castle his residence between 1058-1093. The city's oldest and smallest chapel is located in the castle and was made in honour of Malcom's wife, Margaret. Also of note, Mary Queen of Scots resided in the castle and gave birth to her son James, who would later become the Scottish and English King who unified the crowns of Scotland and England in 1603. The last known monarch to reside within the castle was Charles I in 1633, who lived there before his coronation as King of Scots.

Given the frequency and outbreak of war, Edinburgh Castle was also used as a strategic military post. Many times, the castle changed hands between the Scottish and the English and it was also used as a garrison that held many prisoners of war throughout history. Between the years of 1757 to 1814, the castle housed prisoners from the Seven Years War, The American Revolution and the Napoleonic Wars. During World War Two, German aircraft Luftwaffe pilots who were shot down in battle were housed in the infirmary within the castle. Today, there are many reminders of the castle's military history. One of the oldest and largest canons resides at Edinburgh Castle. Named Mon's Meg, this cannon was given as a gift in 1457 to James II and weighs six-tonnes and could fire a 150kg gunstone for up to 3.2km (2 miles). In honour of Mary Queen of Scot's wedding, Mon let out a blast that is reported to have gone from the Castle to Royal Botanical Gardens!

The castle's rich history and elaborate construction can be viewed today. Many of Scotland's treasures can be found within its walls. The Scot's Crown Jewels are located here as well as the famous Stone of Destiny, which was returned to Scotland in 1996. The place also hosts some great rooms inside such as The Great Hall, a room which saw many famous kings and queens plan their futures as important historical rulers.

Today, Edinburgh Castle is a historical site that houses The Scottish War Memorial Museum and the castle itself became a UNESCO world heritage site in 1995. Located 443 feet above sea level, you can see many other famous Edinburgh treasures such as the Scot Monument, Waverly Train Station and Arthur's Seat – a series of braes and crags to the west of the city. Visited by over one million tourists each year, Edinburgh Castle is a favourite of historians, architects and military enthusiasts who appreciate the vast historical importance of this ancient building. Planning a trip to Edinburgh? Make sure to arrange a visit to this beloved and fascinating piece of Scottish history.

Comprehension Questions

1. Where is Edinburgh castle located?
2. Who was the last monarch to live in the castle?
3. What is the name of the famous cannon located at the castle?
4. Name three things you can see at the castle as a visitor.
5. Why is Edinburgh Castle considered so famous?
6. Would you ever want to visit Edinburgh Castle? If so, why?
7. Name three other countries where you think they might have castles. Explain your thinking.

Extend Your Learning!

1. **Design**
   Draw and design your own castle. Make up an interesting history for it.
2. **Design**
   Design and write a travel brochure for Edinburgh Castle.
   Present it to your classmates or your teacher.
3. **Design**
   Using the coat of arms template provided below, design your own Coat of Arms to go with your new castle's history.

Story CP-12.1: "The Truth About Pirates"

1

What do you imagine when you think of a pirate? You might picture a dirty, evil-looking sailor with a patch on one eye, a wooden leg and a sword in his hand. There are many stories and movies about pirates and some of these stories make pirates out to be funny or heroes of a sort. The truth is that pirates were robbers and they were extremely ruthless and would commit almost any crime to get what they wanted.

Piracy began over 2000 years ago in Ancient Greece when these robbers of the sea would raid ships along the trading routes. The pirates would jump onto ships and loot and steal anything they wanted and if anyone got in their way, they wouldn't hesitate to hurt or even kill people. In truth, these men were merciless and evil bandits. It's curious that the movies would glorify such a horrible type of person.

Piracy was at its peak for about one hundred years, from 1620 to 1720. It was during those years that people rarely felt safe when out at sea. Ultimately, most pirates were always searching for ways to get rich and to give themselves a better life. Often pirates were heavily armed and they would always find new and clever ways to get what they wanted. Pirates were often very superstitious and had some very strange beliefs when they were out at sea. Pirates believed that wearing pierced earrings would save their eyesight. They also believed that having a woman on board their ship was very bad luck. As such, women had to disguise themselves as men to board any pirate ship.

Surprisingly, there was such a thing as a legal pirate. The government recognized the power of pirates and found a way to hire them as "privateers". These privateers were allowed to attack and plunder enemy ships and then share their loot with the government.

There were many famous pirates to sail the seas and to this day, there are still men who attack ships at sea but these are very few and they often are swiftly captured and punished. While the movies show us the shiny side of piracy, it's good to remember that these people were not only robbers of the sea but greedy and ruthless lawbreakers.

Comprehension Questions

1. When and where did piracy begin?
2. How many years was piracy the most prevalent?
3. Why did pirates board other ships?
4. What were some of the strange beliefs that pirates held?
5. What were legal pirates called?
6. Why would governments hire pirates?
7. Have your opinions or thoughts about pirates changed since reading this story? Why or why not?

Extend Your Learning!

1. **Create**
   Create your own pirate treasure map.
2. **Research!**
   Research the most famous pirates. Write about why they were famous and what their worst crimes were.
3. **Design!**
   Design a "Wanted" poster for the most evil pirate from your research.

Story CP-13.1: "The Guinness Book of World Records"

1

Who has the longest beard? Who has the record of being the tallest man ever? All of these plus more can be found in *The Guinness Book of World Records*. This book keeps track of information and records established around the world and many meaningful and sometimes bizarre facts.

The Guinness Book of World Records was first published on August 27, 1955, and came about as a result of an odd argument. The story began at a hunting party in Ireland in 1951, when the managing director of Guinness Brewing company, Sir Hugh Beaver, found himself in an argument about whether or not the golden plover was Europe's fastest game bird. He wanted to know if this was true and looked for a book that would give an authoritative answer, but he could not find one. He thought it would be a good idea if someone came up with such a book and decided to remedy this. At the time, someone working at the Guinness Brewing company put Sir Hugh Beaver in touch with the twin brothers Norris and Ross McWhirter, who were running a publishing and fact-finding company in London. These two brothers had an amazing ability to memorize fact and figures and recall them immediately and accurately. Guinness was so impressed by their amazing skills that he commissioned the twins to start a book. *The Guinness Book of World Records* was soon born. The McWhirters were the editors, compilers and spirit behind the book. In 1972, these amazing brothers could be found on TV, on the show Roy Castle's 'Record Breakers', impressing viewers with their ability to reproduce facts and figures on the spot. Unfortunately, Ross McWhirter was shot dead in 1975. Norris continued as editor until 1986 and later retired in 1996.

The Guinness Book of World Records is well loved around the world by adults and children alike for meticulous accuracy and amazing breadth of subjects and, let's be honest, its weird facts! All world records are solemnly checked and authenticated and new records are encouraged, but how does one go about establishing a world record?

In order to get into *The Guinness Book of World Records*, you must meet some criteria or standards. The criteria and standards are carefully outlined on their website but the important thing to remember about these standards is that the records must be able to be measured objectively (by a number or amount), that it must be easily reproduced, that it does not harm anyone or anything, nor can it break the law. It is a rigorous application process and admission requirements are strict, but both individuals and small groups are always encouraged to set new records and achieve their best.

Today, *The Guinness Book of World Records* still continues to be a best seller. It has sold over a hundred million copies and has been translated to 23 languages in over 100 different countries. Ever dreamed of breaking or establishing a new world record? Check out Guinness' website and let the games begin!

Comprehension Questions

1. When was *The Guinness Book of World Records* first published?
2. Who were the two men who first published *The Guinness Book of World Records*?
3. When did Ross McWhirter die?
4. How many copies of *The Guinness Book of World Records* have been sold?
5. Why do people like this book?
6. What does the word remedy mean as used in the story?
7. What type of record would you like to try to break? Why?
8. When did Norris McWhirter retire?

Extend Your Learning!

1. **Create!**
   Create a poster for the best/worst/silliest/hardest world records ever recorded.
2. **Research!**
   Take poll of your family/class about what type of records they would want to attempt. Graph it up and present your information to your teacher/class/tutor.
3. **Create!**
   Create your own "World Records" contest with your friends and family. From your poll, have your family and friends attempt some of the activities. Record your results and pick the winner.

Story CP-14.1: "Black Holes"

1

Have you ever wondered what outer space feels like? We know it is a collection of stars, planets and galaxies, but what about other possibilities? A point of fascination to both scientists and other people is the idea of black holes. We know of their existence, but what exactly is a black hole and how did they come to be? What can we learn from studying them and what future possibilities can black holes hold?

A black hole is a cosmic body of extremely intense gravity from which nothing, not even light, can escape. A black hole can be formed by the death of a massive star. Black holes are so strong that anything that comes close to them disappears because of their intense gravitational force or pull. Albert Einstein first predicted the existence or possibilities of black holes in 1916 with his general theory of relativity. Later, the term black hole was born in 1967 by American astronomer John Wheeler and the existence of the very first black hole was discovered in 1971.

Black holes are extreme gravity forces, but are all black holes created equally? There are three main types of black holes: stellar black holes, supermassive black holes, and intermediate black holes. Stellar black holes are the smallest of the subtypes of black holes. A stellar black hole is created when a large star collapses in on itself and continues to compress. This dead star, or newly formed black hole, is incredibly dense, which gives it a huge gravitational force. This gravitational force then allows it to capture dust and gas and other matter, and it becomes denser and denser, increasing its gravitational force and overall strength.

Supermassive black holes, similar to stellar black holes, are built in the same fashion but their power and force is a billion times more massive than the sun. Scientists think that supermassive black holes may have been formed by thousands of tiny black holes merging together. Because black holes consume and grow from gathering the dust and space material around them, as they consume more, they grow and become more massive and powerful. Thus, a cycle is established and the super massive "giants" continue to grow and build throughout the galaxy.

Intermediate black holes are thought to be somewhere between stellar black holes and supermassive black holes in size and mass. Intermediate black holes are thought to form when stars in a cluster collide and form a chain reaction. Their construction is similar to that of the supermassive black holes but on a lesser scale.

Because black holes are unseen, how do we know they exist? The answer lies in the gravitational field that surrounds these invisible gems. Black holes are detected by the amount of gravitational force that scientists encounter in space. Try to imagine an invisible force that continues to suck in space objects such a dust and gas but never allows anything out. Imagine the amount of heat, radiation and gravity that these massive objects produces. This is what allows scientists to detect the existence of a black hole. Scientists believe that studying black holes is useful because they are a useful tool for discovering fundamental laws about our universe. Scientists believe that by studying black holes we will be able to rethink big picture ideas such as matter, and apply new ideas to the study of physics. Studying black holes may also help people to gain a better understanding as to the nature and the origins of our universe.

Comprehension Questions

1. What is a black hole?
2. How do scientists know that black holes really exist?
3. Who made up the term black hole?
4. What makes a super massive black hole different from a stellar black hole?
5. Why is it important to study black holes?
6. What object would you compare a black hole to? Why?

3

Extend Your Learning!

1. **Create!**
   Create a comic depicting the creation of a black hole.
2. **Research!**
   Research the life cycle of a star and draw a depiction the life cycle.
3. **Create!**
   Create a model of a black hole using the following experiment.
   www.unawe.org/activity/eu-unawe1308/

Just Read! resources

The following are available to make photocopies for your students or can be downloaded and printed from www.pavpub.com/just-read-teachers-manual-resources.

Student name: ______________________

My Rapid Letter Naming Tracking Sheet

Letter Names Per Minute (LNPM)					
100					
95					
90					
85					
80					
75					
70					
65					
60					
55					
50					
45					
40					
35					
30					
25					
20					
15					
10					
5					
Date					
	Rapid Naming (RN-1)	Rapid Naming (RN-2)	Rapid Naming (RN-3)	Rapid Naming (RN-4)	Rapid Naming (RN-5)

My Rapid Letter Naming Goal:

____

How close were you to reaching your goal?

Colour in the circle that most closely matches your total average score.

Bullseye
Goal Reached!

Very Close
Within 5 LNPM

Close
Within 10 LNPM

Student name: ____________________

My Sound Identification Tracking Sheet

Letter Sounds Per Minute (LSPM)					
100					
95					
90					
85					
80					
75					
70					
65					
60					
55					
50					
45					
40					
35					
30					
25					
20					
15					
10					
5					
Date					
	Rapid Sounds 1 (RS-1)	Rapid Sounds 1 (RS-2)	Rapid Sounds 1 (RS-3)	Rapid Sounds 1 (RS-4)	Rapid Sounds 1 (RS-5)

My Sound Identification Goal:

____

Bullseye

Very close

Close

How close were you to reaching your goal?

Colour in the circle that most closely matches your total average score.

Bullseye
Goal Reached!

Very Close
Within 5 SPM

Close
Within 10 SPM

Student name: ______________________

My Phoneme to Phoneme Blending Tracking Sheet

Words Per Minute (WPM)																														
100																														
95																														
90																														
85																														
80																														
75																														
70																														
65																														
60																														
55																														
50																														
45																														
40																														
35																														
30																														
25																														
20																														
15																														
10																														
5																														
Date																														
	Phoneme Blending (ă)					Phoneme Blending (ĕ)					Phoneme Blending (ĭ)					Phoneme Blending (ŏ)					Phoneme Blending (ŭ)					Phoneme Blending (Mixed)				

My Phoneme-to-Phoneme Word Goal:

____

Bullseye
Very close
Close

How close were you to reaching your goal?

Colour in the circle that most closely matches your total average score.

Bullseye
Goal Reached!

Very Close
Within 5 WPM

Close
Within 10 WPM

Student name: ______________________

My Pseudo- Word Reading Goal:

____

My Pseudo-Word Tracking Sheet

Words Per Minute (WPM)	Pseudo-Words (ă)	Pseudo-Words (ĕ)	Pseudo-Words (ĭ)	Pseudo-Words (ŏ)	Pseudo-Words (ŭ)	Pseudo-Words (Mixed)
100						
95						
90						
85						
80						
75						
70						
65						
60						
55						
50						
45						
40						
35						
30						
25						
20						
15						
10						
5						
Date						

Bullseye
Very close
Close

How close were you to reaching your goal?

Colour in the circle that most closely matches your total average score.

Bullseye
Goal Reached!

Very Close
Within 5 WPM

Close
Within 10 WPM

Student name: ______________________

My CVC Word Fluency Goal: ____________

My CVC Word Fluency Tracking Sheet

Words Per Minute (WPM)	Real words (ă)	Real Words (ĕ)	Real Words (ĭ)	Real Words (ŏ)	Real Words (ŭ)	Real Words (Mixed)
100						
95						
90						
85						
80						
75						
70						
65						
60						
55						
50						
45						
40						
35						
30						
25						
20						
15						
10						
5						
Date						

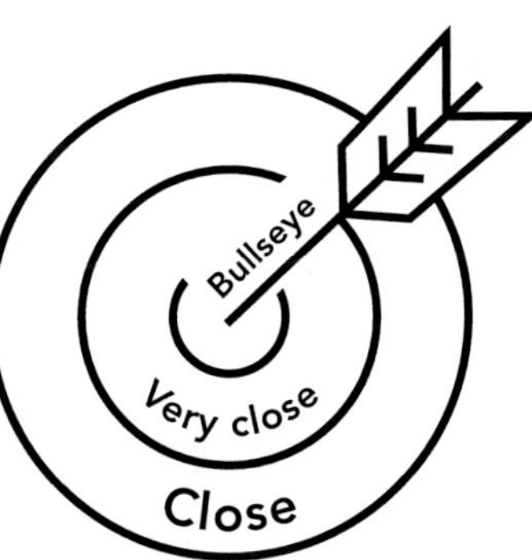

How close were you to reaching your goal?

Colour in the circle that most closely matches your total average score.

Bullseye
Goal Reached!

Very Close
Within 5 WPM

Close
Within 10 WPM

Student name: ______________________

My Word Fluency Tracking Sheet

Words Per Minute (WPM)	Real Word Reading (RWblm-1)	Real Word Reading (RWblm-2)	Real Word Reading (RWblm-3)	Real Word Reading (RWblm-4)	Real Word Reading (RWblm-5)
100					
95					
90					
85					
80					
75					
70					
65					
60					
55					
50					
45					
40					
35					
30					
25					
20					
15					
10					
5					
Date					

My Word Fluency Goal: ______________

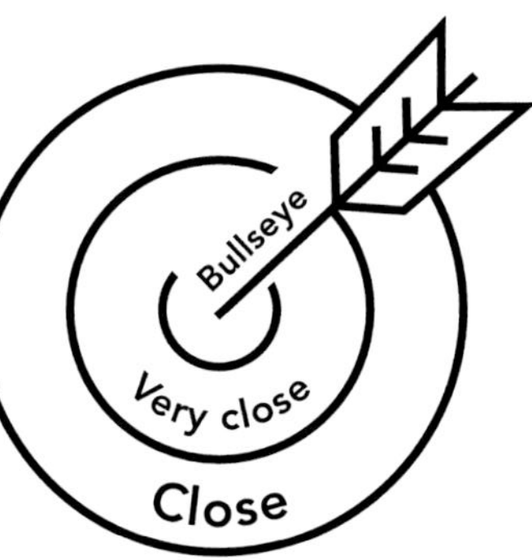

How close were you to reaching your goal?

Colour in the circle that most closely matches your total average score.

Bullseye
Goal Reached!

Very Close
Within 5 WPM

Close
Within 10 WPM

Student name: ____________________ Passage title: ____________________

My Fluency Plus! Tracking Sheet

Words Per Minute (WPM)	
250	
240	
230	
220	
210	
200	
190	
180	
170	
160	
150	
140	
130	
120	
110	
100	
90	
80	
70	
60	
50	
40	
30	
20	
10	
Date	
	Baseline

Words Per Minute (WPM)															
25															
24															
23															
22															
21															
20															
19															
18															
17															
16															
15															
14															
13															
12															
11															
10															
9															
8															
7															
6															
5															
4															
3															
2															
1															
Date															
	Isolated Phonogram Reading					Nonsense Word Reading					Real Word Reading				

Words Per Minute (WPM)					
250					
240					
230					
220					
210					
200					
190					
180					
170					
160					
150					
140					
130					
120					
110					
100					
90					
80					
70					
60					
50					
40					
30					
20					
10					
Date					
	Passage Reading				

My Reading Fluency Goal:

____

Bullseye

Very close

Close

How close were you to reaching your goal?

Colour in the circle that most closely matches your total average score.

Bullseye
Goal Reached!

Very Close
Within 5 WPM

Close
Within 10 WPM

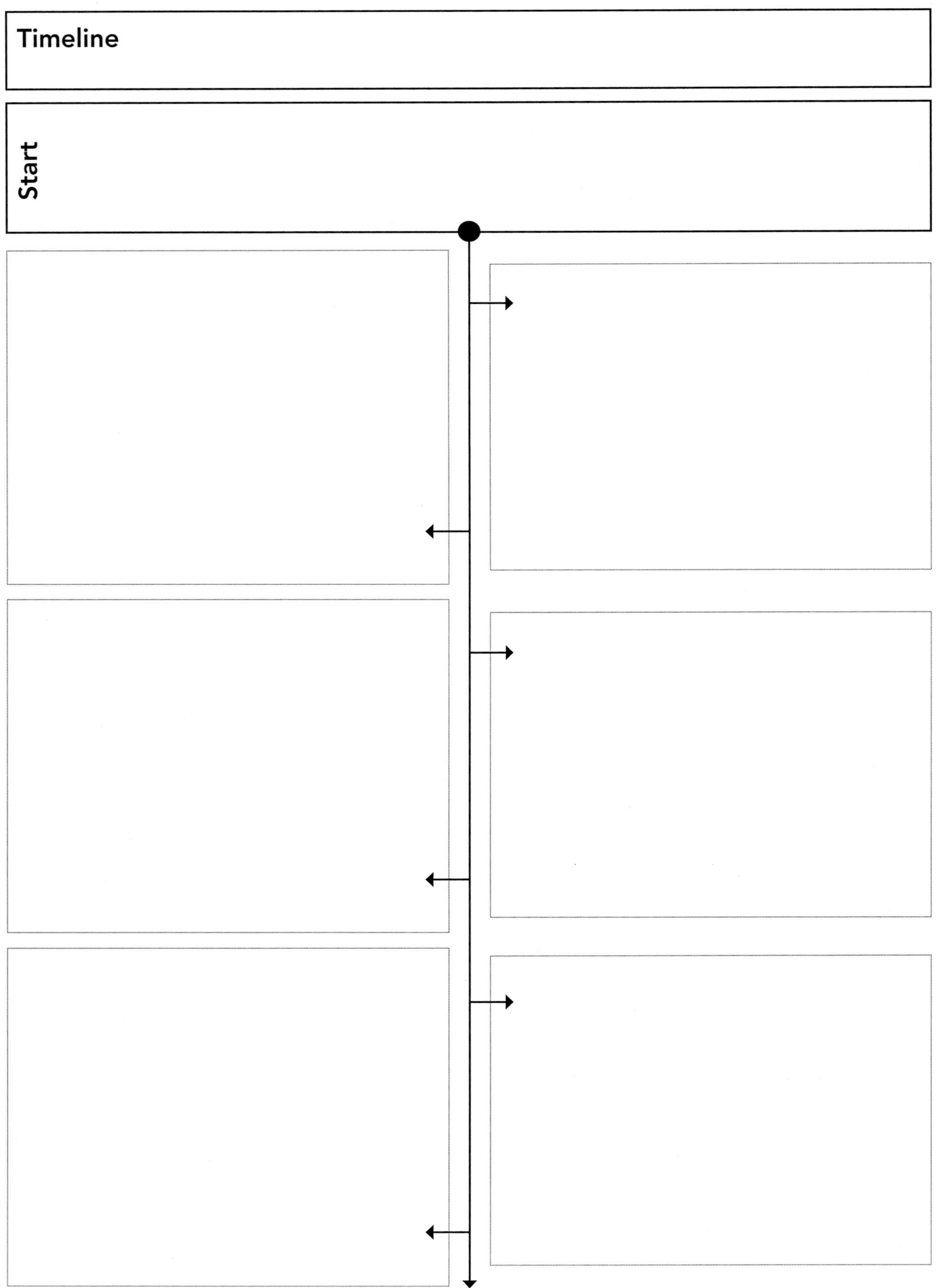
Timeline
Start

Name of My Game:

Reading Fluency Screener

Student information		
Student name:	Age:	Grade:
Testing date:	Assessor's name:	

Recording of scores		
Rapid letter naming	Number of letters identified:	Number correct:
Rapid sound identification	Number of sounds identified:	Number correct:
Non-phonetic reading	Score:	Notes:
Mixed phonetic pseudo-word reading	Score:	Notes:
Mixed real word phonetic reading	Score:	Notes:
Rapid & automatic word recognition	Score:	Notes:
Oral reading fluency scores		
Reading passage administered:	☐ Fluency 1 (Gr.K-2) ☐ Fluency 2 (Gr.2-4)	☐ Fluency 3 (Gr.4-6) ☐ Fluency 4 (Gr.6-8)
Total words read: **Number of errors:**	**WCPM[1]:**	**Accuracy rate[2]:**

1. In order to get your WCPM (word count per minute), take the total number of words read minus the total number of errors.
2. In order to get your accuracy reading, divide the WCPM by the total words read.

Behavioural observations related to reading:		
Fluency indicators	**Yes**	**No**
Does the student attend to punctuation?		
Does the student read with expression?		
Does the student read single words at a time?		
Does the student group words together as they read? (phrasing or chunking)		
Does the student track the text with their finger?		
Does the student have any word attack strategies? (ie: sound out familiar words)		
Does the student skip over or miss whole words?		
Does the student replace words with similar words?		
Does the student read at a rapid pace with no attention to accuracy?		
Does the student read at a slower and/or laboured pace with no attention to accuracy?		
Does the student make several errors that affect fluency? (ie: bus/dus)		
Other behavioural observations		
Does the student appear nervous while reading?		
Does the student appear to be reluctant to read?		
Does the student appear to be distracted while reading?		
When reading becomes more difficult, does the student persevere?		

Rapid Letter Naming

DIRECTIONS: This is a one-minute timed activity. Have your students identify as many letters as they can in one minute. **Mark errors with a slash. Self-corrections do not count as errors.** If a student omits or **skips** a letter, circle the letter and count it as an **error**. If there is a pause of 5 seconds or longer, give the student the letter name, **circle the letter** and count it as an **error**.

Q	w	x	k	M	t	i	H	j	s	10
F	b	a	d	G	R	e	u	O	y	20
V	c	B	Y	S	U	o	P	A	o	30
p	M	l	r	i	X	T	W	b	z	40
g	f	L	h	J	z	n	m	q	Y	50
q	r	f	l	g	V	i	K	l	H	60
e	i	V	d	t	p	o	X	C	z	70
y	G	U	r	D	q	y	H	J	u	80
Q	w	x	k	M	t	i	H	j	s	90
F	b	a	d	G	R	e	u	O	y	100

Total Named:	- # of errors:	= Letters Correct:

Assessor Notes & Observations:

Rapid Sound Identification

DIRECTIONS: This is a one-minute timed activity. Have your students identify as many sounds as they can in one minute. **Score 1 point for every correct sound and 0 points for sounds missed or skipped**. Tally the total number of correct sounds made in each of the following 4 columns and then tally the final score.

Score	Letter	Sound	Keyword
		Vowel Sounds	
	a	/ă/	apple
		/ā/	cake
		/ə/	above
		/ŏ/	walrus
	e	/ĕ/	elephant
		/ē/	we
	i	/ĭ/	insect
		/ī/	bike
		/ē/	radio
	o	/ŏ/	octopus
		/ō/	go
	u	/ŭ/	up
		/yū/	cube
		/ü/	flute
		/ů/	bull
	y	/ī/	cry
		/ē/	candy
		/ĭ/	gym
		Consonant Sounds	
	b	/b/	bat
	c	/k/	cookie
		/s/	city
	d	/d/	dog
	f	/f/	feather
	g	/g/	goat
		/j/	gentle

Column 1 Total ________

Score	Letter	Sound	Keyword
	h	/h/	horse
	j	/j/	jam
	k	/k/	kite
	l	/l/	leg
	m	/m/	mat
	n	/n/	nap
	p	/p/	pig
	qu	/kw/	quick
	r	/r/	rat
	s	/s/	snake
		/z/	nose
	t	/t/	table
	v	/v/	van
	w	/w/	wagon
	x	/x/	ax
	y	/y/	yo-yo
	z	/z/	zebra
		Digraphs and Trigraphs	
	ck	/ck/	black
	sh	/sh/	ship
	ch	/ch/	chin
		/sh/	chef
		/k/	chord
	th	/th/	thumb
		/th/	bathe
	wh	/w/	when
		/hw/	wheat

Column 2 Total ________

Rapid Sound Identification (continued)

Score	Letter	Sound	Keyword
	dge	/j/	badge
	tch	/ch/	witch
	ph	/f/	phone
Vowel Digraphs/r-controlled vowel sounds			
	er	/ər/	her
	ar	/är/	car
		/ȯr/	war
		/ər/	regular
	or	/ȯr/	corn
		/ər/	humor
	ir	/ər/	bird
	ur	/ər/	church
	ai	/ā/	nail
	ay	/ā/	hay
	ee	/ē/	tree
	ey	/ē/	key
	oa	/ō/	goat
	oe	/ō/	toe
	ue	/ü/	glue
		/yū/	cue
	oi	/oi/	oil
	oy	/oi/	boy
	aw	/ŏ/	saw
	au	/ŏ/	faucet
	ow	/ŏ/	snow
		/au̇/	cow
	ou	/au̇/	house

Score	Letter	Sound	Keyword
	ou	/ü/	soup
	oo	/ü/	spoon
		/u̇/	look
	ea	/ē/	treat
		/ĕ/	bread
		/ā/	steak
	eu	/u̇/	neuron
		/yū/	eulogy
	ew	/yū/	few
		/ü/	screw
	ui	/ü/	fruit
	ie	/ē/	field
		/ī/	pie
	ei	/ē/	ceiling
		/ā/	feign
	igh	/ī/	sigh
	eigh	/ā/	eight
Other Sound Patterns			
	ang	/aŋ/	hang
	ing	/iŋ/	sing
	ong	/oŋ/	song
	ung	/oŋ/	hung
	ank	/aŋk/	bank
	ink	/iŋk/	sink
	onk	/oŋk/	bonk
	unk	/uŋk/	sunk

Column 1 Total __________

Column 2 Total __________

Sound Identification Total Score: __________

Irregular Word Reading

DIRECTIONS: This is a one-minute timed activity. Have your students identify as many words as they can in one minute. **Mark errors with a slash. Self-corrections do not count as errors**. If a student omits or **skips** a word, circle the word and count it as an **error**. If there is a pause of 5 seconds or longer, give the student the word, **circle the word** and count it as an **error**.

I	of	to	do	the	you	was	are	one	two	10
too	who	any	many	put	why	they	have	give	live	20
from	what	were	your	you're	said	some	come	only	very	30
much	such	very	sure	here	there	where	does	goes	don't	40
won't	both	four	once	busy	gone	push	bush	look	took	50
pull	full	bull	done	none	pretty	their	they're	which	every	60
love	above	would	could	should	often	again	against	heart	friend	70
other	mother	another	brother	laugh	month	nothing	people	because	answer	80
front	among	build	built	usual	usually	blood	flood	sugar	listen	90
glisten	woman	women	orange	father	rough	tough	enough	eye	during	100

Non-Phonetic Word Reading Total Score: _____ /100

Assessor Notes & Observations:

Mixed Phonetic Pseudo-Word Reading

DIRECTIONS: This is a one-minute timed activity. Have your students identify as many pseudo-words as they can in one minute. **Mark errors with a slash. Self-corrections do not count as errors**. If a student omits or **skips** a word, circle the word and count it as an **error**. If there is a pause of 5 seconds or longer, give the student the word, **circle the word** and count it as an **error**. Mark the types of errors and the number of those errors on the error analysis box below.

yub	caz	lom	fiv	rej	kib	zat	mej	puz	gov	10
ped	baz	ruv	sig	hej	kem	lod	vup	yax	fet	20
glub	prex	skib	remp	pust	glusk	splast	strift	twand	sweft	30
frob	plend	hest	streg	swimp	blesp	jelt	bluft	prist	vont	40
strock	quip	blutch	vidge	bleck	squiv	pelch	shast	potch	mudge	50
vexrip	ponjub	rixvem	pidfoz	prixcot	slibfuz	swigrop	glutfib	bistpub	helbix	60
strame	plibe	vope	rube	gordilp	lang	ponkrid	tring	larpeet	benflab	70
brimeful	lorpoot	spute	hibely	monepill	swi	blu	plotube	trigabe	fring	80
bucle	vife	brafle	vockle	mickest	twickle	punkle	hestle	cratube	zemple	90
jougrip	blaypin	quaip	strewbix	strigh	yixtume	splinge	beurop	jieb	fleigh	100

Mixed Phonetic Pseudo-Word Reading Total Score : _____ /100

Error Analysis:

____ Single consonants ____ ng, nk, all ____ Closed Syllable ____ c'le Syllable

____ Short Vowels ____ qu ____ v-e Syllable ____ Vowel Team Syllable

____ Beginning Blends ____ v-e Error ____ Open Syllable

____ Final Blends ____ Digraphs ____ r-controlled Syllable

Assessor Notes & Observations:

Mixed Phonetic Real Word Reading

DIRECTIONS: This is a one-minute timed activity. Have your students identify as many pseudo-words as they can in one minute. **Mark errors with a slash. Self-corrections do not count as errors**. If a student omits or **skips** a word, circle the word and count it as an **error**. If there is a pause of 5 seconds or longer, give the student the word, **circle the word** and count it as an **error**. Mark the types of errors and the number of those errors on the error analysis box below.

fun	cab	fax	kiss	dug	pin	jazz	fed	cod	lap	10
bless	brisk	spot	end	lamp	bond	dusk	swept	mist	flat	20
limp	strand	swift	splint	jump	bask	cuff	twist	punt	blunt	30
quack	botch	wedge	shop	chimp	clock	thud	latch	squid	shed	40
bake	tube	pitch	lodge	pine	spoke	lathe	game	theme	kite	50
ring	trunk	strung	link	bonk	thank	stall	long	pink	bring	60
quake	try	horn	spite	first	he	purse	farm	probe	term	70
sky	sweet	house	crow	boot	treat	mail	tray	coil	toy	80
crackle	rifle	marble	whistle	table	simple	candle	maple	thimble	bottle	90
boiler	played	twinkle	jousting	happy	jumped	boastful	swiftly	bursting	hunted	100

Mixed Phonetic Real Word Reading Total Score : _____ /100

Error Analysis:

____ Single consonants ____ ng, nk, all ____ Closed Syllable ____ c'le Syllable

____ Short Vowels ____ qu ____ v-e Syllable ____ Vowel Team Syllable

____ Beginning Blends ____ v-e Error ____ Open Syllable

____ Final Blends ____ Digraphs ____ r-controlled Syllable

Assessor Notes & Observations:

High Frequency Instant Word Reading

DIRECTIONS: This is a one-minute timed activity. Have your students identify as many high frequency words as they can in one minute. **Mark errors with a slash. Self-corrections do not count as errors.** If a student omits or **skips** a word, circle the word and count it as an **error**. If there is a pause of 5 seconds or longer, give the student the word, **circle the word** and count it as an **error**.

the	of	and	a	to	in	is	you	it	he	10
was	for	on	are	as	with	his	they	I	at	20
be	this	have	from	or	one	had	by	word	but	30
not	what	were	we	when	your	can	said	there	use	40
an	each	which	she	do	how	their	if	will	up	50
other	about	out	many	then	them	so	some	her	would	60
make	like	him	into	time	has	look	two	more	write	70
go	see	number	no	way	could	people	my	than	first	80
been	call	who	oil	its	now	find	long	down	day	90
did	get	come	made	may	part	over	new	take	only	100

Mixed High-Frequency Word Reading Total Score : _____ /100

Assessor Notes & Observations:

* Sourced from "*The Reading Teacher's Book of Lists*" Pg.95 Fry's List of High Frequency Words

Rapid Letter Naming

Q	w	x	k	M	t	i	H	j	s
F	b	a	d	G	R	e	u	O	y
V	c	B	Y	S	U	o	P	A	o
p	M	I	r	i	X	T	W	b	z
g	f	L	h	J	z	n	m	q	Y
q	r	f	l	g	V	i	K	I	H
e	i	V	d	t	p	o	X	C	z
y	G	U	r	D	q	y	H	J	u
Q	w	x	k	M	t	i	H	j	s
F	b	a	d	G	R	e	u	O	y

Rapid Sound Identification

a	e	i	o	u	y	b	c	d	f
g	h	j	k	l	m	n	p	qu	r
s	t	v	w	x	z	ck	sh	ch	th
wh	tch	dge	ph	er	ar	or	ir	ur	aw
ai	ay	ee	ey	oa	oe	ue	oi	oy	aw
au	ow	ou	oo	ee	eu	ew	ui	ie	ei
igh	eigh	ang	ing	ong	ung	ank	ink	onk	unk

Irregular Word Reading

I	of	to	do	the	you	was	are	one	two
too	who	any	many	put	why	they	have	give	live
from	what	were	your	you're	said	some	come	only	very
much	such	very	sure	here	there	where	does	goes	don't
won't	both	four	once	busy	gone	push	bush	look	took
pull	full	bull	done	none	pretty	their	they're	which	every
love	above	would	could	should	often	again	against	heart	friend
other	mother	another	brother	laugh	month	nothing	people	because	answer
front	among	build	built	usual	usually	blood	flood	sugar	listen
glisten	woman	women	orange	father	rough	tough	enough	eye	during

Mixed Phonetic Pseudo-Word Reading

yub	caz	lom	fiv	rej	kib	zat	mej	puz	gov
ped	baz	ruv	sig	hej	kem	lod	vup	yax	fet
glub	prex	skib	remp	pust	glusk	splast	strift	twand	sweft
frob	plend	hest	streg	swimp	blesp	jelt	bluft	prist	vont
strock	quip	blutch	vidge	bleck	squiv	pelch	shast	potch	mudge
vexrip	ponjub	rixvem	pidfoz	prixcot	slibfuz	swigrop	glutfib	bistpub	helbix
strame	plibe	vope	rube	gordilp	lang	ponkrid	tring	larpeet	benflab
brimeful	lorpoot	spute	hibely	monepill	swi	blu	plotube	trigabe	fring
bucle	vife	brafle	vockle	mickest	twickle	punkle	hestle	cratube	zemple
jougrip	blaypin	quaip	strewbix	strigh	yixtume	splinge	beurop	jieb	fleigh

Mixed Phonetic Real Word Reading

fun	cab	fax	kiss	dug	pin	jazz	fed	cod	lap
bless	brisk	spot	end	lamp	bond	dusk	swept	mist	flat
limp	strand	swift	splint	jump	bask	cuff	twist	punt	blunt
quack	botch	wedge	shop	chimp	clock	thud	latch	squid	shed
bake	tube	pitch	lodge	pine	spoke	lathe	game	theme	kite
ring	trunk	strung	link	bonk	thank	stall	long	pink	bring
quake	try	horn	spite	first	he	purse	farm	probe	term
sky	sweet	house	crow	boot	treat	mail	tray	coil	toy
crackle	rifle	marble	whistle	table	simple	candle	maple	thimble	bottle
boiler	played	twinkle	jousting	happy	jumped	boastful	swiftly	bursting	hunted

High Frequency Instant Word Reading

the	of	and	a	to	in	is	you	it	he
was	for	on	are	as	with	his	they	I	at
be	this	have	from	or	one	had	by	word	but
not	what	were	we	when	your	can	said	there	use
an	each	which	she	do	how	their	if	will	up
other	about	out	many	then	them	so	some	her	would
make	like	him	into	time	has	look	two	more	write
go	see	number	no	way	could	people	my	than	first
been	call	who	oil	its	now	find	long	down	day
did	get	come	made	may	part	over	new	take	only

Screening Passage K-2 "Spot the Lost Dog"

DIRECTIONS: This is a one-minute timed activity. Have your students read the passage below for one-minute. **Mark errors with a slash. Self-corrections do not count as errors**. If a student omits or **skips** a word, put a line through the word and count it as an **error**. If there is a pause of 5 seconds or longer, give the student the word, **put a line through the word** and count it as an **error**. Mark specific errors in the error analysis box below.

Spot the dog was lost. Spot ran to his back deck but his mom and dad 16
were lost too. He did sniff the deck and did fret but at last he did hunt 33
for some prints. He set off on a quest to help find his mom and dad. 49
Quick and fast, Spot did run up the hill of the back to a flat spot. He did 67
tramp in the muck. He was hot and stiff but did not quit. At last, he met 84
his bud Quack who said he sent Spot's mom and dad back to his deck. 99
Spot did rant and yell, but ran back quick and fast. On the back deck, 114
Spot did smell and sniff his mom and dad. He felt his bum wag and he 130
did hum. At last, his mom and dad did stand next to him on the deck. 146
They were glad at last to see Spot. 154

Total Words Read:	- # of errors:	= Words Correct:

Enter the number of errors for each concept:

____ ck   ____ short vowels   ____ non-phonetic words   ____ qu

____ initial blends   ____ final blends   ____ other

Check all the boxes that apply to your student:

☐ student has no word attack strategies

☐ student sounds out every letter in a word

☐ student can read whole words automatically

☐ student disregards punctuation

☐ student reads with very little expression

☐ student has some phrasing and chunking

If a student makes 5 or more errors on any one concept listed above in the box, start working with them at the Decoding Plus Story 1.

Spot the Lost Dog

Spot the dog was lost. Spot ran to his back deck but his mom and dad were lost too. He did sniff the deck and did fret but at last he did hunt for some prints. He set off on a quest to help find his mom and dad. Quick and fast, Spot did run up the hill of the back to a flat spot. He did tramp in the muck. He was hot and stiff but did not quit. At last, he met his bud Quack who said he sent Spot's mom and dad back to his deck. Spot did rant and yell, but ran back quick and fast. On the back deck, Spot did smell and sniff his mom and dad. He felt his bum wag and he did hum. At last, his mom and dad did stand next to him on the deck. They were glad at last to see Spot.

Screening Passage 2-4 "A Fish Wish"

DIRECTIONS: This is a one-minute timed activity. Have your students read the passage below for one-minute. **Mark errors with a slash. Self-corrections do not count as errors**. If a student omits or **skips** a word, put a line through the word and count it as an **error**. If there is a pause of 5 seconds or longer, give the student the word, **put a line through the word** and count it as an **error**. Mark specific errors in the error analysis box below.

Slash is a fish with just one wish. He would like to swim in a big pond. In 18
his very small tank, Slash swims all day long. He is glum and sad but will 34
not give up his wish to swim in a big pond. With a big push, Slash and his 52
bud Chad the crab bump and fall when they jump up from the tank. 67
The tank is too tall to jump from, and they fall back into the small tank. 83
One day, Slash plans a big jump. He tells all of his pals and they think it is 101
the best plan. Chad the crab sits on the small rock and all of the other 117
pals stack on top of him. One by one, they sit still and do not fuss until 134
Slash can get on top.The small tank shifts and spills and all of them think 151
it will tip and spill. They think they must stop but Slash will not. At last, 166
Slash catches himself and sits on the very top of the bunch. He can just 181
tap the top of the dish when he shifts and lands on all of his pals. They 198
jump off the rock and end up in a big clump of sand and dust. They are 215
all very sad that the plan had to stop and that Slash did not get his wish. 231
They all said that one day Slash's wish must come to be. 243

Total Words Read:	- # of errors:	= Words Correct:

Enter the number of errors for each concept:

____ short vowels ____ consonant digraphs ____ non-phonetic words

____ initial blends ____ final blends ____ ng/nk ____ other

Check all the boxes that apply to your student:

☐ student has no word attack strategies

☐ student sounds out every letter in a word

☐ student can read whole words automatically

☐ student disregards punctuation

☐ student reads with very little expression

☐ student has some phrasing and chunking

If a student makes 5 or more errors on any one concept listed above in the box, start at story ______ in Fluency Plus!

A Fish Wish

Slash is a fish with just one wish. He would like to swim in a big pond. In his very small tank, Slash swims all day long. He is glum and sad but will not give up his wish to swim in a big pond. With a big push, Slash and his bud Chad the crab bump and fall when they jump up from the tank. The tank is too tall to jump from, and they fall back into the small tank. One day, Slash plans a big jump. He tells all of his pals and they think it is the best plan. Chad the crab sits on the small rock and all of the other pals stack on top of him. One by one, they sit still and do not fuss until Slash can get on top. The small tank shifts and spills and all of them think it will tip and spill. They think they must stop but Slash will not. At last, Slash catches himself and sits on the very top of the bunch. He can just tap the top of the dish when he shifts and lands on all of his pals. They jump off the rock and end up in a big clump of sand and dust. They are all very sad that the plan had to stop and that Slash did not get his wish. They all said that one day Slash's wish must come to be.

Screening Passage 4-6 "The Lone Hawk"

DIRECTIONS: This is a one-minute timed activity. Have your students read the passage below for one-minute. **Mark errors with a slash. Self-corrections do not count as errors**. If a student omits or **skips** a word, put a line through the word and count it as an **error**. If there is a pause of 5 seconds or longer, give the student the word, **put a line through the word** and count it as an **error**. Mark specific errors in the error analysis box below.

Fleet was a man who prayed all day long in an extremely quiet hallway. 14
When he would pray, he would often get a pain in his neck as it was 30
tilted for too long. One day, while Fleet was praying, he saw an amazing 44
thing in front of his eyes. He realized that a hawk had gained its way into 60
the hallway and landed on top of an old green box. Fleet had not ever 76
seen the hawk, but it was pretty unusual to see birds inside buildings. Fleet 89
sat still and waited for the hawk to fly away. The hawk remained quite 105
still and watched Fleet. Fleet made an attempt to remain in prayer but 117
he became a bit confused and couldn't regain his focus. The hawk sat 129
completely still and watched Fleet as he prayed. It just waited and 141
waited. At last, Fleet became stiff from so much praying and he got up 155
to leave. The hawk sensed his moving and shifting and lifted up its wings 169
to fly away. From the back of the hallway, Fleet watched the hawk fly to 184
the front lawn. It landed in a tree close by and gazed at the distant sea. 200

Total Words Read:	- # of errors:	= Words Correct:

Enter the number of errors for each concept:

____ short vowels ____ consonant digraphs ____ vowel digraphs

____ open syllables ____ non-phonetic words ____ initial blends

____ final blends ____ ng/nk ____ other

Check all the boxes that apply to your student:

☐ student has no word attack strategies

☐ student sounds out every letter in a word

☐ student can read whole words automatically

☐ student disregards punctuation

☐ student reads with very little expression

☐ student has some phrasing and chunking

If a student makes 5 or more errors on any one concept listed above in the box, start at story ______ in Fluency Plus!

The Lone Hawk

Fleet was a man who prayed all day long in an extremely quiet hallway. When he would pray, he would often get a pain in his neck as it was tilted for too long. One day, while Fleet was praying, he saw an amazing thing in front of his eyes. He realized that a hawk had gained its way into the hallway and landed on top of an old green box. Fleet had not ever seen the hawk, but it was pretty unusual to see birds inside buildings. Fleet sat still and waited for the hawk to fly away. The hawk remained quite still and watched Fleet. Fleet made an attempt to remain in prayer but he became a bit confused and couldn't regain his focus. The hawk sat completely still and watched Fleet as he prayed. It just waited and waited. At last, Fleet became stiff from so much praying and he got up to leave. The hawk sensed his moving and shifting and lifted up its wings to fly away. From the back of the hallway, Fleet watched the hawk fly to the front lawn. It landed in a tree close by and gazed at the distant sea.

Screening Passage 6-8 "The Class Party"

DIRECTIONS: This is a one-minute timed activity. Have your students read the passage below for one-minute. **Mark errors with a slash. Self-corrections do not count as errors**. If a student omits or **skips** a word, put a line through the word and count it as an **error**. If there is a pause of 5 seconds or longer, give the student the word, **put a line through the word** and count it as an **error**. Mark specific errors in the error analysis box below.

It was the last day of class and everyone was so excited. They had worked so 16
hard the entire year and they would now get their class party. Each student 30
was allowed to invite a special guest and bring them to school for the whole 45
day and have them be a part of their class. Cassy was especially excited 59
because she was going to bring her cousin Beth, who was also her best friend. 74
The night before the party, Cassy couldn't sleep because she was so excited. 87
What was the party going to be like? Who would be there? Would her other 102
classmates bring their best friends too? The morning of the party, Cassy's 114
mother made chocolate cupcakes for everyone. On the top of each 125
cupcake was a glow in the dark letter. The letter was for their name. Cassy 140
wanted to walk to school with her cousin Beth, but her mother insisted on 154
driving them because of the heavy load of cupcakes. When they got out of 168
the car and said their goodbyes, both Cassy and Beth saw so many students in 183
line. It was true! Everyone had brought their best friends and the class line was 198
so long and loud. Beth and Cassy stood at the back of the line and tightly 214
held on to their cupcakes. Everyone else had enormous bags of chips and 227
party stuff and everyone was really excited. When the bell rang, they all filed 241
into the classroom and their teacher was standing at the front of the room. 255
She had set up a dance square in the corner of the room and had set up a 273
huge party table in the other corner. The kids arranged all of their food on the 289
table. They were hungry and excited all at the same time. The teacher put on 304
their favourite music and announced that the party had started. It was the 316
best school day ever! 320

Total Words Read:	- # of errors:	= Words Correct:

Enter the number of errors for each concept:

____ short vowels ____ consonant digraphs ____ vowel digraphs

____ closed syllables ____ r-controlled syllables ____ open syllables

____ non-phonetic words ____ initial blends ____ final blends

____ ng/nk ____ other

Check all the boxes that apply to your student:

☐ student has no word attack strategies

☐ student sounds out every letter in a word

☐ student can read whole words automatically

☐ student disregards punctuation

☐ student reads with very little expression

☐ student has some phrasing and chunking

If a student makes 5 or more errors on any one concept listed above in the box, start at story ______ in Fluency Plus!

The Class Party

It was the last day of class and everyone was so excited. They had worked so hard the entire year and they would now get their class party. Each student was allowed to invite a special guest and bring them to school for the whole day and have them be a part of their class. Cassy was especially excited because she was going to bring her cousin Beth, who was also her best friend. The night before the party, Cassy couldn't sleep because she was so excited. What was the party going to be like? Who would be there? Would her other classmates bring their best friends too? The morning of the party, Cassy's mother made chocolate cupcakes for everyone. On the top of each cupcake was a glow in the dark letter. The letter was for their name. Cassy wanted to walk to school with her cousin Beth, but her mother insisted on driving them because of the heavy load of cupcakes. When they got out of the car and said their goodbyes, both Cassy and Beth saw so many students in line. It was true! Everyone had brought their best friends and the class line was so long and loud. Beth and Cassy stood at the back of the line and tightly held on to their cupcakes. Everyone else had enormous bags of chips and party stuff and everyone was really excited. When the bell rang, they all filed into the classroom and their teacher was standing at the front of the room. She had set up a dance square in the corner of the room and had set up a huge party table in the other corner. The kids arranged all of their food on the table. They were hungry and excited all at the same time. The teacher put on their favourite music and announced that the party had started. It was the best school day ever!

References

Breznitz Z (2012) *Fluency in Reading Synchronization of Processes*. Psychology Press, New York.

Garnett K (2011) *'Fluency in Learning to Read: Conceptions, Misconceptions, Learning Disabilities and Instructional Moves'*. In: Judith R. Birsh (Ed) Multisensory Teaching of Basic Language Skills (3rd edition). Brookes Publishing Co, Maryland, 2016.

Kress, J.E, Fry, E.B (2016) *The Reading Teacher's Book of Lists* (Sixth Edition). Jossey Bass, US.

Meyer, M. (2012) 'Repeated Reading: An Old Standard is Revisited and Renovated'. In: L. C Moats, K. E. Dakin and R.M Joshi (Eds) *Expert Perspectives on Interventions for Reading: A Collection of Best Practice Articles from the International Dyslexia Association*. Published by the International Dyslexia Association, Baltimore, Maryland, 2015.

Nagy, W.E. and Anderson, R.C. (1984) How Many Words Are There in Printed School English. *Reading Research Quarterly*, 19, 304-330. New York.

Torgensen JK, Rashotte CA and Alexander AW (2001) *Principles of Fluency Instruction in Reading: Relationships with Established Empirical Outcomes in Dyslexia, Fluency and the Brain*. Edited by Maryanne Wolf. York Press, Maryland, 2001.

Wolf, M., & Obregon, M. (1992). Early naming deficits, developmental dyslexia and the specific deficit hypothesis. *Brain and Language*, 42, 219-247